Advance Praise for *Food at Sea*

"A scintillating smorgasbord of seafaring fare over the centuries from the *Odyssey* to the *Titanic*, featuring mouth-watering, if at times stomach-churning, briny tidbits for old salt and land-lubber alike. Simon Spalding is delectably versed in dietary arcana from galley slaves to submarine divers, poop deck to engine room. Cast-iron literary digestion is a gastric must for the author's recipes of lobscouse, dandyfunk, bilge rat, and boiled baby, washed down or thrown up with jungle juice." —**David Lowenthal**, emeritus professor of geography, University College London

"A unique book that concerns longue durée, from the earliest period of shipping until the recent, the design of ships and boats, and the ways those changes in design made for different eating habits aboard those ships. I would recommend it for anyone interested in the history of food aboard ships." —**Ruthi Gertwagen**, University of Haifa, Israel

"The author's engaging text has created an entertaining and scholarly introduction to life at sea. This book should be at home in all libraries from universities to cruise ships. Learn about, and learn how to make, "lobscouse," burgoo," plum duff," "dandyfunk," "spotted dog," "collops," and wash them down with "grog," "kai," or a "cup of joe." —**Craig Lukczic**, president of the Archaeological Society of Delaware; adjunct professor, Delaware State University

"The story of food at sea is far more complex than the smorgasbords provided by modern cruise ships. Granted, people often take cruises for the nonstop eating possibilities and for the great variety of foods they can try. Yet the true story of food at sea is a narrative about the design, development of ships, and evolution of ships from row galleys to cruise and container ships, and how these vessels spread the culinary traditions of the world. Simon Spalding's *Food at Sea* reminds us that of our modern gastronomic customs—and modern preferences for food such as salsa, biscotti, curry, or even lamb—derive in part from ships and the sea." —**Gene Allen Smith**, professor of history at TCU in Fort Worth, Texas; author of a number of books on naval and maritime history

"In his book *Food at Sea: Shipboard Cuisine from Ancient to Modern Times*, Simon Spalding serves up in gratifying fashion an authoritative answer to one of the most often asked question about life aboard ships: What did they eat? He gives insight not only to the food itself, but the industry, technology, and cultural developments behind the availability and choices of sea fare as they changed both ashore and in the maritime trades. Further, he traces the thread of seafaring traditions in those choices. Through wooden ships to steel ones and from salted fish and meat to the convenience of refrigeration, sailors still look for the 'bread barge' to sate that gnawing hunger when on watch in the middle of the night. Full of information for the curious, this book is a must read for any maritime re-enactor, living historian, or anyone interpreting a maritime site." —**Michael J. DeCarlo**, Esq., is a member of the naval living-history organization Ship's Company, Inc., and portrays the ship's cook on board the USS *Constellation* in Baltimore, Maryland, the last remaining U.S. Civil War–era all-sail sloop-of-war

"Throughout history, everyone who ever set sail on a long voyage faced the problem of how to feed passengers and crew. They approached that problem with every food preservation and cooking technique at their disposal, and developed ingenious preparations in the process. Simon Spalding has written a book like no other, the first comprehensive examination of the ways that the ancient Greeks in their oared galleys and Polynesians in outrigger canoes survived on the unknown oceans, the diet of Henry VIII's sailors facing the French, and the routines of modern cruise ship and naval chefs who cater thousands of meals on a daily basis. Though some parts of this story are less than appetizing—nobody will envy the meals of a crewman in Nelson's navy—this book is an absorbing read and recommended to anyone with an interest in nautical or culinary history." —**Richard Foss**, culinary historian and author

"For those who have read almost all about shipbuilding, sea battles, and navigation, now is the time to learn more about one of the most important things onboard supertankers, Viking ships, steamers, and submarines—the food. Simon Spalding take us to the seven seas and through more than a thousand years of dry food, salt food, and bad food, as well as all the improvements to keep the crew alive, and happy, on men-of-war, East Indiamen, steamers, and submarines. It is a 'must have' for everyone interested in the shipping history." —**Hans-Lennart Ohlsson**, director, Swedish Maritime Museum

Food at Sea

The Food on the Go Series
as part of the Rowman & Littlefield Studies in Food and Gastronomy

General Editor: Ken Albala, Professor of History, University of the Pacific
(kalbala@pacific.edu)

Rowman & Littlefield Executive Editor: Suzanne Staszak-Silva
(sstaszak-silva@rowman.com)

The Food on the Go series

The volumes in this series explore the fascinating ways people eat while getting from one place to another and the adaptations they make in terms of food choices, cutlery, and even manners. Whether it be crossing the Atlantic in grand style on a luxury steamship, wedged into an airplane seat with a tiny tray, or driving in your car with a Big Mac in hand and a soda in the cup holder, food has adapted in remarkable ways to accommodate our peripatetic habits. Eating on the go may be elegant or fast, but it differs significantly from everyday eating and these books explain why in various cultures across the globe and through history. This is the first series to systematically examine how and why mobility influences our eating habits, for better and worse.

Food on the Rails: The Golden Era of Railroad Dining, by Jeri Quinzio (2014)

Food at Sea: Shipboard Cuisine from Ancient to Modern Times, by Simon Spalding (2014)

Food in the Air and Space: The Surprising History of Food and Drink in the Skies, Richard Foss (2014)

Food at Sea

Shipboard Cuisine from

Ancient to Modern Times

SIMON SPALDING

ROWMAN & LITTLEFIELD

Lanham • Boulder • New York • London

Published by Rowman & Littlefield
A wholly owned subsidiary of The Rowman & Littlefield Publishing Group, Inc.
4501 Forbes Boulevard, Suite 200, Lanham, Maryland 20706
www.rowman.com

Unit A, Whitacre Mews, 26-34 Stannary Street, London SE11 4AB

British Library Cataloguing in Publication Information Available

Library of Congress Cataloging-in-Publication Data
Spalding, Simon.
  Food at sea : shipboard cuisine from ancient to modern times / Simon Spalding.
      pages cm
  Includes bibliographical references and index.
    ISBN 978-1-4422-2736-1 (cloth) — ISBN 978-1-4422-2737-8 (electronic)
    1. Cooking on ships—History. I. Title.
  TX840.M7S67 2014
  641.5'753—dc23   2014024370

Printed in the United States of America

To Sara Kirtland Spalding,
my in-house editor, my muse,
and my best friend.

Contents

Acknowledgments

I wish to acknowledge and thank the following people for all the help they gave me with this project:

My wife, Sara Kirtland Spalding, who navigated the Chicago Manual of Style and publisher's guidelines; proofread, edited, and made my ramblings on virtual paper into a book manuscript;

Richard Foss, friend and adviser, who initially contacted me about this project, advised me along the way, helped me purchase menus, took photographs, and much more;

Sharon Sheffield, who prepared the index;

Ken Albala, who conceived the Food on the Move series, and took a chance on a writer he'd never heard of to write about food at sea;

Suzanne Staszak-Silva, Wendi Schnaufer, Kathryn Knigge, Andrea Offdenkamp Kendrick, Karen Ackermann, and Flannery Scott at Rowman & Littlefield, for all their guidance and help;

Leigh Russell and Denise Meyerson of Pamlico Community College, for help in borrowing obscure books on even more obscure topics;

Chris Roche, mariner, scholar, and singer, who traveled to Portsmouth to photograph HMS *Warrior*.

I would also like to thank the following people, who have helped in many diverse ways: Gina Bardi of the San Francisco Maritime National Historical Park; Dr. Fred Hocker of the Vasa Museum; Dr. Lawrence Mott of the University of Minnesota; Dr. Ruthy Gertwagen of the University of Haifa; Beth Ellis of the P&O Heritage Collection; Michael P. Dyer of the New Bedford Whaling Museum; Craig Bruns and Josh Fox of Independence Seaport Museum in Philadelphia; David McKnight of the restored frigate HMS *Trincomalee*; Dr. Gerry Prokopowicz of East Carolina University; Dr. Richard Unger and Dr. Adam Jones of the University of British Columbia; Dr. Paula Rahn Phillips of the University of Minnesota; Bruce Vancil, Chris Butler, Gerard Mittelstaedt, Tracy Justus, Peter Kasin, Andy Bradshaw, Thom Rolston, the late Glenn Kaiser, Del Sprague, Frank Fiederlein, Jagoda Salzman, and Hans and Lorraine Westermark.

All these people have contributed in ways too numerous to name: any errors or omissions in my work are not theirs but my own.

I would like to thank those patient men and women of the sea who have patiently pointed me along the way, in particular Richard Worthington, the late Stan Hugill, Captain Eric Rice, Captain Andrzej Drapella, the late Captain David Hiott; and finally a great sea cook and wonderful shipmate, Andrzej "Arni" Przybek.

Simon Spalding
New Bern, North Carolina, March 2014

Introduction

This is a book like no other. It is a history of food at sea: the food that sailors, passengers, and others have consumed, stored, and prepared while they were on the water.

This book is not like any other book on culinary history. The history of food at sea is the history of mankind and the sea. Much of this book concerns changing designs of ships and boats, and the ways those changes in design made for different eating habits aboard those ships. Readers who buy books on culinary history for their recipes will surely enjoy some of the recipes included here, but they will probably choose not to try others. The author is not a culinary writer by trade, but a scholar/sailor who has worked, cooked, and eaten on schooners, a sloop, a brig, and a barque, in sheltered waters and on the Baltic Sea and Atlantic Ocean.

This book is not like any other book on maritime or naval history. Few books that discuss the cruiser *Olympia* are more concerned with her ice maker than her guns, and few books on nineteenth-century sailing ships say more about the shapes of their pantry shelves than the cut of their sails. Focusing on food tells a different story of human seafaring than a more general study of the subject.

Telling the story of food on ships requires the telling of the story of the ships themselves. Changes in the ships have brought about changes in how people ate at sea. The evolution of the warship from an oar-driven ram into a sailing gun platform changed the fundamental nature of naval warfare, creating new eating habits for fighting men at sea. Changing passenger travel from sail to steam changed how those passengers ate, especially the immigrants purchasing the least expensive fares.

Subtle changes in shipboard design and procedure have changed the way seafarers have eaten. Nineteenth-century sailor Charles Abbey shipped in clipper ships with stunsails, and had very little time for anything but work and sleep. Shipping in the clipper *Intrepid* without stunsails, Abbey found time to catch fresh fish and eat them. The development of the propeller, the triple-expansion engine, and the steam turbine shortened the time it took to cross the Atlantic by steamship, which in turn changed the transatlantic experiences of all classes of passengers.

Seafaring has changed the way people ate ashore. When the Vikings colonized Iceland, they found the perfect combination of a low-fat fish, cold temperature, and constant wind that created stockfish, the Friday meal for most of medieval Europe. The development of refrigeration ships made New Zealand lamb a worldwide staple. The *biscotti* that modern coffee drinkers dunk in their morning beverage take their name and heritage from the iron ration of thirteenth-century galley rowers. British passengers to other countries were introduced to Indian cuisine by steamship cooks from Goa, and those dishes became part of the British culinary tradition.

The marine environment has shaped the diet and the implements used to eat at sea. The tables on eighteenth-century warships were unlike contemporary tables ashore. The design of nineteenth-century merchant sailor knives made them a workable substitute for a fork. The pantry shelves of sailing ships used special designs to reduce breakage in heavy seas. Steamers making passages through the Red Sea and Indian Ocean adapted the Indian *punkah* to their dining saloons. Polish ships favor coffee mugs without handles, to reduce breakage and save space.

We will read the words of sea travelers of many eras. Some are familiar names, such as John Smith, Charles Dickens, Herman Melville, and Mark Twain. Others are less famous, but have important tales to tell: eighteenth-century sailor Jacob Nagle, nineteenth-century sailor Frederick Pease Harlow, architect Arthur Davis, and a sampling of poets and songwrights from the fifteenth century to the present.

The story of food at sea is full of surprises. Dutch Navy crewmen of the eighteenth century used a fish sauce that was suggested by a French royal cook four centuries earlier, and endorsed by John Smith in 1627. Columbus sailed without a cook: Iberian ships did not employ sea cooks well into the seventeenth century, while Northern Europeans had done so for 600 years or more. The twentieth-century sailing *proas* of Puluwat Atoll use a cooking stove virtually identical to those used by Columbus and Magellan—made from military equipment left by the Japanese in World War II.

For these and many more tales of food at sea, read on.

ONE

The Ancient and Medieval Worlds

They that go down to the sea in ships,
That do business in great waters,
These see the works of the Lord,
And his wonders in the deep.

—The Bible, King James Version, Psalm 107: 23–24

Mankind has ventured out on open water for millennia. In many prehistoric cases the exact form of the vessels used may be unknown, but the transport of human beings, human artifacts, and plant and animal species over water is indisputable. The settlement of islands thousands of years ago stands as living proof of mankind's early maritime adventures.

In examining the food early mariners consumed at sea, it is useful to consider three different methods by which mariners in small, relatively open craft have sustained themselves during their journeys.

- Early mariners may have brought food along on their journey that resisted spoilage and required no cooking prior to consumption.
- They may have gone ashore during the voyage to prepare food carried aboard, possibly supplemented by food acquired ashore. This usually required mariners to bring some equipment for cooking with them, and

possibly firewood as well. The cooking fire was made ashore rather than on the vessel.

• It is also possible that they cooked aboard their vessel. This required permanent or temporary structures to contain a cooking fire where food was cooked or heated.

Case One: Voyaging Without Cooking

The first case was common in the past, and remains common throughout the world today. The voyaging canoes used to settle the inhabited islands of the Pacific, mostly double canoes with dugout hulls and a platform connecting them, offered limited facilities for cooking. The ancestors of modern Pacific islanders, lacking metal to make a firebox, probably brought food with them that required little or no preparation. Scottish small-boat fishermen brought their "piece" with them; a sandwich, pasty, bannock or scone that could be eaten when out on the water. Small boat sailors still do this, taking a snack and some drinking water on even a short outing on the water. A day sail today is usually accompanied by a cooler of picnic-style food and a supply of drinking water or other beverage.

The stage of maritime cuisine in which there is no cooking during the voyage should not be considered in any way primitive. Islands have been settled and goods transported by people who traveled hundreds of miles over open water without cooking on their journeys. In the case of the peoples of the Pacific, the voyagers brought plant and animal species with them, to guarantee a food supply in their new homes. In the Arctic, similar migrations of people, also bringing animal species with them, used hide-covered *umiaks* in which it would have been virtually impossible to cook. The more developed the mariners' techniques of preserving and storing food, the less necessary it is to gather and/or cook food during the journey.

Case Two: Going Ashore to Cook

The second case, in which the voyagers bring cooking implements and materials with them, going ashore on distant shores en route to cook their food, has occurred at many times and in many places. Fire is a great danger on board any kind of ship, and the danger is particularly acute when the vessel is small and combustible. Many early voyagers needed to make stops in their longer voyages to supplement their supply of drinking water. It must have occurred to early mariners, in different parts of the world, that when they went ashore with containers for drinking water, they could just as easily bring food and a pot with them, and cook food on the beach. Lacking a pot, fish caught at sea and/or game caught ashore could be roasted on improvised spits.

Case Three: Cooking On Board

The third stage of food preparation, of cooking food on board the vessel, requires cooking equipment which can be used while the vessel is under way or at anchor. The fire must be sufficiently insulated from the deck and hull as not to set them on fire. In parts of the world where wood is scarce, firewood or other fuel must be carried on board. In some cases the design of the vessel itself may need to take on-board food preparation into account. This stage appears to have occurred at different times in different places. Evidence suggests that on-board food preparation may have developed earlier in the Mediterranean than it did in northern Europe.

Mesolithic Maritime Trade

There is strong evidence for Mesolithic trade in stone tools, and probably more perishable commodities as well. It was in this period that the Isle of Man was colonized by people from Ireland using the Tardenoisian stone tool culture. There is also the intriguing find of a stone "trancher" axe or pick of the Maglemosian culture found in a trawl in the southern North Sea, suggesting that it may have been lost from a dugout canoe. Dugout boats of the Maglemosian people have been found in Danish peat bogs, and it is possible that this tool was lost at sea.[1] Mesolithic polished stone axes from northeastern Ireland have been found in western Scotland and in several places in southern England, and there are five asymmetrical cutting-edge stone tools (possibly adze blades) from Wales found in Cornwall, one of them found in a dugout canoe.[2] It is probably safe to say that if these Mesolithic mariners brought food with them in their dugout canoes, they ate it cold.

"Neolithic Argonauts"

The section title originates from E. G. Bowen's *Britain and the Western Seaways*, and it is illustrative of the evident expansion of travel and trade over water in the New Stone Age. This is the era of megalithic constructions such as the giant stone sarsens and lintels of Stonehenge (an elaboration of a Mesolithic wood and smaller-stone site), the Avebury stones, menhirs in

Brittany, and stone circles in Scotland. The distribution of megalithic gallery graves and passage graves strongly suggests maritime movement between the coastal peoples of northern and western Europe.[3] What is particularly intriguing is the distribution of megalithic passage graves, suggesting affinities, migration, or regular trade between such far-flung and mostly coastal areas as the southern and western coasts of Iberia, the Biscay coast, and St. Malo area of France, three areas in Ireland, coastal North Wales, the Isle of Man, the Moray Firth of Scotland, all of Denmark and adjacent areas in what is now Germany, and the southwest coast of Sweden.[4]

What sort of boats the "Neolithic Argonauts" of northern Europe used, is open to speculation. It is likely that their craft were still paddled and not rowed or sailed; but it is possible that like the *umiak* of the Inuit people, they had begun to improve the size and seaworthiness of their craft by stretching hides over a frame. Some surviving dugouts from this era are larger and more complex than a simple hollowed-out log, with shaping of the logs after thinning them, and additional planks sewn on to create a larger hull.[5]

In the Pacific, the dugout canoe lasted longer, and evolved to a higher complexity. The dugout hull was connected with either a second hull or an outrigger, and a platform built on the booms that connect them. Double-hull and outrigger canoes have been fitted with sails of pandanus matting for centuries. In Europe the dugout canoe was replaced by hide-covered craft and by wooden hulls stitched or pegged together.

Through the Neolithic period, it is likely that mariners brought food with them that required no preparation.

The Bronze and Iron Ages in Northern Europe

The distribution of different types of bronze axes and other types of tools indicates even greater maritime activity in northern and western Europe. Rock carvings of boats in Scandinavia are open to interpretation, but may portray paddled vessels similar to umiaks. The Hjortspring boat, found in the Danish island of Als and dating to circa 200 B.C., is constructed of wood in a manner that suggests it was modeled on a hide-covered boat. It was over forty-three feet long, six feet wide, and was probably paddled.[6] A bronze razor from Honum in Denmark shows a boat with what might be a mast and sail, though it could be a leafy branch held up to catch the wind from astern.[7]

During the Bronze Age, there is evidence for expanded maritime activity in northern Europe. Irish curraghs, probably rowed and possibly sailed, carried Irish gold and bronze artifacts across the Irish Sea and possibly much further.[8] The first-century B.C. Irish gold model boat known as the "Broighter Boat" may represent a seagoing curragh with a mast and yard, thwarts, fourteen oars, and a steering oar.[9]

Meanwhile in the South

Pictures of boats found in Nubia and Egypt are believed to be over 6,000 years old. These pictures are challenging to interpret, but are believed by many to represent boats made of papyrus bundles, propelled by paddles. By the period 3400–3000 B.C. there is evidence of boats of wood in addition to those of papyrus. Some of these have bipod masts stepped well forward, supporting a single square sail. The earliest Egyptian vessels of wood employed an extraordinary method of construction: short planks were fastened edge-to-edge with hour-glass-shaped wedges and pegs. This was probably a way of using local wood, which was from relatively small acacia and sycamore trees. Later on, the Egyptians imported wood in longer billets from what is now Syria and Lebanon.[10] It has been suggested that pegged-and-wedged wooden vessels of this type were built on the Nile, then dismantled, transported in pieces overland, and reassembled and launched in the Red Sea, perhaps sailing on to the Arabian Sea.

Oars are an important evolutionary step forward from paddles, as the use of a fulcrum on the gunwale of the boat allows more efficient transfer of energy to the water. Oars and sails appear on Egyptian bas-reliefs of their boats in the period 3400–3000 B.C.[11]

By the Dynastic Period in Egyptian history (from ca. 3100 B.C.) the Egyptians were building sailing vessels, and were trading with other Mediterranean and Asian peoples. There are models of Nile boats from this period, some boats from near the pyramid of Sesostris III known as the Dahshur boats, and a magnificent 43.4-meter boat (about 142 feet), built of long planks of Lebanese cedar, found buried disassembled south of the pyramid of Cheops, known as the "Cheops Boat."[12]

Meanwhile, in the Aegean there appears to have been cultural interaction between Crete and the Greek mainland as far back as 3400 B.C. Pictures and models have been found dating back as far as 2800 B.C., which may represent a shaped dugout with sides stitched on.[13] Around 3300 B.C. the Dorians arrived in Greece in narrow rowed galleys, with iron weapons and tools. Around 1400 B.C. Crete was invaded from the mainland, and the survivors fled to Cyprus and other parts of the eastern Mediterranean. From at least this point on there is a thriving Cypriot maritime culture, represented by shipwrecks as well as other evidence.[14]

Cooking Ashore in Homer's Odyssey

Homer's *Odyssey* suggests that during the age when this oral epic was written down, Greek vessels routinely stopped at islands to replenish their water supplies and to prepare food, probably by cooking it on the beach. In Book Ten, when Odysseus's ship was blown back to Aeolus's island a second time, the crew went ashore and brought back water. They ate a quick meal "beside the ships." After all of them had something to eat and drink, Odysseus set off for Aeolus's palace.[15] While he does not specifically say the quick meal was cooked, this seems logical, as they went ashore to eat it. It would appear that in Homer's day, ships regularly made landfall to replenish their drinking water, cook, and eat.

The Phoenicians

From circa 1500 to 70 B.C., a mercantile empire based in what is today the coast of Lebanon thrived in Mediterranean trade. Lebanese cedar and other commodities were carried in Phoenician merchant ships, which were protected by fleets of fighting galleys. Little is known of the food on these ships, but it probably resembled that aboard Cypriot vessels of the same era.[16] An early Phoenician shipwreck, a Late Bronze Age vessel that sank around 1200 B.C. near Cape Gelidonya, Turkey, yielded a variety of personal items in the stern. These included a Canaanite terracotta oil lamp, a merchant's seal, measuring weights, a knucklebone, and olive pits, evidently spat into the bilge by the crew.[17]

Carthage, a Phoenician satellite colony on the northern coastline of Africa, continued to be a thriving competitor to the Romans, until destroyed by them.

Shipwrecks in the Aegean

From circa 1300 B.C. on, there are additional shipwrecks to study from the Aegean and Mediterranean seas, and these offer some clues of what sort of food might have been eaten, and how and where prepared, on these voyages. The basic Mediterranean diet in that era was based on wheat, barley, olive oil, cheese, and wine. These foods, supplemented with fresh fish caught at sea and possibly fresh game killed ashore, are the likely staples of shipboard food in the ancient Mediterranean and Aegean.

The Uluburun shipwreck, found off the southwestern coast of Turkey, appears to have been carrying treasure or tribute, as its cargo includes luxury goods from such diverse origins as Sicily, Egypt, and the Baltic. Dendro-chronology and the presence of Egyptian scarabs in the cargo suggest a date sometime after 1305 B.C. It is believed that the Uluburun ship left a Cypriot or Phoenician port, possibly headed for a Mycenaean palace in mainland Greece. The vessel was between 15 and 16 meters (49–53 feet) long, con-structed of Lebanese cedar in a shell with reinforcing lateral frames added later, and probably carried a sail.[18]

The cargo included copper and tin ingots; jars containing glass beads, olives, Pistacia resin, and glass beads; glass ingots, precious stones, Baltic am-ber, a gold scarab, blackwood (ebony), elephant ivory, hippopotamus teeth, ostrich eggshells, Cypriot pottery and oil lamps, a trumpet, assorted weapons, pan balance weights, assorted foodstuffs and much more. The food materials included almonds, pine nuts, figs, olives, grapes, safflower, black cumin, su-mac, coriander, whole pomegranates, and a few grains of charred wheat and barley. The cereal grains at least are likely to have been food intended for consumption on the trip, while the more luxurious food items and spices are more likely to have been part of the valuable cargo.[19]

A sixth-century B.C. shipwreck of a laced-together Hellenic vessel off the coast of Pabuç Burnu, Turkey, yielded grape and olive pits that were probably cargo, but also some ceramic bowls, cups, and pitchers which were probably used for food by the vessel's crew.[20]

A later shipwreck is the fifth-century B.C. wreck known by its find-place, an Israeli coastal kibbutz, as the Ma'agan Michael ship. The wreck was excavated and conserved by the University of Haifa. This vessel, of Cypriot origin, was about thirty-seven feet long, built with Cypriot copper nails, and carried an elegant single-fluke anchor. Among the many ceramic items recovered from the wreck are a water jar, a ceramic cooking pot, and remnants of food, including grape, fig, olive, and barley. The food items are believed to have originated in southwestern Turkey; while they may have been cargo, there is a strong possibility that some of the food, and possibly the water jug and ceramic cooking pot, were for the use of the crew during the voyage.[21]

Another shipwreck of this era was found near Chios, in the Aegean Sea near the Turkish coast, and is believed to date to around 350 B.C. Chios has been the site of naval battles, massacres, and other dramatic events spanning several millennia. This particular shipwreck is interesting in that the vessel sank with a cargo of wine and flavored olive oil. The olive oil was in large amphorae, and thus was more likely to have been cargo than crew food; but the oil, originating in Cyprus and containing oregano, might have been something that Cypriot mariners of this era ate at sea. It has been suggested that the oregano may not only have imparted flavor to the oil, but helped it keep longer as well.[22]

One of the most famous early shipwrecks is the "Kyrenia Ship," also Cypriot, a sailing vessel about forty-seven feet long. This vessel appears to have sunk around 300 B.C., when the vessel had enjoyed a service life of about eighty years. The Kyrenia cargo included over 400 amphorae of wine, evidently from Rhodes, Samos, and elsewhere, 29 millstones and about 9,000 almonds. The crew probably fished for at least some of their food, as about 300 fishing weights were found in her bow. There are cooking implements, consisting of a bronze cauldron and a "large casserole pot." Apparently these were used in cooking crew food ashore, in the manner suggested by Homer's *Odyssey*. There are also eating implements: four wooden spoons, four oil jugs, four salt dishes, and four drinking cups. It would appear that the crew numbered four on her final voyage, and that each had a spoon, oil jug, salt dish, and drinking cup.[23]

The Kyrenia ship was excavated in the 1960s and is displayed in Kyrenia, Cyprus. Several replicas have been constructed, and the Kyrenia ship is shown on Cypriot coins. She is probably one of the best known of ancient ships.

The evidence up to this time in the Mediterranean and Aegean seas suggests food prepared ashore, at least for vessels under sixty feet long. There are indications that the Romans may have built cooking galleys into some of their small vessels, for example "Chretienne C," a small merchantman fifteen to sixteen meters (49 to 53 feet) long from the second century B.C., which apparently had a tile-roofed galley in the bow.[24] This is support for the idea that constructions for preparing food on board date back to at least this date.

The Romans built sailing cargo-carrying vessels much larger than these, and it seems likely that they built on-board cooking facilities on their large vessels. Enormous sailing ships were built to carry grain from North Africa, Egypt, and Asia Minor to Imperial Rome; these are believed to have ranged in size from 340 to 400 tons by around A.D. 200. These ships carried the grain that allowed Rome to issue a *dolus* (origin of the English expression "the dole") or distribution of free bread to 200,000 male citizens of Rome, many of whom were probably the sons of out-of-work small farmers.[25] The big grain ships would have had plenty of space for cooking facilities. In the absence of more Roman archaeological evidence, the question of on-board cooking arrangements for Roman ships remains an intriguing mystery.[26]

At the time of writing, the Roman shipwreck found in the mud of Varazze, an Italian fishing village near Genoa, is still an intriguing mystery. The wreck includes amphorae full of food articles, still sealed with their pine-and-pitch caps intact. Chances are that these are cargo rather than food for the crew, but it will be interesting to see what else comes to light as this wreck is investigated.[27]

The Yassi Ada Shipwreck: A Conclusive Ship's Galley

Conclusive evidence of a ship's galley comes from a vessel of the Byzantine period. This vessel was found near an older fourth-century shipwreck off the island of Yassi Ada in the southeastern Aegean, near the Turkish coast. Coins found in the wreck indicate that her last voyage occurred around 625 or A.D. 626. The vessel was built in the planks-first method of older shipwrecks in the region, with an unusually fine bow and a rather sleek beam-to-length ratio of 1:4. She was about twenty-and-a-half meters (67 feet) long, and is estimated to have been about sixty tons burden.

For Byzantine vessels of this era, there is more documentary evidence available than is the case for earlier maritime activity. The seventh-century or slightly later Rhodian Sea Law laid down guidelines for different crew members and their pay. These included a *naukleros*, shipowner or captain, who received two shares of the profit. Next came the *kybernetes*, or helmsman; the *proreus*, or "prow-man" (perhaps a lookout, fisherman, or anchor handler), the *naupegos* or ship's carpenter; and the *karabites*, or boatswain. Each of these received a share-and-a-half. The *nautai*, or seamen, each received a single share. Last, and indeed least in terms of pay, was the *paraskharites*, the keeper of the hearth or grill, who received but half a share of the profit. Some scholars have questioned whether the *paraskharites* was indeed a cook, but it seems logical, especially in the case of a vessel such as the Yassi Ada vessel, which had an on-board galley.[28]

Several of these ranks are mentioned in literature earlier than A.D. 600. Some ranks specific to oared galleys, such as the *keleustes*, who was responsible for commanding the strokes of the galley oarsmen; and the *epibatai*, marines or warriers; *toicharchoi* or side-chiefs who were probably the stroke oarsmen on both sides; and *auletes* or *trieraules*, who played the *aulos* or other musical instrument to synchronize the oar strokes.[29]

The galley of the Yassi Ada vessel had an ingenious and intricate construction, which suggests that it may have been the product of a long evolution. The galley occupies a space in the stern, surmounted by a little deckhouse from which the smoke could exit the hold. The galley occupied a deck area just three by one-and-a-half meters (10 by 5 feet). The cooking facility was a wooden platform covered with about twenty-five hearth tiles twenty-three to twenty-four centimeters square. The tiles were found in association with iron bars that may have formed a grill to hold the cooking pots off the fire, or could have served to hold cauldrons in place. The hearth tiles, like the ceramic pantiles that covered the deckhouse, are mismatched, and appear to be scrounged from a variety of sources. A charming detail of one hearth tile is a partial footprint of a human infant. The hearth is estimated to have been one by three-quarters of a meter, big enough for two large cauldrons found in the wreck.[30]

This vessel probably carried passengers, as more than twenty cooking pots, some blackened by fire, were found near the galley tiles.[31] The likelihood of this vessel carrying passengers as well as cargo would explain why a significant part of the vessel was dedicated to on-board food preparation.

Sailing Curraghs

When the Vikings arrived in the Faeroe Islands late in the eighth century, there were Irish clerics already there, who had introduced sheep to the islands.[32] Something similar occurred in the Shetlands and in Iceland. The Irish presence lingers in these locations in place names that include "pap" or "papar," the Norse name for Irish monks. According to the legends of St. Brendan, the Irish settlement of these and other far-flung islands was accomplished in sailing curraghs, hide-covered boats that were rowed and sailed. The 1976–1977 voyage of Tim Severin and his companions in the sailing curragh *Brendan II* drew attention to the possibilities of colonizing voyages by Irish clerics. What food the Irish curraghmen of this remote age ate remains a mystery, but is likely to have included grain and probably some dairy products as well. It is very unlikely that any cooking was done on hide boats, but there is the possibility of these Irish clerics going ashore to cook.

The Viking Age

The Vikings, raiders and traders who came swooping out of Scandinavia in the early Middle Ages, are known by several ship burials, as well as other ship finds. The Nydam and Kvalsund boats, both slender clinker-built (where the edges of the planking overlap) rowing vessels of the fourth and seventh centuries, represent the evolution of the Viking longship.[33] The Oseberg ship, a magnificently decorated ninth-century vessel probably intended for relatively sheltered waters, was the sarcophagus of a wealthy woman, and is filled with rich grave goods intended for the afterlife of the deceased. Among these is a folding iron tripod and riveted iron cauldron.[34] A more seaworthy burial ship is the tenth-century Gokstad ship, the vessel most people imagine when they visualize a "Viking Ship." A replica of the Gokstad ship, built in 1893, sailed the Atlantic in twenty-eight days.[35]

The Oseberg and Gokstad ships are the best-known Viking vessels, but there are others. Later Viking vessels show a greater degree of specialization, with sleek narrow longships that carried sail but were designed primarily for fighting under oars; and, pictured and described though rarely found, deeper and beamier craft, called *knarr* or *knorr*, for carrying cargoes long distances under sail.[36]

Matsveina: A Viking Sea Cook

This Norse term, usually translated as "journeyman cook" is a term that appears in the eleventh century. Eyrbyggerne's saga stated that the men would draw lots to see who was to prepare food for the ship: "in those days it was not the custom for traders to have journeyman cooks, but those who ate together cast lots every single day as to which of them should prepare food." Later in the same century, the job was given to one specific man, who earned wages for this work. By that time, many vessels towed an "afterboat" or tender astern, and the *matsveina*, possibly joined by a few assistants, could row ashore in the tender, taking a cooking pot, perhaps a tripod, and empty water casks. If the shore was not wooded and there was no driftwood available, they would have needed to bring firewood as well. Food could have been cooked on the beach while some of the shore party searched for fresh water to refill the water casks. Norwegian legal regulations specify three trips ashore per day for the cook: one to collect water, and two to prepare meals.[37]

On the ships, it was customary to keep a lidded water trough, from which the crew could take water, a normal consumption of at least four liters per man per day. Casks were used to bring the water on board, and it has been suggested that for longships and early Viking vessels, these needed to be relatively small to fit in the available shipboard spaces. Royal ships sometimes carried beer, but water was the normal beverage on most Viking-age vessels.[38]

It would appear that the normal procedure for Scandinavian trading/raiding vessels of the Viking era was, like Odysseus and probably the crew of the Kyrenia and other early Aegean and Mediterranean vessels, to make regular stops on islands or coasts, replenishing water supplies and cooking food on the beach. Collecting and carrying firewood would have been more essential in the north than in southern Europe, as wood was scarcer on northern beaches. When raiding or trading within the British Isles, there were plenty of islands in the Shetlands, Orkneys, Hebrides, and elsewhere where the Vikings could anchor, haul up on the beach and/or send an "after-boat" ashore to collect fresh water and cook hot food.

That firewood was used is made clear in the Greenland Saga. When Bjarni Herjolfsson and his crew were blown off course on their way to Greenland in 985 or 986, they found a coast "covered with small wooden knolls," and later a country "level and well wooded." These were probably places in North America. Bjarni's crew, wanting to go ashore, "claimed they were short of wood and water." He insisted they wanted for neither, and refused to go ashore. The fact that his crew wanted to go ashore for firewood as well as water indicates that they planned to do some cooking; if not on board, then perhaps at the next landfall.[39]

Foods

Food eaten on Viking voyages was called *nest*, *farnest* (voyage-food), or *hafnest* (sea-food, i.e., food eaten at sea). This was cooked in a riveted pot, like the one found with a tripod aboard the Oseberg ship burial. According to Magnus Erlingsson's saga this included porridge, flour, and butter. Sometimes dried slices of fatty halibut, dried cod (probably *skreidh* or *hardhfiskur*, different versions of stockfish, air-dried cod), and bread were carried as well. The crew was to receive a ration of barley meal and butter, equivalent to 880 grams of meal and 285 grams of butter.[40]

Long-Distance Voyaging

There remains the question of what Scandinavians did when sailing to and from Iceland, Greenland, and North America, where there are few small islands to visit on the way. For the vessels used for these voyages, there are fewer examples of actual ships to study. Skuldelev 1, one of five vessels deliberately sunk to form a barrier in Roskildefjord, Denmark, in the eleventh century, is the only surviving example of a deep-draft seagoing Viking-age Scandinavian sailing vessel. Skuldelev 1 shows no evidence of a galley. Vessels on these long voyages must have carried greater water capacity than longships and coasting traders; whether larger water casks or a greater number of small ones.

The Viking Ship Museum in Roskilde, Denmark, hosts not only the five eleventh-century vessels recovered from the fjord, but an active program of building replicas of these vessels and others from the Viking era. In an intriguing piece of experimental archaeology, Anton Engbert and other crew members of *Bialy Kon* (White Horse), a reconstruction of the tenth-century Slavic vessel Ralswiek 2, placed a large cauldron, like the one found aboard the Oseberg ship burial, on the ballast stones, then lit a fire inside the cauldron, and cooked food in a smaller cauldron set inside the large one. Using this method, the crew succeeded in cooking their food without burning themselves or their vessel.[41] This technique can be used only in relative calm, and there is no direct evidence that it was in use in historical times. However the fact that it can be done, in a vessel and with a cooking pot of Viking-era design, suggests that it might have been tried, when there were no islands available on which to go ashore and cook a meal on the beach.

If the cauldron-as-firebox-set-on-ballast-stones method of the *Bialy Kon* crew was used on the long trips to Iceland, Greenland, and North America, it would explain why Bjarni Herjolfsson's crew wanted to collect firewood on the mysterious shore they sighted.

The Lateen Sail

Meanwhile in the Mediterranean, a new sail design evolved. In the Roman era some vessels, mostly smaller ones, were equipped with fore-and-aft sails of "spritsail" or triangular type.[42] Yassi Ada I, the fourth-century vessel found near the Byzantine vessel with a galley, is probably the earliest wreck that evidences lateen rig. After the fall of the Western Roman Empire, the square sail was gradually replaced in these waters by the triangular lateen sail. The lateen sail allowed sailing vessels of all types to sail closer to the wind, that is to make more headway into the wind. This trait, though at the expense of performance before the wind, made the lateen sail the preferred design in Mediterranean and Arabian waters for several hundred years.[43]

Arabian Dhows

Among the craft built with lateen sails is the dhow of Arabia. Arabian dhows and other craft have carried cargos in the Persian Gulf and the Indian Ocean for centuries. Using foods similar to those in use in the ancient Mediterranean, and using navigation techniques that incorporated elements of astronomy, Arabian seafarers may have ventured as far as the coast of China. A voyage of this nature was made in 1980–1981 by Tim Severin. In the *Sohar*, a recreated ninth-century dhow built in Oman, Severin and his crew sailed to India and then to Canton, China.

Polynesian and Micronesian Voyagers

The settlement of the islands of Polynesia and Micronesia ranks as one of the most outstanding accomplishments of early mariners. Excavations in the Ha'atuatua Valley of Mika Hiva in the Marquesas Islands offer a detailed picture of life of early Polynesian settlers there, who arrived some time between 130 B.C. and A.D. 370. It is evident that these pioneers brought the pig, the dog, and (perhaps inadvertently) the rat with them. It is possible that they brought the jungle cock, valued for its bright feathers, as these were present in Mika Hiva by A.D. 1100. Coconuts, taro, yams, and breadfruit were evidently brought with them as well, as the Ha'atuatua Valley artifacts include tools to process these. Fishbones and the shells of edible shellfish litter the site, along with mother-of-pearl fishhooks and red, unpainted pottery. Some of these foods may have been eaten on the journey, and in any case all of them were cargo for the early Polynesian settlers of the Marquesas.[44]

Certain island people have continued to make long interisland trips in traditional sailing outrigger canoes, and it is interesting to study the list of materials taken on board. On Puluwat Atoll, Caroline Islands, in the 1960s and until the present, these include an open iron box (usually scavenged from wrecked Japanese World War II equipment) for cooking fish caught at sea. This is filled with sand on shorter trips, or left empty on longer ones. Dried coconut husks are carried for cooking fuel. Fishlines and hooks are carried, both for trolling and for use as handlines. A large bottle or glass float is filled with emergency drinking water. The foods carried on voyages are familiar foods ashore: fresh taro and fresh breadfruit pounded and packed in big breadfruit leaves the morning of departure; preserved breadfruit (for a long trip); ripe, unopened coconuts to eat; and younger green coconuts primarily to drink.[45] When sailing to Pikelot, the voyagers bring three-to-six live turtles back home with them. Fish is considered the property of the crew that caught it, but in Puluwat the turtle meat is regarded as community property, divided by the traditional senior chief among all the households and any visitors on the island.[46]

The sheet metal box to cook fish is a remarkable piece of gear, one that would have been instantly familiar to the crews that accompanied Magellan and Columbus, who also cooked in metal fireboxes filled with sand. Of course the metal is a postcontact material, which poses the question of how, or if, pre-contact Pacific Islanders might have cooked the fish they caught. It is possible that pre-contact voyaging canoes did have provision for cooking fires, even before sheet metal was available. A seventeenth-century European drawing of a large double canoe off the Tuamotu Islands (in present-day French Polynesia) clearly shows a cooking fire on the forward end of the platform.[47] If this picture is accurate, it suggests that Polynesians sometimes cooked food on large double canoes.

Javanese Mariners

A carved frieze on a ninth-century A.D. Buddhist temple in Borobodur, Java, shows what appears to be an enormous canoe or vessel with an outrigger. A vessel this size certainly carried a substantial food supply, and could have carried equipment for cooking on board. This would certainly be a fruitful field for some scholar to research.[48]

The Catalan-Aragonese Fleet in the War of the Sicilian Vespers

Galleys, narrow fast rowed vessels designed to ram and board their opponents, continued to dominate naval warfare in the medieval Mediterranean, as they had since Classical Antiquity. Between 1282 and 1293, fleets of Catalan-Aragonese galleys battled Charles of Anjou's galleys over control of Sicily and nearby strategic areas, in the War of the Sicilian Vespers. The records of the Catalan-Aragonese fleet were meticulous, and many of them survived, offering a detailed picture of medieval galley warfare.

The galleys themselves were much like Classical Roman galleys: long, low, and lean. They had a ram in the bow; and in this era, a pair of steering oars rather than a single stern rudder. The stern rudder was a Northern invention whose adoption in the Mediterranean was gradual. The shape of the sail, lateen now rather than square, was the most obvious change from the galleys of a millennium before. A more subtle change is that most of the soldiers aboard were now crossbowmen. In this period, service at the galley oars was a form of military service performed by free men; the practice of enslaving captured enemies to row galleys came later, in the sixteenth century. The typical Catalan-Aragonese galleys had 116 oars, and a crew of 150.[49]

The Catalan-Aragonese fleet kept detailed records of food aboard their galleys in this campaign. The food issues are fairly typical of those in other Mediterranean fleets of the thirteenth century. The food issue to crewmen was divided into three parts:

1. Potu: drink.
2. Panatica: Biscuit.
3. Companagius: cheese, meat, *salsa*.[50]

The drink was red or white wine, varying a great deal in its alcohol content and source. It appears that the Catalan and Sicilian galley crews were more temperate than their Angevin counterparts. During this campaign, the Catalan-Aragonese crews received a wine ration between 0.3 and 0.4 liters of wine a day, while their adversaries were issued over two liters of wine a day.[51]

The biscuits deserve some special mention, as they were a staple of shipboard food in this era, and for centuries to come. Known as *biscotti* because they were baked twice, they were a concentrated hard bread that would keep a long time at sea. The delicious mildly sweet *biscotti* modern Italians dip in coffee, as well as military hard tack, pilot crackers, and various forms of dry hard bread, are all descended from the *biscotti* of the Medieval Mediterranean. Biscuit (as *biscotti* came to be called in French and English) is described as "a very light bread for transport because it is baked twice and lasts longer than others and does not spoil." The *biscotti* were kept in cloth bags that were "painted," perhaps a waterproofing to make the bags something like oilcloth, with special ties called *guarniti*.[52]

The remaining issue probably varied from day to day, as it did on the "meat days," "fish days," and "cheese days" in Spanish service three centuries later. A fourteenth-century *Consolat del Mar* specifies a system in which the men received meat on Sunday, Tuesday, and Thursday; on the other days they received *companatge*, defined as "cheese, or onion, or sardines or other fish."[53] Another system of alternation specified that on some days, half the crew received meat, the other only meat broth: on Sunday everybody receiving meat. Fish are hardly mentioned in the Sicilian Vespers accounts, so it may be that fresh fish were caught, or dried, or purchased. In some cases, the men received meat in their *salsa* on Fridays and Saturdays.[54]

The cheese was probably something like *pecorino sardo*, an uncooked hard cheese made from fresh whole sheep's milk, curdled with lamb or kid rennet, lightly smoked, and then kept in cool cellars to ripen, and baked to produce a rind.[55]

The *salsa* deserves special mention as well. This was nothing like the fresh tomato-based *salsa picante* that is a feature of Mexican and other Latin American cuisines today. The *salsa* served aboard thirteenth-century galleys was more of a stew, combining fava beans (also known as horse beans or broad beans), chickpeas, olive oil, garlic, onions, salt, and spice (possibly ginger, or perhaps whatever was available). On some days, it also included a small (about ten grams per man) issue of salt meat, which probably obviated the salt.[56] The *salsa* is interesting as well because the fava beans were cooked together with the other ingredients, something which appears not to have been the practice in thirteenth-century Spain ashore.[57] In the extremely crowded conditions aboard fighting galleys of that time, cooking was probably performed in a single pot over a single fire, which caused the beans, inedible without cooking, to be combined with the other ingredients of the *salsa*.

Salt meat was a staple of the galley crews, probably beef or pork soaked in brine. On days when they did not receive meat, some galley crewmen were usually issued "cheese, or onion, or sardines or other fish."[58]

Rowers in the Mediterranean required prodigious amounts of water, esti-mated at eight liters a day. Water spoilage was a problem for the Christian galley fleets: there are accounts of water spoiling on trips of only sixteen days. The combination of high water consumption by rowers and water spoilage limited the range of medieval galley fleets, and was a significant factor in strategic and tactical planning. In this regard, Muslim fleets of this period had an advantage, as they still used ceramic amphorae for their water supply. The *vegetes* or water butts used by the Christians may have been lighter and less fragile, but they did not keep water fresh as long as the Muslim amphorae.[59]

It is clear that even in the extremely cramped conditions of a thirteenth-century galley, the *salsa* was cooked on board. The cooking facilities must have had capacity sufficient to cook *salsa* for 150 men at a time. Whether similar to the tiled platform of the Yassi Ada wreck six centuries earlier, or more like the sheet-iron firebox of Columbus's caravels 200 years later, the galleys of the Catalan-Aragonese fleet (and presumably the Angevin fleet as well) must have had facilities for on-board cooking. Fourteenth-century merchant galleys had dedicated brick hearths on the main deck, and it could be that a similar arrangement prevailed in the war galleys of the previous century.

The State Archives of Venice include fourteenth-century decisions and decrees of the *Consiglio dei Rogati*, many of which touch on the problems of manning and provisioning the galley fleet. Shortages of *biscotti* were chronic, with biscuits coming from as far away as Bulgaria. It has been estimated that in the Venetian campaign in the Bosporus in the 1350s, something like 56 percent of the cost of the entire campaign was spent on provisions.[60] This no doubt contributed to the decline of the rowing galley following the inflation of food prices in Europe during the second half of the sixteenth century.

Developments in Sailing Ship Design

While rowing galleys remained little changed from their early medieval form, European sailing ships continued to evolve. In the Mediterranean, ships were built by "carvel" construction, with a keel, stem- and sternposts, then frames or "ribs": the planking was then laid on edge to edge. In northern Europe, square sails predominated along with clinker construction, in which the planks were overlapped, and ribs added afterward. The stern rudder replaced steering oars in northern Europe from circa 1200, gaining acceptance more slowly in the Mediterranean. By this time most sailing vessels had their hulls covered by a full-length deck, with platforms added at the stern and sometimes the bow. These platforms eventually merged with the hull to become fore and after decks or "castles." By circa 1400 vessels were built with more than one mast, which often combined square and lateen sails, for better performance before or on the wind.[61]

The Hanseatic League and the Cog

Several German trading towns banded together around 1200 to form a merchant association which dominated northern European trade. The Hanseatic ports used a variety of different vessels, but most typically the cog, a vessel with straight stem- and sternposts, a deep capacious hold, fore- and after-castles on the larger and later examples, and a single mast with a square sail. Documents relating to the crews of cogs specify a cook who cooked for both watches; in one case he is the eleventh of an eleven-man crew. Excavated cogs show evidence of a cooking hearth, a narrow wooden chest filled with clay. The horizontal surface of this chest is sometimes found covered with a layer of bricks on which the fire was built, and on which ceramic or metal cooking pots were placed. Thus we see in the thirteenth and fourteenth centuries a well-established northern European tradition of a designated cook in the crew list, and a permanent cooking hearth built into vessels of middling or larger size.[62]

Icelandic Stockfish

Atlantic cod is a versatile fish for long-term storage. Because of its lack of fat, it does not spoil as quickly as other fish, which makes it an excellent candidate for air-drying. It is no surprise that once Vikings established a colony in the North Atlantic in Iceland, they developed a way to preserve cod which requires no salt, a commodity in short supply for the Icelandic settlement. Stockfish, called *skreidh* in Old Norse and Icelandic, is cod which has been cleaned and filleted; the fillets are hung outside to be dried in the wind, sun, and air. There are variations on the process, for example *hardhfiskur*, a traditional Icelandic delicacy.

The eating habits of Christian Europe made Iceland a viable supplier of food to much of Medieval Europe. Observant Christians ate no meat on Friday, usually eating fish instead. Those with local sources of fresh fish used them, but much of Europe depended on stockfish from Iceland. Both the

Hanseatic League and the English engaged in regular trade with Iceland, bringing back shiploads of stockfish for Europe's Friday meals. Stockfish, a long-lasting dry food, also became a staple of food consumed at sea by Europeans, particularly in the north.[63]

This fifteenth-century English poem, "Libelle of Englyshe Polycye" is about the Iceland trade. As the poem states, "there isn't much to say about Iceland, except concerning stockfish." "By needle and by stone" refers to a magnetic compass, its iron needle magnetized by a lodestone.

> Of Yseland to wryte is lytill need
> Save of stokfischc; yit for soothe in ded
> Out of Bristow and costis many one
> Men have practised by nedle and by stone
> Thiderwardes wythine a lytel whylle,
> Withine xij yeres, and wythoute parille,
> Gone and comen, as men were wonte of olde
> Of Scarborough, unto the costes colde.[64]

The Hundred Years War Between England and France

Provisioning records exist for both sides during this protracted conflict, which included the sea battle at Sluys in 1340. An account of French naval expenditure from 1346 includes payments to nearly fifty small victuallers who brought supplies to Calais.[65] Rouen was a major center of French naval supply, and documents from 1355 to 1385 include supplies of eating, cooking, and drinking utensils; biscuit, water or other beverage; oil, barley, candles, and dressings for wounds. The officers and crossbowmen also received beef, pork, wine, salted or dried fish, dried peas and beans, salt, onions, and garlic. Twenty-one ships from Harfleur, one from St. Valery, and thirty-two Spanish ships received one or two barrels of biscuit per ship in 1385.[66] While most of the French accounts and records concern biscuit, Jean d'Hopital's account for 1346–1347 also mentions fifty small cheeses.[67]

During the reign of Henry V of England, Southampton was built up as a center of English naval supply.[68] English ships at that time were victualed (provisioned) with bread and flour, beef, mutton, salt meat, salt and fresh fish, beer and wine. Thomas Gylle of Dartmouth, commissioned by Henry VI to make a voyage to Gascony in 1440 in the *Christopher* with a crew of ninety-three, documented the following provisions: flour, fifty-four pipes (barrels) of beer, twenty-seven beef carcasses, salt fish including ling, hake and chelyng, some extra salt, and four bushels of oatmeal.[69]

These accounts suggest some differences between French and English food preferences at sea. The English provisions include beer or wine, while the French specify wine. Onions and garlic appear in French provisions, and oatmeal in English ones.

Zheng He and the Chinese Treasure Fleets

China experienced periods of greater and lesser maritime activity, and the Chinese produced large seaworthy vessels during the Tang (A.D. 618–907) and Song (A.D. 960–1279) dynasties, which carried cargoes to and from Southeast Asia and even the Indian Ocean. The design of Chinese ships and sails made them perform better before the wind than on the wind; but as the seasonal monsoons in East Asian waters often blow in opposing directions, it was possible to plan long trips so that most of the winds would be favorable on both legs of the voyage.

During the Ming Dynasty (1368–1644), large fleets commanded by the admiral Zheng He and others sailed into the Indian Ocean, bringing back live giraffes and other cargo from the east coast of Africa. Gavin Menzies has proposed the Chinese may have gone much further afield in the 1420s, a thesis that could explain many archaeological and cartographical mysteries that defy other explanation. Whatever the scope of their exploration and discovery, the Ming Dynasty fleets are said to have developed ingenious methods of providing fresh food on long voyages, such as sprouting soybeans, and keeping ginger plants in pots. Fresh ginger is an excellent antiscorbutic, rich in vitamin C and A; it is also reputed to be effective against motion sickness. The Chinese carried fruit: pomelos (also known as shaddock) and other fruit. They are believed to have brought trained otters which worked in pairs to drive fish into nets, and to have kept frogs in tubs and other livestock in pens. Unpolished rice is rich in vitamin B1, which would help to prevent beri beri.

The Chinese have a long tradition of preserving vegetables, which would have been very helpful on long voyages. Debate continues on just how far the Ming Dynasty fleets traveled, but it is clear that fifteenth-century Chinese capacities for feeding crews on long voyages were equal to the task. From a dietary standpoint, Chinese mariners of this era were probably better prepared for long voyages without landfall than were their European counterparts.[70]

The Demise of the War Galley

During the sixteenth century, war galleys became larger and larger in the Mediterranean. Instead of one man per oar, massive oars were operated by five rowers apiece, which made life particularly miserable for the man on the inboard end of an oar. Christian (mostly Spanish, Venetian, and Genoese) and Muslim galley fleets clashed, most famously in the Battle of Lepanto in 1571, in which the Christian fleet defeated the fleet of the Ottoman Turks. In this period, it became common (though not universal) to use enslaved captives as oarsman; thus, a large portion of the rowers in Christian galleys were Muslim, and vice versa. Galley rowers were quartered ashore in barracks or *bagni*: the *bagno* of Algiers included room for Christian services, while the *bagno* of Livorno included a mosque.[71]

The food of galley crews in the sixteenth century differed little from that of the thirteenth. In 1538, the prescribed rations for a *ciurma* (oarsman) in the Sicilian galleys of the Spanish fleet consisted of twenty-six ounces of *biscotti* per day, four ounces of meat three times a week, substituted by a *salsa* or stew on the remaining four days. The price of food rose steadily throughout sixteenth-century Western Europe. The meat ration declined as the century wore on; and as the price of food increased, galley fleets became increasingly expensive to maintain. For this and other reasons, the rowed ramming warships that dominated the Mediterranean and Aegean for over four millennia were replaced by warships of new design.[72]

Salt Herring and Salt Cod

Herring bones have been found in Danish sites from circa 3000 B.C., so herring has a long history in the North European diet. Because of its fattiness, herring must either be consumed or salted quite soon after it is caught. In or about 1350, the Dutch developed a technique of pickling herring in brine, according to legend the invention of Wilhelm Beuckelzon, a fisherman or fishmonger from Zeeland or from Flanders.[73] Whether packed in dry salt or pickled in brine, the herring industry created an enormous demand for salt. In medieval Denmark, Finland, and elsewhere, salt was produced by evaporating seawater into a dense brine, then boiling the brine to produce crystal salt. In the late Middle Ages, the Hanseatic League controlled salt supplies and in some cases traded salt for salted herring.

The Baltic herring stocks waned during the Middle Ages, and the herring shoals of the North Sea took on more importance, with both the Dutch and the English developing fleets of specialized fishing craft for this seasonal catch. The Dutch called their long, narrow herring craft *buises*, (usually anglicized as "buss"). These vessels caught the fish in drift nets, then processed them and packed them in barrels on board. The herring busses doubled as small cargo-carriers between herring seasons. The Dutch purchased salt produced from seawater in the time-honored manner of evaporating and boiling, from Portugal and from salt-works in Fife on the east coast of Scotland. Herring busses were resupplied by herring *jagers* (hunting boats) that would purchase the packed herring from the busses, and resupply them with barrels, salt, and provisions.[74] An English pamphlet from 1614 describes the provisions of a Dutch herring buss as beer, bread, butter, bacon, and peas.[75] It is likely that the herring fishermen also ate fresh herring, and any edible by-catch (other species of fish) they found in their nets.[76] Competition and conflict between the Dutch and English herring fleets flared into open warfare during the mid-seventeenth century.[77]

Atlantic cod, air-dried into stockfish in Iceland, was a staple of the medieval European diet. During the Middle Ages, Basque fishermen began catching and salting cod. By the fourteenth century salt cod was a European staple, an alternative to air-dried cod from Iceland. Cook Guillaume Tirel, better known by his nickname "Taillevent," was head chef to Philip VI and Charles V of France, making him one of the most influential *gastronomiers* of the era. Taillevent recommended that salt cod be eaten with mustard sauce or with melted fresh butter. He also advised that salt cod must be soaked to desalinate it, but not for too long.[78]

Crusaders and Pilgrims

Starting in 1095, a series of Crusades, "one of the most miscellaneous, most unruly movements in history" from Western Europe headed to Palestine with the stated objective of freeing the holy places there from the Seljuk Turks.[79] Most of these Crusaders traveled from the south of France in typical Mediterranean merchant sailing craft. In the early Crusades, these were large two-masted lateen-rigged vessels with a pair of rudders, one to a side. The provisions on board were probably similar to those aboard the Aragonese and Angevin galleys of the thirteenth century.

Another populous and colorful genus of medieval passengers were pilgrims, usually people of adequate means who traveled to distant holy places ostensibly for the good of their souls, and then to return home enlightened or at least invigorated by the journey. One can recognize in accounts of medieval pilgrims some elements of tourism in later eras. Chaucer's *The Canterbury Tales* opens with a colorful description of how spring rains make the land come alive, and stir in the human breast the urge to "maken pilgrimages." Chaucer's pilgrims traveled overland to Canterbury, but many medieval pilgrims traveled by sea. The shrine of St. James in Santiago de Compostela in

Galicia, northern Spain, was a favorite from the tenth century on, and many medieval pilgrims wore the scallop shell of a Compostela pilgrim.

Cooking for a ship full of pilgrims aboard a medieval sailing vessel must have been a challenge. One may assume that the cooking area was expanded from those found aboard Hanseatic cogs, possibly a large brick hearth deep in the hold as found in the sixteenth-century *Mary Rose*. Cloth or wood partitions would subdivide the hold for the pilgrims' sleeping quarters. A fifteenth-century English poem, *The Pilgrims Sea-Voyage and Sea-Sickness*, describes a ship of pilgrims setting out for Santiago de Compostela. Once the sails are set, the master calls for the cook to prepare food for the crew, even if the pilgrims arc too seasick to eat. He calls for beer, which he receives from the steward. Meanwhile, the seasick pilgrims are throwing up into their bowls, calling out for hot wine to ease their discomfort. It is doubtful that all seasick pilgrims disposed of all the results of their nausea over the side; which is probably why the smell of the issue from the bilge pump was so awful. One hopes that the pilgrims found their sea legs, and their appetites, before arriving in Spain.

Haul the bowline! Now veer the sheet!
Cook, make ready anon our meat!
Our pylgrymms have no lust to eat
I pray God give them rest.

Go to the helm! What ho! No neare[r]!
Steward, fellow! A pot of beer!
Ye shall have, Sir, with good cheer,
Anon all of the best.

Thys mean'whyle the pylgrymms lie,
And have their bowls all fast them by,
And cry after hot malvesy—
"Their health for to restore. "

For when that we shall go to bedde,
The pumpe was nygh oure beddes hede,
A man were as good to be dede
As smell therof the stynk.[80]

TWO

The Age of Exploration

Beginning in the fifteenth century, Europeans began to move beyond their home waters and explore the seas beyond the familiar coasts they had plied for centuries. Spanish, Portuguese, and later French, English, and Dutch explorers sought new routes to India, the East Indies, China, and Japan.

For centuries, goods from these areas were carried by Javanese, Arab, and other mariners to western Asia, where they were carried overland to the Levant (modern Israel/Palestine and Lebanon), and purchased by Venetian and Genoese traders. The supply of costly South, Southeast, and East Asian goods passed through Venetian and Genoese hands on its way to the rest of Europe. Pepper, cloves, cinnamon, and other highly prized spices came to Europe only by this route. In addition, most of Europe's gold and ivory supplies came from Africa, in a trade monopolized by these same two Italian city-states.

In the fifteenth century, Prince Henry of Portugal resolved to undercut the virtual monopoly the Venetians and Genoese enjoyed in Asian and other exotic goods. Exploring the coast of Africa beyond Cape Bojador, the Portuguese hoped to undercut the Italians in the sale of gold, ivory, and black pepper, while also searching for a sea route around Africa into the Indian Ocean. The Portuguese colonized the Cape Verde Islands, and proceeded to explore more and more of the African coastline. In the process, they did find a new type of black pepper, melegueta pepper (*Aframomum melegueta*), which they sold to the rest of Europe.

Figure 2.1. Sixteenth-century depiction of Columbus leaving Spain in 1492 by Theodore de Bry, 1528-1598. Though the clothing and ships are a century later in style, this illustration conveys a good sense of what Columbus's departure was probably like. Reproduction Number: LC-USZ62-102010 in Collection: Miscellaneous Items in High Demand. Courtesy of Library of Congress. http://www.loc.gov/pictures/resource/cph.3c02010/.

South of the equator, there were navigation problems. The Pole Star, used as a celestial signpost for latitude, dipped below the horizon. In the late fifteenth century, the Portuguese learned to take the sun's altitude at noon, and then apply the sun's declination from the equator on that day, to determine latitude. Portuguese explorers such as Vasco da Gama found a sea route around India; and the Spanish sent Columbus, Magellan, and others westward to find an alternate route.

Iberian Maritime Traditions

There are good reasons why it was the Iberians from Spain and Portugal who began to explore new sea routes in the fifteenth century. They had inherited much of the best of shipbuilding, sail design, and navigation techniques from both northern and southern Europe. Vessels like the caravel and navigation manuals such as *Arte de Navegar* by Martin Cortes combined Mediterranean with North Atlantic/Baltic practice in ways that broadened Iberian, and eventually European, horizons.

By the fifteenth century Iberian vessels often carried a box or tray of sheet iron in which cooking fires could be made safely in fair weather. These were called *fogón* in Spanish, which is usually translated "firebox" in English. Loose bricks could be laid over the deck and the firebox laid on it with a layer of sand in it; a cooking fire could then be safely made. It is likely that cooking in caravels was accomplished using a *fogón*, which was set somewhere on deck, and only in mild weather.[1]

Columbus and other leaders of Iberian exploring voyages list a steward in the crew. The steward was a petty officer responsible for the distribution of food, drink, firewood, sandglasses, candles, and lanterns. In some ships the steward was also responsible for training the boys to turn the sandglass every half hour and call out the time, recite the points of the compass, and other duties.[2]

Columbus's accounts of his crew fail to mention a cook. It appears that on his 1492–1493 voyage, and other Spanish vessels of this era, there was not a designated cook. Perhaps the men took turns, or each watch appointed one of their number to prepare the food.[3]

Spanish and Portuguese vessels carried the well-established staples of seafaring cuisine: beef and pork pickled in brine, and ship's biscuit. In Portugal, the baking of ship's biscuit was a royal concern, and the ovens for this purpose were located near the royal palace in Lisbon. Salted flour was also carried, and could be baked into bannocks in the ashes of the fire, a practice still current with Arabian sailors.[4] Cheese, onions, dried peas, beans, and chickpeas also appear in lists of provisions.[5]

Fruit was carried as well; Columbus stocked up on fruit in the Canary Islands before heading west. Sir John Hawkins in the sixteenth century carried oranges on his long voyages, which no doubt contributed to the health of his crews. Dried fruit was carried in some cases, though it may have been a luxury item for the officers.[6] Preserved fish were carried by Iberian explorers. These would have been sardines and anchovies, as well as salted Atlantic cod. Northern explorers probably brought stockfish (dried cod), salt cod, and salted herring.

Columbus wrote in his journal of provisioning the *Santa Maria* and his two *caravelas* in the Canary Islands. On September 3, 1492 he recorded that they had stowed all the wood and water they needed. Columbus listed some provisions as already procured, including salt, wine, molasses, and honey. Other supplies he records as not yet ready, resulting in a few days' wait.[7] The following day Columbus recorded the loading and stowage of dried meat, salted fish, and fruits. He commented that the fruit would have to be consumed early, as it would spoil if the voyage exceeded three weeks. The day after this they loaded their supply of biscuits.[8] The wood would have been for fuel to cook in the fireboxes. The salt suggests that he provided for the salting down of meat or fish for the return voyage. The fruit was apparently fresh.

Fresh fish were caught on lines or speared along the way: this practice must have been common on long voyages in medieval times, as Columbus brought the equipment for both on his first voyage across the Atlantic.[9] Columbus's crew availed themselves of fresh seafood on both legs of their journey. On the outward bound leg of the journey in September 1492, the crew of the *Nina* harpooned a porpoise.[10] On the return trip in January 1493, fishing from the ship was extremely important due to diminishing food supplies. On January 25, Columbus's journal records that some of his crewman killed a porpoise and a very large shark. Both were eaten, as apparently the available food stores were limited to bread, wine, and *ajes* they had brought back from the islands they visited.[11]

Ajes were probably yucca or sweet potato.[12] From the beginning, European ships sailing to the New World and around Africa to the Indian Ocean replenished their food supplies with locally available foods. The ajes that sustained the men of the *Pinta* and *Nina* (the *Santa Maria* ran aground and had to be abandoned) on their voyage home were the first in a long list of foods that European explorers stocked up on when making landfall on distant shores.

New Foods from the New World

After European animals had been introduced to the West Indies, sun-dried or smoked beef and bacon became a favorite commodity there. The Taino Indian technique they called *barbacoa* was applied to these new meats. Barbacoa, which became known as barbeque in French and English, was a technique of slow-cooking/smoking by putting the meat on a wooden frame, called a *boucain* in French. This led to renegade Europeans who lived on the islands becoming known as "buccaneers."[13] The technique of barbacoa spread quickly to Jamaica, where it became known as jerking meat: jerked chicken and beef have remained staples of Jamaican cuisine ever since.[14] Slow-roasted meat has become known as barbeque the world round.

Cassava (*Manihot esculenta*) was one of the great food discoveries in the West Indies. While it requires rather elaborate preparation, cassava flour can be used to make sturdy biscuits that keep very well at sea. Cassava was successfully transplanted to distant regions of the globe, where it became a staple of local diets, and of seafarers seeking provisions.

For a description of cassava and one way of preparing it, here is a later account of the preparation of cassava, from an eighteenth-century sailor whose ship was in Rio de Janeiro:

> "Good living" as is call'd in that country, jerk beef and farenia, which is made out of a tree that is call'd manyoke [manioc, or cassava]. When planted, it grows about 10 feet high and is not fit for use under sixteen or eighteen month. Then the roots grows much like a yam or a potatoe but much larger; they then [are] scraped clean and grated as we do horse redish [radish], but they have mils for that purpose, as they make a great quantity. Then it is pressed to take the juice out of it and then sifted through two or three sives, then hove into large earthen pans made for that purpose with fiers under them and parch it. It is then fit for use.[15]

The process of grating and pressing removes the harmful cyanogenic glucosides of bitter cassava, and makes the cassava safe to eat. Jacob Nagle, the source of the quotation, enjoyed his "good living" on jerk beef (barbacoa) and cassava loaves, both foods that lasted well, and provided welcome replenishment of ship's stores.[16]

Yams were an available foodstuff on the coasts of Africa, and they could be kept a good while. These were a welcome food for at least a few weeks after going ashore in Africa. The native New World yam, the yampee (*dioscorea trifida*) is tasty but quite small. The Guinea or African yam (*dioscorea rotundata* and *dioscorea cayenensis*) was therefore introduced to the West Indies by the Spanish. In the seventeenth century, the even larger great yam (*dioscorea alata*), native to India, was introduced to Africa and then the West Indies, where it became a staple of the local diet.[17]

The carrying of livestock on board for slaughter and consumption during the voyage, other than chickens, was not yet common in the fifteenth century. Thus long-distance voyagers of the fifteenth and sixteenth centuries were deprived of the fresh meat their successors enjoyed on long voyages. A Spanish edict of 1621 forbade the carrying of livestock, which suggests that during the years preceding, some Spanish ships probably tried to carry animals larger than chickens, for slaughter at sea when provisions ran low.[18]

On small vessels such as Columbus's two *caravelas*, it could be essential to fill empty casks with sea water, to ballast and trim the vessel. Columbus records that he did this, in his journal entry for February 14, 1493.[19] This became standard practice on long voyages, particularly the much longer voyages the Portuguese made around Africa and into the Indian Ocean.

Columbus's 1492–1493 voyage entailed reasonably short periods between landfalls. The really deadly voyages of this era were those from Europe around the Cape of Good Hope, into the Indian Ocean to India, the East Indies, China, and Japan. Supplies ran low, and dietary deficiencies sapped the health of the crews. Scurvy and other deficiency-related ailments were constant dangers on the voyages around Africa to the Indian Ocean. When Vasco da Gama and other Portuguese explorers sailed around Africa to India from 1497 on, a large proportion of their crews died of scurvy, more than from any other cause.[20]

The Portuguese Carreira da India

The dangers of the voyage did not deter the Portuguese from sending enormous carracks to India and other destinations around the Horn of Africa, establishing a center of trade in Goa. These large vessels carried a crew of over 120 men, and a number of passengers and supernumeraries. Experienced sailors were scarce, and a great deal of training was carried on along the way. One despairing Portuguese shipmaster hung a string of onions on the starboard rail, and a string of garlic on the port rail, to help his inexperienced hands tell them apart.[21]

On these crowded ships, there were boys to see to the lanterns, carry messages, and work the pumps; three to four pages to sing out the change of watches every four hours and announce the auction of deceased persons' goods at the mainmast; and yet there is no mention of a designated cook. It appears that everyone was issued basic foodstuffs; a daily issue of wine, water, and bread, and a monthly issue of salt meat, oil, vinegar, salt, and onions. A stove in the waist, at the foot of the mainmast, was lit by a *merinho* (petty officer) in the morning, and this was watched by two sentries. The fire was put out at 4:00 p.m. Apparently everyone cooked for himself. Perhaps some men would mess together informally, and send one of their number to the cooking hearth to cook their food.[22]

The *fidalgos*, young gentle-born adventurers, probably had their servants cook for them. There were rowdy celebrations when they crossed the Equator, a tradition which continues up to the present day. They would also feast (with what foodstuffs they had) on rounding the Cape of Good Hope. Many died from scurvy and disease on the trip; the early Portuguese trading voyages were fatal to a high proportion of those brave enough to make the trip.[23]

Locating a large cooking hearth deep in the waist of the ship was good for stability, but entailed some discomfort and risk. The smoke was left to find its own way out through the hatches: not until later centuries was a chimney added to the shipboard cooking hearth. Everyone below decks must have been breathing smoky air when the fire was lit. In addition, an out-of-control galley fire in this location could be disastrous. The Portuguese appointed two *merinhos* to watch the fire and extinguish it, even though they did not appoint a ship's cook.[24]

Mary Rose

In 1545, the French attacked the English coastal city of Portsmouth, in response to the English attack on Boulogne the previous year. During the battle, one of Henry VIII's proudest warships heeled over and sank in the shallow water of the Solent, carrying most of the crew to their deaths. Cannons were recovered from the wreck over the centuries, and in 1982 the surviving section of the hull was raised. The wreck is displayed in Portsmouth in a museum which displays artifacts, along with reconstructions of how these items may have appeared when new.

The *Mary Rose* was a particularly significant find, in that she sank in battle with a full complement of sailors and soldiers aboard. It is also fortunate that she settled into the mud of the Solent, so that most of the hull, with much of its contents, survived to be recovered. The *Mary Rose* has dramatically improved modern understanding of many aspects of shipboard life in 1545, from longbows and tankards to cannon and ship construction. The *Mary Rose* was not a vessel of exploration, but a warship operating in home waters. She represents the most detailed picture available of life aboard ships of the sixteenth century, a time capsule of the maritime world of 1545.[25]

Skeletal remains of crew members were recovered with the *Mary Rose*. The *Mary Rose* was not on a long voyage, during which dietary deficiency could be expected. Nonetheless, many crew members suffered from malnutrition, showing evidence of scurvy, rickets, and other conditions caused by dietary deficiency. It may well be that these deficiencies were caused by insufficient diet ashore (especially in the case of archers, who were not permanent members of the crew), and a diet that was routinely low in vitamins, common in many working class people of the time period.[26]

Nine barrels were recovered from the *Mary Rose* that contained beef and pig bones. This indicates that cattle and pigs were butchered, cut up, and stored. Being stored in barrels, it is highly likely that the beef and pork were pickled in brine. Fish bones were found in baskets, which suggest that they were carried dry; either salt cod or wind-dried stockfish.[27]

The *Mary Rose* had a cook who was paid on the same scale as the master carpenter and the master gunner. Some incised graffiti on a tankard and a bowl suggest that the cook may have been named *Ny Cop* or *Ny Coep*.[28] The ship had two cooking hearths deep in the hold, each with a very large brass

Figures 2.2. Wooden tankard found on the *Mary Rose*. Courtesy of Peter Crossman, *Mary Rose* Trust. 2009. Wikimedia Commons. http://commons.wikimedia.org/wiki/File:MaryRose-wooden_tankard1.JPG.

cauldron. This design may have already existed for some time in large sailing vessels, and it certainly lasted for the next 200 years or so (with some modifications) until replaced with iron stoves in the same location.[29]

Martin Frobisher and Other English Explorers

English as well as Dutch explorers searched for navigable Northwest and Northeast passages to the Far East. While unsuccessful in this object, expeditions such as those of Stephen Borough in 1553 and 1556, and of Martin Frobisher in 1576–1578, established trade relations with Muscovy (Russia), and provided the foundation for English footholds such as the port of St. John's in Newfoundland. Lists of provisions exist for these and similar voyages, listing such provisions as biscuit, wheat, beans, beer, cider, beef, and fish in one case; beer, bread, beef, fish, bacon, peas, butter, cheese, vinegar, oatmeal, aquavita, wood, and water in another.[30] Sebastian Cabot in 1553 required that the steward and cook of each ship make a weekly accounting of such victuals as meat, fish, biscuit, bread, beer, wine, oil, and vinegar.[31]

Martin Frobisher's search for the Northwest Passage and gold in 1576–1578 (Frobisher is one of the earliest and most famous prospectors to confuse iron pyrites or "fool's gold" for the real thing) served plenty of beer to the crew: Frobisher specified an issue of eight pints of beer per man per day.[32] Frobisher's second voyage of 1577 has left particularly detailed records of food issues: a daily ration of one pound of biscuit and one gallon of beer per man; one pound of salt beef or pork per man on flesh days and one dried codfish (stockfish) for each four men on fast days. The issue of stockfish to four men must have been common in English ships, as it was cited in just this way in the dietary complaints of the crew of the *Golden Lion* in 1587. Frobisher specified that oatmeal and rice were to be issued on fast days if the stockfish supply was depleted; a quarter-pound of butter and half a pound of cheese per man per day; as well as honey for sweetening. Frobisher provided a hogshead of "sallet oyle" and a pipe of vinegar to last 120 men the voyage. This was to be supplemented by fresh fish and wild fowl and game as available.[33]

An Alternate Location for the Cooking Hearth

In 1578 Sir William Wynter, surveyor of the ships for Queen Elizabeth of England, recommended that the galley should be relocated from the middle of the ship to the forecastle.[34] This position had advantages and disadvantages. The forecastle was not yet the customary crew accommodation as it became in later merchant vessels, and being up above the main deck, the smoke would tend to blow away. An out-of-control fire in this location would not set fire to stores in the hull, though it could become very dangerous if it spread to the tarred fore shrouds (the tarred standing rigging that braced the foremast against the sides of the hull). Two big disadvantages are that the weight of the bricks would now be up high, making the ship less stable; another is that in this period the lower yards were lowered when not in use, and the fore-halyard usually passed through a knighthead (stationary block on a reinforced post) inside the forecastle. A brick cooking hearth in the forecastle could complicate the handling of this important line.

A payroll for an English galleon of 500–800 tons, from 1582, specified a cook. While the master, the boatswain, the quartermasters, the coxswain, the steward, the carpenter, the master gunner all had one or more mates, and even the surgeon had "His Man," the cook apparently did his work alone.[35] The cook could, at his discretion, allow crewmen to dry their clothing or themselves by the fire.[36]

Drake's Raid on Cadiz

In 1587, Spain was preparing "The Enterprise of England." A mighty fleet was to set sail for the English Channel, fight off any English ships, rendezvous with barges carrying the Spanish troops in the Low Countries under the prince of Parma's command, and escort them across the North Sea where it meets the English Channel to attack and conquer England. The plan had many flaws, but it was a matter of grave concern to England. Therefore, in 1587 Francis Drake led a preemptive raid against Cadiz, where ships were gathering to comprise and supply the Armada.

Drake's raid on Cadiz took place between April 29 and May 1, 1587. Drake arrived with about twenty-six ships. Four of them were Queen Elizabeth's ships, large sailing warships—the *Elizabeth Bonaventure*, the *Golden Lion*, the *Dreadnought*, and the *Rainbow*. There were three big ships from the Levant Company of London, also large and well-armed. In addition Drake had seven smaller armed ships, and eleven or twelve small scouting vessels. Cadiz was defended by eight galleys, which proved unable to defeat Drake's sailing vessels. This action was a demonstration that galleys could not outmatch nimble sailing vessels when the latter were well handled. The galleys recaptured a Portuguese caravel from Drake's squadron, and Drake's ships sank a large armed "argosy," a Genoese-owned or -chartered vessel that challenged the English squadron. The English did not land, which was not their objective. Instead, they picked through the majority of the vessels in harbor, many of which were carrying stores intended for the Spanish Armada. In all, Drake's raid captured or destroyed something between twenty-four (the Spanish figure) and thirty-seven (Drake's figure) vessels in Cadiz harbor, a major setback for the impending Spanish enterprise against England.[37]

The ships Drake's men burned in Cadiz harbor were mostly carrying supplies and provisions for the "Enterprise of England." On their way back to England, Drake's squadron stopped in Portugal, capturing Sagres Castle, the fortified monastery of St. Vincent, and Valliera Castle, along with guns and supplies. The English destroyed over a hundred fishing boats (crippling the local tuna/tunny fishery), and a large number of coastal cargo carriers, many of them carrying barrel staves.[38] These barrel staves were probably intended to be coopered into the barrels and casks that were to carry provisions for the Armada. The loss of these barrel staves was of strategic importance. Seasoned barrel staves could not easily be found to replace those Drake burned, and much of the Armada's food and drink were carried in barrels made of green—that is unseasoned—wood. Many of the barrels leaked, much of the supplies spoiled, and the ships of the Armada experienced critical shortages of food and drink while they sailed around the British Isles back to Spain.[39]

Food Issues Aboard English and
Spanish Ships, 1587–1588

The spoilage experienced by the Spanish Armada in 1588 is an important event concerning food in naval history. Drake's destruction of the barrel staves in 1587 contributed significantly to the failure of the Spanish Armada the following year.

All was not happy in Drake's squadron of ships that raided Cadiz in 1587. The crew of the *Golden Lion* mutinied and returned to England. The mutineers singled out insufficient food when writing in their defense:

> What is a piece of Beefe of halfe a pounde amonge foure men to dynner or halfe a drye Stockfishe for four dayes in the weeke, and nothing elles to helpe withal—Yea, wee have helpe, a little Beveredge worse than pompe water. . . . You make no men of us, but beastes.[40]

This passage offers an interesting snapshot of crew food aboard Drake's squadron. It would appear that aboard the *Golden Lion* in 1587, the crew was organized into messes of four men. Their fish ration was stockfish, which is to say, air-dried cod. It also suggests that all was not always well with the food in English ships. Sir Richard Hawkins estimated that 10,000 Englishmen died of scurvy alone during twenty years of Elizabeth's reign.[41]

The following year, the Spanish Armada sailed for England, notwithstanding the Spanish supply of food and drink being stored in barrels made of unseasoned staves. Certainly some Spanish ships were short of provisions, whether this was the case when they left Lisbon and Coruna, or whether because they had discarded much of their food due to spoilage. While both fleets were in the English Channel, the *San Salvador*, one of the Spanish galleons, was partially disabled by an explosion of gunpowder in her stern, and fell into the hands of the English. The *San Salvador* had 64 seamen and 319 soldiers aboard. To provide for this company *San Salvador* had, when captured by the English, fifty-three barrels of wine, but only three casks of beef, already going bad, and one cask of beans.[42]

In the English fleet, there was an official ration for the men who served them, though the actual issues were often less, a four-man ration going for five or six:

> Meat Day—One pound of biscuit, a gallon of beer, two pounds of salt beef.
> Fish Day—One pound of biscuit, a gallon of beer, cheese, a quarter of dried cod.
> Once a week—one pound of ham, one pint of peas.[43]

Aside from the addition of biscuit, ham, and peas, this fare resembles the rations issued aboard the *Golden Lion* the previous year. The peas could have been any number of different varieties, some rare today, which were customarily cooked into pease porridge, a thick pea soup that was an English, and indeed northern European staple, often flavored with ham or bacon. It is no surprise that the issue of ham is found with the issue of peas.

Chaplain, geographer, and author Richard Hakluyt wrote in 1598 about the mariners of his time, "No kinde of men of any profession in the common wealth passe their years in so great and continuall hazard . . . and . . . of so many grow to gray heires . . . a hard cabin, cold and salt meat, broken sleeps, mouldy bread, dead beer, wet clothes, want of fire."[44] As Hakluyt points out, one of the greatest hardships of sea life in this era was the food, sometimes of poor quality, and sometimes eaten cold.

Location of Cooking Hearth, and a Possible "Mess Kit"

The cooking hearth locations in English ships could be any one of at least three: the false orlop deck, deep in the hold before the mainmast, or in the forecastle. The Swedish royal ship *Vasa*, which sank in Stockholm harbor in 1628, had a cooking hearth deep in the hold, similar to the cooking hearths in *Mary Rose*. One of the bricks in the *Vasa's* cooking hearth bears the footprints of a small pig. An interesting find in the *Vasa* was a barrel containing a large communal bowl, a *stånka* or large coopered tankard, and seven wooden spoons. The staff of the Vasa Museum believes that this represents the issue "mess kit" of a "backlag" or mess of seven men, an early example of a naval kit for one mess. Mess kids were found as well; a "kid" is the naval term for a container for transporting a mess's food to and from the galley. Smaller lathe-turned wooden eating bowls were found aboard *Vasa*, but these were marked with individual owner's marks, and thus were probably the private property of individual sailors. There were civilian contractors still aboard the *Vasa* when she sank, so it is possible that this chest and its contents represent a mess kit for contractors rather than for the crew; however the "crew mess kit" interpretation is generally accepted.[45]

Despite William Wynter's suggestion, English shipwrights continued to put the cooking hearth deep in the hold, as it is in the *Vasa*. An English treatise on shipbuilding dating to about 1620, and quoted in Peter Kirsch's *The Galleon: The Great Ships of the Armada Era*, also places the cooking area deep in the hold:

> Abaft the mast down under the steerage are two other partitions, the one for the bread room, the other for the steward room. All the rest of the hold serves for stowage of victuals, only in some of the King's ships the cook room is also contrived upon the false orlop in the hold.[46]

Figure 2.3. A mess "kid," with a stånka (spouted coopered can), common bowl, and spoons for seven men from the *Vasa*, a Swedish royal ship from 1628. This appears to be an early example of issued equipment for one mess. Courtesy of Anneli Karlsson, photographer; Vasa Museum, Stockholm, Sweden.

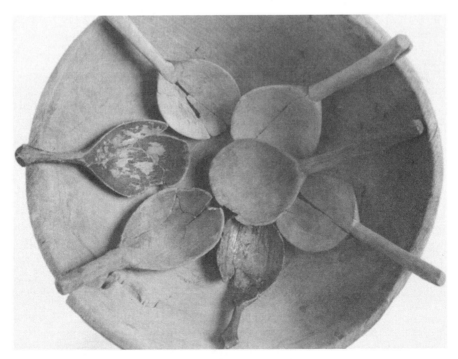

Figure 2.4. Detail of spoons from the *Vasa*. Courtesy of Anneli Karlsson, photographer; Vasa Museum, Stockholm, Sweden.

Northern European vessels continued to place large cooking hearths deep in the hold for centuries to come.

Food in Spanish Royal Galleons Circa 1600

The provisioning of Spanish Royal Fleets (Armadas) was overseen by purveyors (*proveedores*) in charge of each fleet.[47] The Spanish shipboard diet in royal galleons was similar to that on Columbus's ships: ship's biscuit, water, wine or cider, salt pork or ham, dried beef, salted codfish, cheese, rice, fava beans, chickpeas, olive oil, and vinegar. These items were rationed in specific quantities. Fresh items including garlic, onions, and peppers, while not part of the regular ration, were sometimes carried and allotted to the men.[48] Spanish documents relating to provisioning show the inflation in food prices, fivefold in the case of ship's biscuit, during the sixteenth-century, which as described in the last chapter, may have played a key role in the demise of the rowing galley as a practical warship.[49] Other items such as salt pork from Flanders and olive oil and vinegar from Andalusia rose in price less radically, in both cases by 2.5 times.[50] In Spanish voyages to the Indies, chickpeas, fava beans, and rice figure prominently. Rice was grown in Valencia, and may have come from there. Fish, usually dried and salted cod, *bacallao*, was a staple on Spanish ships.[51] For Spanish vessels traveling to the Americas, local products were regular replacements for the stocks they consumed. While Columbus mentioned only ajes as food brought from the New World on his first return voyage, by 1600 Spanish ships returning from the Americas replaced their biscuit stores with loaves of *casaba* (cassava), and their meat supplies with *tortuga* (turtle).[52]

Spanish ships on long voyages regularly topped up their water supply with rainwater; arranging sails, awnings, and other cloth to collect it.[53] Ships bound for the Indies carried live hens, whose eggs were a delicacy for officers and for the sick. When supplies of biscuit ran low, broken bits of biscuit were sometimes cooked with whatever else was available to make a stew or gruel called *mazamorra*.[54] Another dish served in Spanish ships of this era was a *menestra* of rice and legumes, usually fava beans or chickpeas.[55] *Menestra*, as well as oil and vinegar, accompanied the issue of fish on the fish days: Wednesdays, Fridays, and Saturdays.[56] Sunday, Monday, Tuesday, and Thursdays were customarily meat days.[57] Cheese was carried in lesser quantities than fish or meat, and was customarily issued when battle was expected, or on days when the weather did not permit cooking.[58] Beer was only carried by ships provisioned from the Low Countries, and was considered a substitute for cider. Wine was a more usual issue, including French wines as well as Spanish. A Spanish captain-general in 1557 observed that French wines did not keep as long as wines from Navarre, and should therefore be issued first.[59]

There remains some mysteries about food preparation aboard Spanish ships in the 1620s. Royal ships built for long voyages in the 1620s were equipped with only two *fogones*, the sheet metal fireboxes used by Columbus and his contemporaries. Two of these for 200 men seems an impossibly small cooking capacity.[60] Perhaps by then Spanish galleons carried brick cooking hearths like their Portuguese, English, and Swedish sisters, so that the two *fogones* were only a supplemental cooking facility. Spanish royal galleons of this period carried big copper cauldrons weighing forty to forty-five pounds each, which also suggests a more substantial cooking hearth than a portable sheet metal *fogón*. Perhaps by the 1620s *fogón* had come to take a broader meaning, as it has in modern usage, to include a brick cooking hearth.

Provisioning on English Voyages to and from Virginia

The English began to establish a foothold in North America in the late 1500s. English settlement and habitation of Virginia began with an exploratory venture by Philip Amadas and Arthur Barlowe in 1584 and military expeditions led by Richard Grenville and Ralph Lane in 1585–1586. The English established their first settlement in the New World on Roanoke Island in 1587 in what was then known as Virginia. This colony, under Governor John White, did not flourish and there was an unsuccessful attempt by White to reprovision or rescue what became known as the "Lost Colony" in 1590. During this period, English ships on their way to and from Virginia used the West Indies as a place to restock with fresh water and food. Most late sixteenth-century accounts of journeys to the new colony of Virginia describe visits to the islands where sailors stopped to collect fresh water and salt and restock food stores. In 1584, Amadas and Barlowe, who had been at sea since April 27 of that year, reached the Canary Islands by May 10 and the West Indies by June 10. While they found the islands themselves to be "unwholesome," they used them to refill their supplies "so that having refreshed ourselves with sweet water & fresh victuall, we departed." [61]

Finding fresh water was a vital concern for Virginia explorers, and the West Indies were a good place to stop to collect the necessary supplies. In 1585, Richard Grenville reported that they "came to an anker at Cotesa . . . neere to the Iland of S. John, where we landed, and refreshed ourselves all that day."[62] Refreshing oneself often meant a hard slog, from island to island, in search of a good water source. There were times when a promising prospect for fresh water was a disappointment, and the English mariners either had to keep searching or take their chances and drink bad water. On the 1587 Roanoke settlement voyage, John White's men did not find an acceptable water source at Santa Cruz and so resorted to drinking contaminated water in

> a standing ponde, the water whereof was so evill, that many of our company fell sicke with drinking thereof: and as many as did but wash their faces with that water . . . their faces did burne and swell, that their eyes shut up, and could not see for five or six dayes, or longer.[63]

When they finally found fresh water, they did so by splitting up their foraging group and when one of the groups finally found "a very fayre spring of water," they brought back three bottles to the rest of the settlers to sample it.[64] However, before they found the good water source, White writes, "wee drank the stinking water of the pond."[65] White's men continued to look for fresh water as they island hopped through the West Indies. At the island of St. Johns, they spent three days looking for water without finding any and used up other supplies in the process: "spending in the meane time more beere then the quantitie of the water came unto."[66] Sailors often had to dig for their water. In 1590, on the return trip to resupply the Roanoke colony, White's men were completely out of fresh water. On Hatteras Island (on the North Carolina Outer Banks), the sailors dug "in those sandie hills for fresh water whereof we found very sufficient."[67] When they reached the Roanoke site and found it deserted, before sailing on to look for the colonists in another location, they left a "Caske with fresh water on shoare in the Iland" for future use if and when they returned.[68]

The English sailors often encountered Spaniards in the West Indies. In many cases, the interactions were hostile. Sometimes diplomacy won out: if the Spanish were convinced that the English were only in search of water and food, no blood was shed. There could have been a confrontation when Richard Grenville's men came upon Spanish horsemen on May 22, 1585, at Cotesa, but when the Spaniards were told that the Englishmen's "principal intention was onely to furnish ourselves with water and victuals, and other necessaries . . . with faire and friendly meanes" they met the English requests with "large promises of all curtesie and great favour."[69]

English ships were also in constant need of salt. On May 26, 1585, Grenville's men went to the southwest side of St. Johns to "fetch salt."[70] Master Ralph Lane departed in one of the frigates with 20 men to collect salt and "intrenched himself" on the sands of the shallow coastal waters which happened to be "compassing one of their salte hils within the trench."[71] A troop of Spanish horsemen saw what happened and watched from a distance while Lane and the men "caryed their salte aboord and laded his Frigat," returning to join Grenville's fleet three days later.[72] Grenville's men followed any lead they could get to find salt, even from foreigners. On June 9, they landed at Caicos to search for "salte-pondes" on the "advertisement and information of a Portugall."[73] Searching for salt often led the English on other avenues of food acquisition. On July 6, 1587, White's men were searching for salt on the island of Caicos, but were also able to hunt for waterfowl, including swans.[74]

Virginia explorers also used the coastal waters to store freshly caught fish for their journey. Grenville reported that his men "caught in one tyde so much fish as would have yeelded us twentie pounds in London."[75] White's settlers of 1587 caught "five great Torteses" at Santa Cruz and they were so big that "sixteene of our strongest men were tired with carying of one of them but from the sea side to our cabbins."[76] On White's return trip in 1590, he may have led his men to fish in some of the same waters, both in the West Indies and Virginia. In August 1590, near the "Virginia" (modern North Carolina) coast, they "tooke in some fresh water and caught a great store of fish in the shallow water."[77]

Ships that reached the West Indies would have been able to incorporate a fair amount of fruit into their diets as well, a boon for avoidance of scurvy. John White's drawings of 1585 include pictures of pineapple, "horn plantain" and "mammee apple."[78] Earlier, in 1584, Amadas and Barlowe, as they first encountered Virginia, "manned their boats" and explored the new land where they found it "full of grapes, as the very beating and surge of the Sea overflowed them."[79] Sometimes they came to grief over their choice of fruits in their excitement to consume it. In 1587, on the island of Santa Cruz, John White reported that "some of our women and men, by eating a small fruit like greene Apples, were fearfully troubled with a sudden burning in their mouthes, and swelling of their tongues so bigge, that some of them could not speake."[80] Although this problem lasted only twenty-four hours, it also affected breastfeeding babies: "Also a child by sucking one of those womens breasts, had at the same instant his mouth set on such a burning, that it was strange to see how the infant was tormented for the time."[81] Undeterred by this experience, White's settlers collected "yong plants of Oranges, Pines, Mameas, and Plantanos" to plant in Virginia.[82]

Once in Virginia, English captains used local resources to restock for the trip back to England. On August 18, 1587, the ships unloaded the goods belonging to the planters (settlers) and "began to take in wood, and fresh water, and to new calke and trimme them for England."[83] On the way back to England, the ships also ran short of food and water. English ships repeated the process, stopping over in the West Indies to reprovision. On the abortive 1590 expedition, White's ships also stopped in the West Indies for "fresh water, and some other fresh victuals."[84]

Ships also ran low on supplies out on the open ocean on the return trip. After leaving the ill-fated Roanoke colonists in mid-August, 1587, the flagship was low on fresh water due to a leakage problem. The sailors used all the liquid on board to combine "all the beverage we could make, with stinking water, dregs of beere, and lees of wine which remayned, was but three gallons, and therefore now we expected nothing but famine to perish at Sea."[85] Fortunately for White and the crew, they landed in western Ireland where they met another ship that provided them with "fresh water, wine, and other fresh meate" before completing the journey to England.[86] The three-gallon cocktail of stinking water and the dregs of beer and wine casks must have been revolting.

John Smith: Life at Sea in English Ships Circa 1600

The most detailed description of life at sea in English ships of this era comes from John Smith, an adventurer of broad experience and knowledge. Smith is best known for his command of the Jamestown colony, but his long career as a professional soldier, explorer, and leader took him to Eastern Europe, France, and the Netherlands, and earned him, among other honors, the title of Admiral of New England. Even accounting for embellishment and exaggeration, he led an extraordinary life. His *Sea Grammar*, published in London in 1627, offers the most detailed account of English seafaring practice of this era. Smith wrote in great detail about English shipboard life, with many interesting observations about seafaring traditions which probably go back to medieval times. Here is what he has to say about the feeding, training, and disciplining of the ship's boys:

> The boyes the Boatswaine is to see every Munday at the chest, to say their compasse, and receive their punishment for all their weekes offences, which done they are to have a quarter can of beere, and a basket of bread, but if the Boatswaine eat or drinke before hee catch them, they are free.[87]

This is a very interesting insight into the training of young sailors, illustrating a tradition that continued unbroken into the twentieth century, and a curious tradition of English seafaring in this era. Boys or apprentices have been "saying their compass," reciting the thirty-two points of the compass right up to the early twentieth century. While compasses have been marked in degrees as well as points since the eighteenth century, the system of steering by points rather than degrees endured until World War II in most traditions. Whether "saying" the compass in 1627 or 1927, the recitation sounded something like this:

- North, North by East, North-Northeast, Northeast by North, Northeast, Northeast by East, East-Northeast, East by North,
- East, East by South, East-Southeast, Southeast by East, Southeast, Southeast by South, South-Southeast, South by East,
- South, Sou' by West, Sou'Sou'west, Sou'west by South, Sou'west, Sou'west by West, West-Sou'west, West by Sou',
- West, West by Nor', West-Nor'west, Nor'west by West, Nor'west, Nor'west by Nor', Nor'Nor'west, Nor' by West, North.

The detail about the punishment of the boys for offences is fascinating; if the boatswain begins to eat before punishing them for the previous day's infractions, they are forgiven. It is likely that the punishment consisted of blows to the offender's back with a wooden rod. The "can" referred to is a coopered mug made of a base, staves, bands, and usually a hinged lid, as found in multiple examples aboard the *Mary Rose*. The "basket of bread" appears to be the forerunner of the bread barge, about which we will hear more in the following two chapters.

Petty Officers and Their Duties: The Steward

Smith describes the duties of the steward, quartermasters, cooper, and cook. In so doing, he reveals a great deal about the storage, distribution, and preparation of food in English ships: "The Steward is to deliver out the victuals according to the Captaines directions, and messe them foure, five, or six, as there is occasion."[88] It would appear that the steward in this case distributed the food to the crew, as well as probably bringing it to the master and mates. What is profoundly illuminating about this passage is that it shows that the organization of the crew into "messes" who ate together, a convention which survived for centuries in the naval tradition, was already established practice on English ships in 1627.

The Quartermasters

Quartermasters in 1627 were responsible for the stowage in the hold, which affects the trimming of the vessel; and it appears that they functioned at that time something like watch-keeping mates.

The quarter Masters have the charge of the howle (hold) . . . and of their squadrons for the watch, and for fishing to have a Sayne [a seine or net], a fisgig, a harpin yron, and fish hookes, for Porgos, Bonetos, Dolphins [the fish, not the cetacean], or Dorados, and rayling lines for Mackrels.[89]

Smith refers to the "watch" as the four-hour time period and the work duty performed therein, while he calls the men who perform this duty "squadrons." In the centuries to follow, the men as well as the duty period became known as "watches."[90] The "fisgig" is a barbed trident, from Spanish *fisga*; the "harpin yron" is a harpoon. A small barbed trident for spearing frogs is still called a "gig" today. With these instruments, fishhooks, and a seine or net, a vessel provisioned as Smith recommends would be well equipped to supplement its food stores with fresh-caught fish and other sea creatures.

The Cooper

The cooper was responsible for barrels and anything on board with a barrel-like construction. Coopered containers held "wine, beare, sider, beverage, fresh water, or any liquor."[91] In 1627, the ship's cooper was bound to be a busy man, as there are not only a multitude of casks aboard, but "steepe

Figure 2.5. "The Old Whaler," from Gordon Grant, *Sail Ho: Windjammer Sketches Alow and Aloft* (New York: William Farquhar, 1930, 78). This illustration, while much later, shows the technique of spearing fish from the martingale shrouds with a *fisga* or grains-iron. The technique was no doubt similar for the crewmen of Columbus and Smith.

tubs" (for desalinating salt beef by soaking in fresh water, a forerunner of the "harness cask" of later sailing vessels), the coopered cans the men drank from, and any number of other articles. The beverages likely to be carried in cask on an English ship of 1627 included wine and cider as well as beer and fresh water.

The Cook

Here we have the cook, a position in the crew that was missing from Columbus's crew list, and from the Portuguese carracks sailing to India. In northern Europe, crews of midsize and larger vessels had included a dedicated cook since the eleventh century.

> The Cooke is to dresse and deliver out the victual, hee hath his store of quarter cans, small cans, platters, spoones, lanthornes, &c. and is to give his account of the remainder.[92]

Smith refers in several places to "boiling the kettle," a phrase still used in British English in preparing to make tea. One of these cases is during a lull in a sea battle; it seems that Smith wants the crew to have something hot to eat or drink whenever it is safe to boil the kettle.

Organization of the Crew

Smith, in his customary detail, explains how the crew is to be divided into watches:

> How they divide the company at sea, and set, and rule the watch . . . The Captaine or Master commands the Boatswaine to call up the company; the Master being chiefe of the Starboord watch doth call one, and his right hand Mate on the Larboord doth call another, and so forward till they be divided in two parts . . . and then devide them into squadrons according to your number and burthen of your ship as you see occasion; these are to take their turnes at the Helme, trim sailes, pumpe, and doe all duties each halfe, or each squadron for eight Glasses or foure houres which is a watch.[93]

The process Smith describes continued on merchant vessels into the 1920s: the crew is assembled, and the two watch leaders (master/captain and mate in Smith's day; first and second mates in the nineteenth and twentieth centuries) take turns choosing men for their watches, already called the starboard and larboard watch in 1627. Smith then describes watch duties, and confirms that four-hour watches, "watch on and watch off" were normal in his day. Each man in the crew "is to chuse his Mate, consort, or Comrade, . . . but care would bee had there be not two Comrades upon one watch because they may have the more roome in their Cabbins to rest."[94] It would appear that "hot-bunking," in which two men from opposite watches share the same sleeping accommodation, was normal in 1627. Hammocks were not yet in general use, so it appears that the two "comrades" share a bunk or similar bed, sleeping in it alternately when the other stands watch.

Smith goes on to describe how the crew is organized regarding the distribution of food: "The next is, to messe them foure to a messe, and then give every messe a quarter Can of beere and a basket of bread to stay their stomacks till the Kettle be boiled."[95] Smith suggests four to a mess, which appears to have been standard practice aboard English vessels in 1587 and 1588 as well. The mess became institutionalized in the navies of successive centuries, though its numbers could be greater than four. The basket of bread or biscuit functioned just as the wooden "bread barge" in following centuries: the men can help themselves to biscuit while they wait for hot food. The Swedish royal ship *Vasa* has evidence of a similar organization of the crew regarding food. Smith continues:

> that they may first goe to prayer, then to supper, and at six a clocke sing a Psalme, say a Prayer, and the Master with his side begins the watch, then all the rest may doe what they will till midnight; and then his Mate with his Larboord men with a Psalme and a Prayer releeves them till foure in the morning, and so from eight to twelve each other, except some flaw of winde come, somme storme or gust, or some accident that requires the helpe of all hands, which commonly after such good cheere in most voyages doth happen.[96]

This passage speaks volumes about the organization of manpower and time, as well as about mealtimes, aboard English vessels of the early seventeenth century. The master's starboard watch and the mate's larboard watch work the ship in alternation. The changes of watch occur at midnight, 4:00 a.m., 8:00 a.m., noon, 6:00 p.m., and then again at midnight. This watch routine resembles the watch organization of following centuries, except that instead of two short dog watches 4:00–6:00 p.m. and 6:00–8:00 p.m., there is a long, six-hour watch from noon to 6:00 p.m., then another six-hour watch from 6:00 p.m. to midnight. This routine of five watches a day still "dogs" or rotates which of the two watches, starboard or larboard, stands a given watch. In following centuries, two dog watches made seven watches, still an odd number, per day. The meal times coincided with changes of watch, 8:00 a.m., noon, and 6:00 p.m. As Smith points out, all ease and relaxation is by the board when "All Hands!" is called to shorten sail when the wind increases or a storm is on the weather horizon.

Smith gives a commander's-eye-view of a ship-to-ship engagement with a Spanish vessel. After some exchange of shot, night falls. As day breaks, the commander enjoins the cook to prepare breakfast: "And Cooke see you observe your directions against the morning watch, Boy, Holla Master Holla, is the kettle boiled, yea, yea, Boatswaine call up the men to prayer and breake fast. Boy fetch my cellar of bottles, a health to you all fore and aft, courage my hearts for a fresh charge."[97] After this they rejoin the battle.

This passage, like others in A Sea Grammar, is partially comprised of dialogue, but without quotation marks. The captain advises the cook to prepare breakfast so that it may be served to both watches at 8:00 a.m., and he has the boy check that the kettle is boiling, and hot food is on the way. The boy confirms that the kettle is boiling with his, "Yea, yea," much like the "Aye, aye" that became customary in English-language seafaring use later. The captain commands that drink from his store of bottles (probably wine or liquor) be shared with officers and men alike, and bids them take courage to rejoin the fight.

Smith takes commanders to task who take insufficient concern for the dietary well-being and comfort of their crew. He says that some do not think it is important to have pleasant food for the crews, but Smith feels it is important for a commander to keep a "petty tally" or little account of the following:

Fine wheat flower close and well packed, rice, Currands, Sugar, Prunes, Cynamon, Ginger, Pepper, Cloves, greene Ginger, Oyle, Butter, Holland cheese, or old cheese, Wine vineger, Canarie sacke, Aqua vitae, the best Wines, the best waters, the juice of Limons for the scurvy, white Bisket, Oatmeale, gammons of Bacon, dried Neats tongues, Beefe packed up in vinegar, Legs of Mutton minced and stewed, and close packed up, with tried sewet or butter in earthen pots.[98]

These are the "extras" that Smith feels a wise commander will lay in a store of, with which to supplement the men's rations: white flour, rice, currants, sugar, prunes, spices, oil, butter, cheese, vinegar, fortified wine, liquor, clear water, biscuit made of white flour, bacon, dried neat's tongues, beef in vinegar. All these would certainly have kept crew morale in fighting trim, if used occasionally to supplement the standard fare. Two items are worthy of special attention. The legs of mutton minced and stewed, was to be packed up in earthen pots sealed with rendered suet or butter, which would help keep it some time out at sea. The use of leg meat, and the whole preparation, presages the "portable soup" of the eighteenth-century British Navy. This early precursor of portable soup could be part of a special meal after a week or two at sea. The lemon juice for scurvy is also noteworthy. Most commanders at sea felt that it was a dietary deficiency that caused scurvy, and there were those like Smith who recognized the value of citrus in assuaging or even preventing the disease. John Hawkins, for example, carried oranges on his long voyages. It is regrettable that sailors continued to die of scurvy for almost two hundred years after John Smith suggested this remedy. Smith also suggests that a sea commander stock "To entertaine strangers Marmalad, Suckets, Almonds, Comfits and such like." These are dainties with which to entertain distinguished guests on board.

Smith reminds his readers that more English sailors have died because of starvation, disease, or diet deficiency than have been killed in battle since 1588, and he goes on to describe some dainties that he feels should be provided to sick crewmen, or to all the crew from time to time: "a dish of buttered Rice with a little cynamon, ginger, and Sugar, a little minced meat, or rost Beefe, a few stewed Prunes, a race of greene Ginger, a Flap-jacke, a can of fresh Water brewed with a little Cynamon, Ginger, and Sugar." The flapjack is of course a pancake. The drink of water with cinnamon, ginger, and sugar is interesting: tea, coffee, and cocoa were not yet generally available. Since it is served in a "can," a coopered wooden tankard, Smith implies that this drink was served cold, not hot. These are the treats that could be offered the crew on special occasions.

Smith continues with a description of the normal fare aboard English ships in Smith's day:

> a little poore John, or salt fish with oile and mustard, or bisket, butter, cheese, or oatmeale pottage on fish dayes, or on flesh dayes salt Beefe, Porke, and Pease with six shillings beere, this is your ordinary ships allowance, and good for them are well if well conditioned, which is not alwayes as Sea-men can (too well) witnesse.

This is probably close to what English sailors were actually issued in Smith's day. "Poor John" can either mean a specific fish, an inferior sort of cod, or more generally, a pejorative term for any dried or salted fish. Note that the salt fish is served with oil and mustard as recommended in fourteenth-century France: Dutch Navy issues of fish in the following century were accompanied by a sauce of butter, mustard, and spice.

> And after a storme, when poore men are all wet, and some have not so much as a cloth to shift him, shaking with cold, few of those but wil tell you a little Sacke or Aqua vitae is much better to keepe them in health, than a little small beere, or cold water although it be sweet.[99]

"Small beer" is the low-strength beer that was a staple of the English diet for centuries. Smith's advice to offer a tot of fortified wine or something even stronger to men who have just worked hard and gotten themselves soaked for their pains, seems to have fallen on at least a few deaf ears in his own day, but was certainly followed in the centuries to come.

Smith goes on to make some important points about provisioning. A wise commander will keep a good store not only of the necessities, but of the luxuries as well. This is not only essential for showing good hospitality to guests, so as to make a good impression of the owners and himself; but, as Smith has set out before, to encourage his men when they need encouragement the most.

Conclusion

It is in this period, from the fifteenth through the early seventeenth century, that much of European and international practice in preserving, preparing, and distributing food at sea was formalized. National differences still remained, such as the Iberian preference against hiring a designated cook. Some nations continued to favor wine, and others beer, as the seagoing beverage of choice. Nonetheless the basic methods of preserving and preparing food at sea by the 1620s were to endure for the following centuries.

This chapter concludes with a few lines from an English ballad about the Spanish Armada of 1588:

> Spain, and Bisque, and Portugal, Toledo, and Granada,
> They all did meet to make a fleet, and called it the Armada.
> When they had got provisioned, as mustard, pease, and bacon.

THREE

Sailing Navies

National navies came into being during the seventeenth century. Naval forces up to this point consisted of a backbone of ships belonging to a monarch, supported by a hodge-podge of privately owned vessels chartered, borrowed, or pressured into participation in a naval campaign. As navies evolved, new administrations evolved to feed the men who sailed in them. New techniques of food preservation and preparation developed to meet the dietary needs of new types of warship, sailing and fighting far from their native shores. This chapter examines the evolution of artillery, of warships, and of the crew of a sailing warship; then turn to the dietary and culinary practices that evolved along with the guns and the ships.

National Navies: The Sailing Warship Evolves

The evolution of the sailing warship is important, and resulted in long-standing naval institutions of food preparation and distribution. Therefore the next few pages are devoted to the evolution of the artillery-firing sailing warship and the evolution of the institutions that grew around it. After having addressed the evolution of the ship type and the institution of national navies, the chapter explores what these meant to the changing character of food at sea.

The evolution of national navies was compelled by the evolution of the sailing warship. Changes in the weaponry of armed vessels inspired this change. Specialized warships existed in Medieval Scandinavia and the Medieval Mediterranean, with the longship and the galley as specialized vessels designed primarily for speed under oars. The galley survived into the seventeenth century as a specialized warship design of the Mediterranean, and only in isolated localities and applications thereafter. Sea battles in medieval northern Europe were fought between vessels that could serve for either mercantile or naval purposes. The addition of archers in the fore and after castles, grappling hooks, and armed men in the waist to fight with a boarding party, could make a warship out of a merchant ship.[1]

Beginning in the fifteenth century, the introduction of artillery changed warship design forever. The process of change was gradual. Initially, artillery was added to existing ship designs. Rows of small guns were added along the deck of the after castle of carracks and other sailing vessels, firing through permanent openings in the upper works. Galleys were adapted to carry a single gun in the bow firing over the ram.[2] As larger guns were developed for use ashore, gunports were fitted to the hulls of vessels that were expected to fight. The basic design of the gunport already existed: some medieval pictures of sailing vessels show hinged ports, probably used for loading and unloading lumber, livestock, and other cargo without having to hoist them through the hatch.[3] The existing design of loading ports was adapted to artillery: ports were cut in the sides of the ship on the lower decks, allowing larger guns to be carried without making the ship overly top-heavy. This invention or adaptation is credited to a Frenchman in 1501.[4] The gunports were hinged on their upper edge, so that they could be closed and caulked during a sea passage, but they could be opened quickly, and the guns run out and fired, in the event of a battle or confrontation at sea.[5] During the first half of the sixteenth century, more and more ships belonging to monarchs, or designed to carry valuable cargoes that could require armed defense, had their sides dotted with gunports.

At the same time, the guns themselves continued to evolve, not only in size but in basic design as well. Most fifteenth-century ordnance was breech loading: a removable chamber was loaded with powder, wadding, and shot (usually stone). This chamber was slid into place behind a forged iron tube, wedged home, and then could be fired. This type of gun did not require being "run in" between shots, but the design limited the size and power available. Increasingly during the first half of the sixteenth century, iron breech-loading guns of this type were replaced by cast bronze muzzle-loading guns. Bronze muzzleloaders offered a better gas seal when the gun was fired; they could be cast with a stronger, thicker breech; and they could be made in larger sizes. By the late sixteenth century, all but the smaller sizes of shipboard artillery were cast muzzleloaders. Bronze guns of Spanish origin often had the Latin motto cast into them, "Ultima Ratio Regis," "The King's Final Argument," which is usually paraphrased, "The Final Argument of Kings."

The muzzle-loading gun transformed sea battles between sailing vessels. Previously, sea battles entailed an exchange of arrows as the vessels approached one another; then grappling and boarding, with the issue decided by fighting hand to hand. The muzzle-loading gun turned battles at sea into artillery duels, in which individual vessels or squadrons of vessels would blaze away at one another with their artillery. The issue could be decided by vessels sinking or blowing up when their powder magazines exploded, or one vessel could strike its colors and surrender to an opposing vessel. Some battles or individual ship-to-ship duels were still decided by hand-to-hand boarding actions, but this was now one of several possible conclusions; before circa 1550 it had been the only way to decide naval battles.[6]

Thus was born the specialized sailing warship. No longer a troop carrier with grappling hooks, it became an artillery platform, with its decks lined with guns and its sides pierced by gunports. The transformation of the sailing warship transformed the roles of the men who served in them as well. The men who served these guns in battle were sailors, not soldiers, and a floating artillery platform demanded a great deal of manpower. Each gun required five or more men to run the gun in and out, as well as to clean, load, and prime the gun between shots. A fighting ship of the early sixteenth century might carry soldiers (mostly archers or arquebusiers) equal in number to the sailing crew. By the beginning of the next century, the ship was manned almost entirely by sailors, the majority of whom worked her guns. A small force of musketeers augmented the crew: they shot at individual enemy combatants from the decks and from the tops—fighting platforms at the doublings of the masts, and the musketeers were useful in final hand-to-hand combat. At other times, these musketeers functioned as seagoing guards or policeman, protecting the officers from mutineers and enforcing discipline. In time these small bodies of musketeers evolved into Marines.[7]

The evolution of the sailing warship as artillery platform was gradual, taking place over the sixteenth century with many transitional types. The transformation in artillery and ship design compelled the evolution of standing navies to protect the overseas commerce of their nations, and it was in the seventeenth century that standing national navies came into being. Sixteenth-century monarchs owned a small number of vessels, armed with guns. These conveyed and protected costly cargoes such as the Spanish silver shipments from the New World.

The Spanish Armada of 1588 and the English Fleet that opposed it were comprised of a small number of royal ships, leading a far greater number of private vessels chartered, purchased, or coerced into joining battle. By the second half of the seventeenth century, France, England, the Netherlands, as well as other countries, had national navies. No longer simply royal ships that supplied the backbone of a fighting fleet of private vessels, these navies were permanent institutions, with permanent crews and considerable administrative and support staff ashore as well. Navies included big "line-of-battle" ships (also called "ships of the line"); smaller, faster frigates; and a number of smaller craft as well.

For the carrying of low-bulk, high-value cargoes, certain ship types evolved that served as a kind of hybrid. The best-known of these is the East Indiaman, a vessel that could carry the costly cargoes of the East Indies back to European waters, while fighting off attempts to capture those precious cargoes. East Indiamen, whether Dutch, English, or French, had a relatively deep hold, and a single covered gun deck that was proportionately higher than the lower gun deck of a warship, leaving more space for cargo. With her guns mounted higher in the hull than those of a man-of-war, the guns of an East Indiaman needed to be somewhat lighter as well. The guns of the *Bonhomme Richard*'s lower deck were eighteen pounders (i.e., they fired an iron ball estimated to weigh eighteen pounds), at a time when most frigates' lower decks were equipped with twenty-four pounders. The *Bonhomme Richard* was an old French East Indiaman, which John Paul Jones purchased on behalf of the American Congress.[8]

Feeding the Men Who Serve the Guns

The manpower requirements of a man-of-war made sailing warships of this era intensely crowded. Most of the crew slept in hammocks slung fore-and-aft in the spaces between the guns, and dined off hanging tables that could be lowered into the same spaces.

Just as the demands of long-distance exploration and commerce placed new demands on the feeding of ship's crews over long distance and long time, the new sailing warship placed new demands in terms of the sheer quantity of food required to sustain the crews of ships crammed with guns and the men who served them. Every morning the men took down their hammocks, lashed them up, and stowed them in a railing over the bulwarks, where the compacted canvas offered extra protection from gunfire. Thus the command for getting up was "Lash and stow!" or "Up Hammocks!"[9] At mealtimes, hanging tables were swung down and chests or benches dragged into place to sit on. These tables, which lasted into the era of steam navies, were a specific naval design. At one end, they hinged or hooked into the side of the vessel. On the inboard end they were suspended from the deck above, by slings initially made of rope, and later made of iron. An optional component

Figure 3.1. Hanging tables on HMS *Warrior*. Photograph by Christopher Roche, 2014. Used with permission.

was a single hinged leg, which could swing down from the inboard end of the table to the deck below. These tables were constructed by the ship's carpenter and carpenter's mates when a new warship was commissioned.[10] With occasional exceptions such as the British Leda-class frigates (e.g., frigate HM *Trincomalee*, still afloat in Hartlepool), which had a mess deck below the guns, most crewmen on sailing warships slept and ate by their guns. Even the frigates with a separate mess deck still preserved the same arrangement of either hammocks slung fore-and aft (to sleep) or thwartship tables swung down into place (to eat).

Establishing a Basic Ration

As standing national navies came into being, there arose a need to establish standards for adequately serving the men who served in them. The administration of food in the British Navy was overseen initially by a Surveyor of Victualling. In 1683 this single officer was replaced by a Board of Victualling Commissioners, more succinctly known as the Victualling Board. This institution, comprised of seven commissioners who met regularly, and seventy-odd clerks, oversaw the supply of comestibles to the fleet. The Victualling Board met regularly and supervised a substantial staff of clerks, bakers, and purchasers abroad.[11] Samuel Pepys, appointed Surveyor of Victualling in 1665, drew up a victualing contract in 1677 which specified the basic ration for seamen.

This basic ration was to be a daily allowance of one pound of biscuit and one gallon of beer; and a weekly allowance of eight pounds of beef; or four pounds of beef, two pounds of bacon or pork with two pints of peas. (The association of pork with peas, which we have already seen in the previous chapter, was to continue in the British Navy.) Meat was served on Mondays, Tuesdays, Thursdays, and Sundays. Wednesdays, Fridays, and Saturdays were fish days, the issue being either fresh cod, stockfish, salt cod, or salt hake. The issue of fish was accompanied by two ounces of butter, and either four ounces of Suffolk Cheese or two and two-thirds ounces of Cheddar cheese.[12] The Suffolk cheese, made from milk "thrice skimmed," caused trouble, not from spoilage but because it was so hard that it was said that even rats could not gnaw it. Eventually the Suffolk cheese could become infested with red worms (cheese worms, *Eisenia fetida*), and so in 1758 the Victualling Board eliminated Suffolk cheese, replacing it with Cheshire, Cheddar, Gloucester, or Warwickshire cheese. While these had a shorter shelf life than the Suffolk cheese, they were more popular.[13]

The basic ration for seamen in the British Navy was updated again in 1733, when the Admiralty published "Regulations and Instructions relating to His Majesty's Service at Sea." The dietary guidelines included in this publication remained in force through the entire period of the sailing navy.[14] Here are the weekly totals:

Biscuit	7 Pounds Avoirdupois
Beer	7 Gallons Wine Measure
Pork	2 Pounds Avoirdupois
Pease	2 Pints Winchester Measure
Oatmeal	3 Pints Winchester Measure
Butter	6 ounces
Cheese	12 ounces [15]

As the British Navy increasingly operated in distant waters, the admiralty came up with guidelines for substituting locally available foodstuffs for those commonly available in home waters. The Admiralty sought to ensure that sailors would receive enough food, and that their diet would still be balanced. They established a system of substitutions, designed to ensure that crewmen on foreign stations received nutrition roughly equivalent to that of sailors in home waters.

"When it may be found necessary to issue any other Species of Provisions or Substitutions for the above, it is to be observed that they are to be furnished in the following proportions, vis.":

- One pint of wine equals a gallon of beer, no more than one quarter of the whole to be issued in wine.
- Four pounds of flour, or three pounds of flour with a pound of raisins, equals four pounds of salt beef.
- Half a pound of currants, or half a pound of beef suet, is equal to one pound of raisins.
- Four pounds of fresh beef, or three pounds of mutton (a fattier meat), are equal to four pounds of salt beef.
- Three pounds of fresh beef or mutton, is equal to two pounds of Pork, if combined with peas.
- One pint of Calavances (chickpeas, or possibly lablab; i.e., hyacinth bean), or "doll" (dal, i.e., lentils), is equal to a pint of peas.
- A pound of rice is considered equal to a pound of bread, a pint of peas, a quart of oatmeal, or a pound of cheese.
- A pint of wheat or barley is equal to a pint of oatmeal.
- 5¾ pounds of molasses are equal to one gallon of oatmeal.
- One pound of sugar is equal to two quarts of Oatmeal, one pound of butter, or one pound of cheese.
- A pint of oil (e.g., olive oil) is equal to a pound of butter, or two pounds of cheese.
- A half pound of cocoa, or a quarter pound of tea, is equal to one pound of cheese.[16]

These substitutions served as guidelines for issuing sailors a balanced ration while serving in the Mediterranean, the Indian Ocean, the Baltic, or elsewhere. A few of the substitutions are questionable in terms of caloric intake, such as a quarter pound of tea for a pound of cheese, but the tea was an expensive luxury, and so cost may play a role in that proportion. The men themselves understood their need for solid food. Jacob Nagle was an American seaman who served in an American privateer during the War of Independence; in privateers, merchant vessels, and in the British Navy thereafter. Nagle wrote in his journal of shortages on the merchant sloop *James*, in the Virgin Islands: "Though we had plenty of coffee and sugar, it did not satisfy hunger altogether."[17]

Substitutions of foods not listed by the Victualling Board were made on an ad hoc basis at the discretion of the captain. For example, yams and potatoes may have been issued in lieu of other foods. Locally caught turtles could be a source of fresh meat as well. Jacob Nagle describes the meat ration aboard the twenty-gun privateer *Brilliant* lying off Santo Domingo in the Caribbean: "While laying here we lived well, fresh beef one day and turkle [*sic*] [turtle] the nex [*sic*]. Amongst those islands fish and turkle [*sic*] is plentiful." Nagle and his shipmates continued to eat turtle on their way home to Scotland: "We had seventy five large turkel [*sic*] on board, but none lived to reach Scotland, the weather being two [*sic*] cold. Therefore we lived well on the passage."[18]

St. Helena and Ascension are two islands that offer a landfall to ships sailing from West Africa around the Cape of Good Hope to the Indian Ocean. St. Helena thus presented an important opportunity for British ships headed around the Cape of Good Hope to stock up on antiscorbutic (curative or preventive of scurvy) watercress, catch fresh fish, and top up their supplies. Jacob Nagle offers us a glimpse of the dietary offerings of that remote little island:

> Every Indiaman is compeled to leave stores on the island on their homeward bound passage. Makeral is plentiful, some beneta [bonito], and albacore. They are the chief fish that is cought here. Water crises [*sic*] [watercress] is numerous, the shiping make use of it, being holesom [*sic*] for the scurvey [*sic*].[19]

The Staff of Naval Life: Biscuit

The single most important ingredient in the diet of the men serving in sailing navies was the hard dense bread known as ship's biscuit. These were baked ashore in enormous naval bakeries in Deptford, Portsmouth, and Plymouth. Additional supplies were sometimes acquired from contractors, and as the design of on-board cooking facilities became more complex they could be baked on board. The recipe was simple, consisting of flour (of the type known as whole wheat flour today), water (about half the volume of the flour, less than that used for soft bread), and a little salt. Molasses can be added to biscuit, but this may shorten its shelf life. Biscuits in the eighteenth-century British Navy could be square, round, or octagonal, and they were usually pricked with a fork and stamped with the "broad arrow" mark of government ownership, and a letter that identified the baker. This process slightly compressed the center, making it harder than the edges. When the edges had been soaked or knocked off, sailors called these hard centers "purser's nuts."[20]

Ship's biscuits were usually too hard to chew as issued. They could be soaked in broth, or water, to soften them, or the edges could be knocked off and slowly sucked. The chief virtue of the biscuit is that it kept a long time. They would eventually acquire "weevils" (in fact a beetle, *Stegobium paniceum*) if kept too long, and a traditional sailor's habit of tapping the biscuit on the table was alleged to remove some at least of the weevils.[21] In the British Navy, it was believed that biscuit would keep longer if the bread room in which it was stored was ventilated; in fact, the moisture that came with the fresh air actually contributed to spoilage. In the Dutch and American navies, biscuit was kept sealed until needed, which made their biscuits last longer. During the War of 1812, American biscuit was observed to be superior to British biscuit, probably for this reason.[22]

The Roast Beef of Old England

The other staple of the naval diet was salt beef. Freshly slaughtered beef was cut into pieces by "randers" (not renders) and "messers," treated with dry salt, and cured in barrels of brine. To conserve the beef properly, the solution had to be strong enough to make the beef float, and it had to be held down below the water level to prevent spoilage. Saltpeter (potassium nitrate) was also added to the brine in the belief that it helped the salt penetrate the meat. The saltpeter may have reduced the chance of botulism. The saltpeter also gave the meat a pink color. If the cask leaked and meat was exposed to the air, it rotted and had to be condemned and discarded.[23] Specific centers of beef production, such as Cork in Ireland, contributed a high proportion of the British Navy's salt beef. British ships and squadrons far from home ran out of salt beef, and purchasing agents acquired whole herds of cattle to supplement the beef supplies of these vessels. The keeping of all sorts of livestock on board, to be slaughtered when needed, was common practice in this period.[24] Pork was pickled in brine in the same manner as beef, and was also a staple of the British and other navies.

Admiral Vernon's Legacy

As noted, wine or spirits could be substituted for the beer ration. Spirits issued alone could be quite intoxicating, and on either August 21, 1740, or on March 24, 1743 (accounts vary), Admiral Edward Vernon ordered the men in his ships to receive their rum together with water. The admiral's nickname was "Old Grog," after his wearing of a "grog" or grosgrain (corded silk) cloak. Grog was therefore what the sailors called the mixture of rum and water. The health of Admiral Vernon's men appeared to benefit from the institution, not surprising as this meant that they drank water with their alcohol. The adoption of lime or lemon juice as a scurvy preventive came later, and gradually. Some commanders parsimoniously issued lime juice as a treatment to men already suffering from scurvy, but not as a preventive to the entire crew. As a result of this false economy, hundreds of scurvy cases continued to dog the British Navy through the first decade of the nineteenth century. To be "groggy" came to mean being less than alert due to alcohol or lack of rest.[25] The proportions of rum and water varied over the centuries, but some combination of water was served in the Royal Navy under the name of grog until 1970.

Rum was also known as "Nelson's Blood," after the Battle of Trafalgar, because Admiral Horatio Nelson's body was carried back to England for burial, preserved in a cask of liquor. In actual fact the cask was filled with brandy; but sailors believed it was rum, and so rum got a nickname in the Royal Navy. Sailors developed their own expressions to describe combinations of water and liquor: "Due North" meant "straight liquor," "Due West" meant "plain water," "Northwesterly" meant "liquor and water in equal proportions," and "Southerly" meant "empty glass."[26]

The issue of grog ration was sometimes announced to the crew by having a fiddler or fifer play the tune "Drops of Brandy." This is a merry tune in 9/8 time, still played throughout the British Isles. In later years, a specific call on the boatswain's whistle, "Up spirits!" signaled the issue of grog.

The Cook and His Galley

The cook in a British warship was a warrant officer (American petty officer), and preference was shown to Greenwich pensioners, who as pensioned-off naval seamen, might be missing a leg, an eye, or some other body part, but had experience at sea. On ships of larger size the cook had mates or assistants.[27]

Salt beef was desalinated by soaking in a steep tub, a piece of gear which was given the more colorful name of "harness cask" in the nineteenth century. After serving out the meat from the copper pots, the "slush" or rendered fat, was scraped from the coppers and kept in a "slush tub." Half of the slush went to the cook, who could use it for any number of tasks; while the other half was reserved for the rigging.[28] Spars were routinely "slushed" with fat to cut down on friction from mast hoops, stunsail booms, and other objects that slid along them. This was done by sailors going aloft with a bucket of slush and a brush, sometimes sitting on the spar as they slushed it. The use of slush as a verb, to rub a surface down with refuse fat, is said to date back to 1807.[29] Later on, the money raised from the sale of discarded or surplus items to pay for little luxuries on a warship was called a "slush fund" in the Royal Navy, the phrase first appearing in print in 1864.[30] Eventually the phrase was applied to funds used for bribery or for reimbursing questionable expenses.

Figure 3.2. "Slushing Down," from Gordon Grant, *Sail Ho: Windjammer Sketches Alow and Aloft* (New York: William Farquhar, 1930, 27). This illustration is over a century after Nelson, but the process and equipment was much the same in the eighteenth century.

Early eighteenth-century British naval vessels' facilities for cooking were much like those found on *Mary Rose* and *Vasa*: a brick hearth with a copper boiler. The most significant improvement from 1545 and 1628 was the addition of a chimney to carry the smoke up to the deck. Iron stoves were introduced as a savings in weight in 1728, and the Navy board recommended dimensions for the stoves of different sizes in 1757.[31] The "coppers" or copper cauldrons, were quite large. Thomas Dring, an American sailor imprisoned aboard the *Jersey*, a former sixty-four-gun ship of the line used as a prison hulk in New York during the War of Independence, estimated the capacity of the *Jersey*'s cauldron at two to three hogsheads, or 120 to 180 gallons.[32] The *Defence*, an American privateer brig excavated in Maine, had a cauldron with a capacity of 68 gallons. These cauldrons usually had fitted lids, which themselves could have holes for small kettles or pots.[33]

A dramatic improvement to food preparation in the British Navy was the Brodie stove, the brainchild of Scotsman Alexander Brodie. Brodie's 1780

Figure 3.3. Stove with copper pots on HMS *Warrior*. Though this is a British warship from the mid-nineteenth century, the design of the stove and utensils is little changed from the forms attained fifty years earlier. Photograph by Christopher Roche, 2014. Used with permission.

patent covers an iron stove of ingenious design, bolted together so that it could be disassembled, and damaged parts replaced. The Brodie stove used a combination of wrought iron, cast iron, and copper, and included a spit big enough for an entire sheep or pig, turned through sprockets and a chain by a fan in the chimney. The spit-turning mechanism somewhat resembled the "clock jacks" used to turn spits in eighteenth-century kitchens ashore. There were cranes, similar to fireplace cranes, with which to swing multiple pots over the fire, a baking oven, and racks for "stewing stoves" which resembled a brazier, in which small pots could be heated by embers from the main fire. Spigots in the boilers allowed fluid to be drained from below, and there was even a condenser which produced a small amount of distilled water. The whole contraption sat on four short legs that held it up off the deck.[34]

Cooking the Ration: Lobscouse, Burgoo, Sea Pie, and Many Variations of Duff

The basic foodstuffs described in the ration were combined in a number of imaginative and not so imaginative ways. The following foods are a few of the most ubiquitous shipboard delicacies from navies of this era.

Lobscouse
The origins of Lobscouse are obscure; the dish and the name are found throughout much of the Baltic region, as well as Norway, England, and Germany. There are several different possible derivations of the name: depending on which you think most likely, the dish could have originated in Latvia and Lithuania, Sweden and Finland, Norway, England, or Germany. It is a standard dish ashore in Scandinavia, where it is made of alternate layers of sliced potato and sliced beef, with onions; seasoned with salt and a good deal of black pepper. Water is added and then the lobscouse is baked in a covered pot. In some versions, the lobscouse is more of a stew, stirred regularly while it is cooked. A similar version is sometimes called "scouse" or "lobby" in England. Lobscouse is often associated with Liverpool, perhaps because of that seaport's intimate relationship with the sea. At sea, chunks of ship's biscuits served in place of the potatoes, and the beef was usually salt beef, fresh from a soak in the steep tub or "harness cask." Lobscouse was a staple of the shipboard diet for centuries. The American favorite, Corned Beef Hash, is essentially a fried, transplanted variation of lobscouse.[35]

Burgoo
This is what oatmeal porridge was usually called when prepared in the British Navy. In its simplest version, it was simple oats and water in 1:2 proportions, with a pinch of salt. Butter, cream, milk, and sugar, in some combination, could be added when it was served.

Sea Pie
Sea Pie is sometimes identified as an alternate term for Lobscouse; but whereas Lobscouse could be prepared more like a stew, Sea Pie was invariably baked. For this reason, the Sea Pie had a layering of the potatoes or biscuit fragments and salt beef; in lobscouse, all the ingredients were usually mixed together. Curiously, some of the surviving Scandinavian versions of lobscouse are baked with sliced potatoes and meat in discrete layers, producing something more like what eighteenth- and nineteenth-century English-speaking sailors would probably have called a "sea pie."

Duff and Its Variations
Duff was suet pudding, usually boiled in a bag. In the British Navy, these bags were usually labeled for each mess. The principal ingredients were flour, suet, and water. In the late eighteenth and early nineteenth century, there were many variations of duff, some with weird, even lurid names. One type of duff was Jam Roly Poly: the dough is rolled out, slathered with jam, then rolled into a cylinder before boiling.[36] Another type was Spotted Dog, in which the

cook would add milk and eggs, season with spice, and stir in dried currants (the spots). This variation still survives in England as "Spotted Dick."[37] Yet another type, and possibly the most luridly named of the Duff Clan, was the Drowned Baby or Boiled Baby. This was duff with sugar, raisins, and a little spice added. Thankfully, this came to be known as "Plum (or Plumb) Duff" by the mid-nineteenth century.[38] The spice for any of these dishes might feature cinnamon, powdered ginger, ground nutmeg, ground cloves, or allspice. Cooks sometimes served them with a sweet sauce, syrup/treacle, or molasses as a topping.

Portable Soup

Portable Soup was a form of concentrated food, allegedly developed by a Mrs. Dubois around 1756. Vegetables were boiled along with shin beef (which contributes to its coagulation) and diced organ meats, cooled and hardened, and then cut into slabs and boxed. When boiled up with water, it made a soup. While it was hoped that the resulting broth would be antiscorbutic, it was not; this was a welcome supplement to salt beef and biscuit on long ocean passages. Portable soup was initially intended for the sick, but it was popular with the men, and soon was issued generally, fifty pounds for every hundred men on ships bound for foreign stations. Captain James Cook spoke highly of portable soup, and it became a standard issue in the British Navy through the late eighteenth and early nineteenth century.[39]

Potatoes and Yams

Potatoes and yams were substituted for the bread ration at foreign stations, in the proportion of two pounds of potatoes or yams for one pound of bread. Potatoes were said to be popular with navy crews, while yams were a less popular substitution.[40]

Breadfruit

Breadfruit was and still is a staple food in the South Pacific. The famous voyage of HMS *Bounty* commanded by William Bligh was primarily for the purpose of obtaining breadfruit seedlings from Tahiti, and planting them in Jamaica. Bligh was successful in gathering the Tahitian seedlings: but after a month was unsuccessful in rounding Cape Horn in an eastward direction, and then the famous mutiny occurred. Bligh and the crew members loyal to him miraculously sailed all the way to the Dutch East Indies in the Bounty's launch, subsisting on minute amounts of ship's biscuit. Breadfruit was eventually transplanted to Jamaica by others.

A Royal Navy Tradition Begins: Cocoa

The issue of cocoa may have started in the West Indies Station. Captain W. Young of the Sandwich wrote to the Controller of the Navy in 1780, "I cannot conceive why in the West Indies the men cannot be allowed sugar, coffee, and chocolate in lieu of oatmeal; they are a better breakfast for the men and a much greater anti-scorbutic." Surgeon Trotter recommended the issue of cocoa to the Channel fleet: "In a cold country it could be singularly beneficial. What a comfortable meal would a cup of warm cocoa or chocolate be to a sailor in a winter cruise in the Channel or North Sea on coming from a wet deck in a rainy morning watch." So, tentatively at first, cocoa became a Royal Navy tradition.[41]

Messes, Mess Cooks, and Mess Kids

John Smith in 1627 described the organization of messes of four men. This system was well entrenched in the Royal Navy, though the number of the mess could vary from four to as many as seven. Crewmen were free to choose which mess they would join, and it was customary to let them change messes on a designated Sunday, about once a month.[42] Within each mess there was one mess cook, rotated about once a week within the members of the mess. The mess cook was responsible for preparing the mess's food for cooking, bringing it in the mess's kid (something like a firkin or wooden container), with the puddings in labeled sacks or nets, to the galley. On most warships, the mess tables were folded up against the sides when not in use. The mess cook arranged the hanging table, and set the benches or chests in place. When the food was ready, the same mess cook then collected the food from the galley in the mess kid, brought it to his mess's table, and distributed the food.[43]

The men's utensils included both issue items and those they acquired themselves. By the eighteenth century the customary wooden plates in naval service were square, with slats nailed to all four edges to create a raised edge. Square trenchers were common in the seventeenth century, and it appears that a simplified version of that design went to sea. The men were known to purchase ceramic or pewter plates of their own, but the wooden plates were always there should the fancier ware become broken or lost.[44] The "bread barge" was a tray or shallow box that held ship's biscuit or soft bread, according to what had been issued. Because the biscuit sat in a "barge," weevils (actually *Stegobium paniceum*, a beetle) were nicknamed "bargemen" in naval slang.[45] Mugs of horn with wooden bases were also issued: reproductions of these, along with square wooden plates, are displayed on the mess tables of HMS *Victory* and HM Frigate *Trincomalee* today. Horn cups work well for water or liquor, but impart a dreadful flavor to any hot drink put in them. One wonders what sort of drinking vessel the men used for issues of tea and coffee. If tin or ceramic drinking ware was not issued, something must have been acquired by the men in some way, if they were to consume any issues of hot drinks.

The mess cook was responsible for distribution of the pieces of meat, distributing them in a ritualized manner. Placing a portion on a plate, he would call out, "Who shall have this?" A blindfolded messmate would call out the name of one of their mess, and the mess cook would pass that "whack" or portion to the messmate named.[46] The mess cook was responsible for washing up after meals, probably feeding the scraps to the shipboard livestock, and dumping anything still left out the heads, openings to the sea in the beakhead forward. Dumping food scraps out the gunports was disallowed. The "tumble home" or inward slant of most warships' sides would cause any food scraps tossed out an open gunport to stain the side of the vessel, and possibly decompose there. It goes without saying that there was probably not a single naval commander of the sailing era who would have knowingly permitted his crew to toss their food scraps out an open gunport.

Mealtime Schedules

These could vary at the captain's discretion, but usually had crew and officers breaking fast at 8:00 a.m., then the crew having dinner at noon and the officers an hour later (sometimes the captain later still); then the crew eating supper at 5:00 or 5:30 p.m. while the officers had supper at 6:00 p.m. This may have allowed junior officers to relieve helmsmen and lookouts during the crew's meal. On some ships, the meal times appear to have been 8:00 a.m., 12:00 noon, and 4:00 p.m. HMS *Revenge* apparently used this schedule.[47] The call to eat was often announced by having a fiddler (usually one of the sailors) or a fifer (attached to the Marines) play the tune "The Roast Beef of Old England."

Officers' Table

The officers ate aft in the wardroom or gunroom; larger vessels had both, with captains or admirals dining alone, the commissioned officers in the wardroom, and junior officers in the gunroom. Smaller vessels had smaller officers' eating quarters, and consequently there would be more consolidation of the ranks. The officers received the same food as the crew, but universally augmented this fare by purchasing wines and delicacies, pooling their resources and entrusting the purchases to a "mess caterer" who could make purchases in ports of call. The tables and chairs were designed to be easily taken apart and stowed when the vessel was cleared for action. This part of the vessel included guns, and during battle the officers would be on deck, so the wardroom was completely transformed into a part of a gun deck when preparing for battle.[48] During the nineteenth century, the wardroom became an area for the surgeon to treat the wounded in battle.

It was usual for the officers to purchase ceramic dishes, serving plates, and other elegant trimmings for their table. There were a number of clever devices they would sometimes acquire to keep dishes and food from sliding around or off the table, such as "fiddles" (baffles and/or railings) on the table; cloth-covered wedges of different sizes to keep dishes upright (useful if heeled over on a reach, not so useful if the vessel is rocking and pitching); pudding bags filled with peas; or wet cloths on the table to discourage plates sliding around.[49]

Officers purchased wine for the wardroom, in splendid variety and quantity. In 1761, Captain Clements of the Argo purchased wine in Italy, resulting in the following inventory:

Messina: 1 butt, and 3 kegs containing 40 gallons each
Port: 2 hogsheads
Cyprus: 2 kegs, 1 demijohn and 2 bottles
Champagne: 6 dozen bottles
Burgundy: 12 dozen bottles
Claret: 12 dozen and 7 bottles
Frontenac: 6 bottles
Montepulciano: 1 chest
Florence: 8 chests and a half
Malvasia: 2 chests
Rum: one dozen and nine bottles[50]

In 1749 the captain of the *Harwich* in the East Indies had the following inventory:

Madeira: 2 pipes, 2 puncheon, 3 1 half-leaguer and 4 third-leaguers
Arrack: 1 puncheon, 3 hogsheads, 1 half-leaguer and 4 third-leaguers
Rum: 27 gallons 2 quarts in bottle and cask
Brandy: 20 gallons[51]

Readers should keep in mind that these supplies were to be shared with guests and with the other denizens of the wardroom, and some may have been purchased to resell or trade.

Twelfth Night Cake in Heavy Weather

A colorful account of eating in the wardroom in heavy weather comes from Henry Theonge, naval chaplain aboard HMS *Assistance* in 1676.[52] Besides being a good account of accepting bad weather in the wardroom, it is an early and detailed description of a king cake or *galette de roi*:

> Very ruff weather all the last night, and all this day. . . . wee had much myrth on board, for wee had a greate kake made, in which was put a beane for the king, a pease for the queen, a cloave for the knave, a forked stick for the coockold, a ragg for the slutt. The kake was cutt into severall pieces in the great cabin, and all putt into a napkin, out of which every one took his piece, as out of a lottery, then each piece is broaken to see what was in it, which caused much laughter, to see our lieutenant prove the coockold, and more to see us tumble on over the other in the cabin, by reason of the ruff weather.[53]

Heavy weather could limit the food men received, and their ability to prepare it. The following comes from Jacob Nagle's early journal, when he was serving in the American privateer *Fair American* during the War of Independence:

> "The gale continued for several days . . . we had no provisions eccepting two or three bags of bread dust and a quart of water, and when that was expended, we received a half pint of flower, but we could not spare the water.[54]

Scurvy

Scurvy, caused by insufficient consumption of Vitamin C for the body to produce the collagen essential for the body's connective tissue, remained a serious danger of long voyages, and of remaining on station a long time without fresh food. Of course commanders would do what they could to prevent scurvy, but it did occur on long passages. John Smith suggested carrying "the juice of Limons for the scurvy" as early as 1627, yet this advice was not followed universally in the early years of national navies. There was a good deal of controversy over the actual cause of the condition. Some thought that scurvy was caused by eating rancid fat, and others believed that eating salt fish caused scurvy.[55] The confusion is understandable: as scurvy occurs when fresh foods containing Vitamin C are not consumed, it is tempting to blame the increasingly limited range of preserved foods that are consumed on a long trip without landfall.

A Scottish naval surgeon named James Lind made a study of scurvy in 1747, and published his "Treatise of the Scurvy" in 1753, after leaving the Royal Navy. He found that eating fresh fruit (two oranges and one lemon a day) was the most effective cure for men suffering from scurvy. Sadly, Lind's work was generally ignored.[56]

Captain Cook is often credited with leading the effort to reduce scurvy in the British Navy, and his record during his first expedition to the South Pacific, 1768–1771, is exemplary. Cook managed not to lose a single man to scurvy on his voyage from England to Java. In part this was through persuading his men to eat citrus fruits. Cook had his men collect edible greens ashore at every opportunity, and he issued these foods in equal quantities to every man and officer aboard HMS *Endeavor*. Most famously, he persuaded his men to eat sauerkraut, pickled cabbage—this was not common in the English diet, but was and still is a dietary staple in Central, Northern, and Eastern Europe.[57]

Initially Cook's men were disinclined to eat the sauerkraut, so Cook resorted to a clever stratagem. Sauerkraut was served to the officers in the wardroom, but was made available to the men's messes only if they wanted it. Within a week, the men decided they wanted sauerkraut, and thenceforward everyone aboard *Endeavor* drew a regular ration of it.[58]

Scurvy did not disappear overnight from the British Navy, however. Jacob Nagle offers a vivid description of scurvy aboard HMS *Sirius* sailing to Australia in 1789:

> Going round the Horn this passage, the ships company was taken with the scurvey [sic] . . . Some died in sight of the Cape of Good Hope, or Table Bay . . . (2 January 1789) The doctor went to town and braught [sic] a quantity of fruit on board to be served out to both sick and well, for even those that were doing there [sic] duty, when biteing [sic] an aple [sic], pare [sic], or peach, the blod [sic] would run out of our mouth from our gums with the scurvey [sic].

After HMS *Sirius* got into Table Bay and purchased mutton, vegetables, and wine, the men began to recover from scurvy: "Crew recovering daily, till all were well and harty [sic]. We shipped hands in lew [sic] of those that died in the passage."[59]

In 1794, at the urging of Dr. Gilbert Blane, an experiment was tried in which two-thirds of an ounce of lemon juice and two ounces of sugar were added to the grog issue aboard *Suffolk*, while making a twenty-three week nonstop voyage to India. This measure was effective in curing scurvy (and represented the next step in the evolution of Royal Navy grog): subsequently lemons were issued often in home waters at least, greatly reducing scurvy in the British Navy. Parsimony or the unavailability of lemons caused the lemon juice to be issued only to men already showing symptoms of scurvy through the 1790s and early years of the nineteenth century, and scurvy continued to afflict seamen in the British Navy. Limes were sometimes substituted for reasons of cost or availability, and the practice of including lime or lemon juice in the issue of grog, for the entire crew as a preventive antiscorbutic, appears to have become general after 1810. Adding the antiscorbutic to the men's grog probably helped ensure that all would actually consume their lime juice ration.[60] Sailors of other nations began calling British ships "Limejuice Ships," and their crewmen "Limejuicers" or just "Limeys." Eventually the nickname was applied to Englishmen generally.

Food of Other European Navies

Food in the French Navy was similar to that in the British Navy, with some interesting differences. Herring and sardines sometimes served as the salt fish ration, which is not surprising as sardines were often caught by fishing vessels based in Brittany near the naval port of Brest. The French Navy's daily ration for the men, as expressed in the *Ordonnances* of 1689, 1747, 1765, and 1786, consisted of one and a half pounds of biscuit, a midday meal of bacon, salt beef, fish, or cheese; and a supper of dried peas or beans, prepared with oil and vinegar. An interesting French feature was a monthly issue of mustard seed for the men to season their food. Soft bread, rice and prunes (a favorite pastry ingredient in the Breton countryside around Brest) were mostly reserved for the sick. The liquor ration was usually red wine. French officers before the revolution were known to set a fine table; the officers subsisting on more Spartan fare in Napoleon's navy. When their Atlantic ports were blockaded, French seamen experienced shortages of foodstuffs, and French prisoners were sometimes suffering from scurvy when captured.[61]

The Dutch Navy seems to have been a great deal like the British one in its food issues, though there are records of pickled herring, pickled cabbage, and onions. Buckwheat (groats) appear in records of food issues for Dutch sailors. A weekly issue of a pound of cheese was normal, as was an ample supply of beer. The issue of fish was sometimes accompanied by a dip made of butter, mustard, and spices: this method of eating the fish ration bears an interesting similarity to the issue of "salt fish with oile and mustard" that John Smith describes as standard shipboard fare on English ships in 1627.[62]

The United States Navy

In the American Navy, the grog ration in the 1790s was usually corn whiskey rather than rum, but this could vary. The messes in some American ships appear to have used a canvas floor cloth rather than mess tables, and metal plates and cups were the rule. Meals in American ships were generally served at 8:00 a.m., noon, and 4:00 p.m.[63]

Here are the prescribed weekly rations for crew members of the American Navy in 1798:

Beef	3 pounds
Pork	3 pounds
Potatoes	2 pounds
Salt Fish	1 pound
Bread	112 ounces
Cheese	12 ounces
Butter	4 ounces
Peas or beans	$1\frac{1}{2}$ pints
Rice	1 pint
Spirits	$3\frac{1}{2}$ pints[64]

Here are the prescribed weekly rations for crew members of the American Navy in 1813, after modifications in 1801, 1805, and 1806:

Beef	$3\frac{1}{2}$ pounds
Pork	3 pounds
Flour	1 pound
Suet	$\frac{1}{2}$ pound
Bread	98 ounces
Cheese	6 ounces
Butter	2 ounces
Peas	1 pint
Rice	1 pint
Molasses	½ pint
Vinegar	½ pint
Spirits	$3\frac{1}{2}$ pints [65]

After the War of 1812, American rations were revised again. The value attached to each issue may be the amount of extra pay each man was entitled to if he did not receive it.

Rations per week per man according to regulations of 1818:

Suet	½ pound	6½ cents
Cheese	6 ounces	6½ cents
Beef	3½ pounds	29 cents
Pork	3 pounds	29 cents
Flour	1 pound	4 cents
Bread	98 ounces	30½ cents
Butter	2 ounces	3 cents
Sugar	7 ounces	7 cents
Tea	4 ounces	12 cents
Peas	1 pint	34 cents
Molasses	½ pint	3 cents
Vinegar	½ pint	2 cents
Spirits	3½ pints	35 cents[66]

The quality of American naval rations was not always the best. Charles Nordhoff, a journalist who served in the United States Navy prior to the American Civil War, recalled:

> I had always fancied that the stories of worm-eaten bread, and water, the smell of which could cause violent nausea, were a little more than apocryphal; but . . . We experienced both. I have seen drinking water pumped out of our tanks, into a butt on deck, which smelt so abominably as to make any approach to it utterly impossible, ere it had stood in the open air an hour or two. . . . And I have seen biscuit literally crawl off the mess cloth.[67]

The reference to a "mess cloth" is interesting. This is probably a cloth, possibly painted or tarred, that was laid on deck, instead of the hanging tables which were customary in the British Navy.

Conclusion

This chapter ends with an ode to Admiral Vernon, his grosgrain cloak, and grog. Dr. John Trotter wrote this commendation of grog aboard the *Burford*, Vernon's flagship, in 1781:

A mighty bowl on deck he drew,
    And filled it to the brink;
Such drank the *Burford*'s gallant crew,
    And such the gods shall drink.
The sacred robe which Vernon wore
    Was drenched within the same;
And hence his virtues guard our shore,
    And Grog derives its name.[68]

FOUR

Nineteenth-Century
Merchant Ships

While national navies came into being, merchant shipping continued to evolve, though slowly and conservatively. Throughout the eighteenth century, food on merchant ships remained more or less as John Smith described it in 1627. The introduction of the potato from the Americas to Europe affected food-ways ashore more than on ships, as potatoes did not keep long at sea.

To bring our story forward to the nineteenth century, it is useful to discuss the personnel changes that occurred over the course of time. An important player in the story of food preservation at sea left the stage, for most purposes, in the nineteenth century. From 1627 through the eighteenth century, most vessels employed a ship's cooper, who repaired and maintained the barrels and casks in which most food and drink was stored. The cooper not only maintained and inspected them, but broke them down and then reassembled them as needed. The cooper was customarily addressed by the title of "Bungs."[1] By the early nineteenth century, most merchant ships no longer employed a cooper, even though wooden barrels were used extensively for food storage. The cook, steward, and if needed the carpenter were responsible for whatever shipboard cooperage was required on nineteenth-century merchant vessels. A dramatic exception to this was whaling: whaling ships continued to employ a ship's cooper, to maintain the barrels in which whale oil was stored for the voyage home. After about 1860, British whalers stored their whale blubber in steel tanks; but American whalers continued

Figure 4.1. Photograph of a painting by Charles S. Morrell of *Balclutha* under British registry. Reproduction Number HAER CAL,38-SANFRA,200—142 in Collection: Historic American Buildings Survey/Historic American Engineering Record/Historic American Landscapes Survey. Courtesy of Library of Congress Digital Collections. http://www.loc.gov/pictures/resource/hhh.ca1493.photos .033556p/.

to employ wooden barrels, and shipboard coopers, into the early twentieth century.

The Cook and His Galley

On nineteenth-century merchant ships, the galley was usually located in a deckhouse amidships, so that the galley fire was above the deck. Most merchant ship galleys of the time were about the size and shape of a modern walk-in closet, with about half that space occupied by the stove. On some merchant ships, this deckhouse also provided shelter to the cook, sailmaker, and/or boatswain—*daymen* whose work took place on a different schedule than the mates and sailors who stood four-hour watches. The berths for the cook and another *dayman* would usually run fore and aft, on the other side of a bulkhead from the galley and its stove. A large wood-burning iron stove served for cooking and baking, mounted thwartship (i.e., side-to-side, at a right angle to the centerline of the vessel). A "Charlie Noble" flue carried the smoke upward, while preventing burning material from reaching the flammable sails and rigging. The Charlie Noble had a sheet metal globe or cylinder atop the flue with vertical slits to let the smoke escape. It was usually free spinning, and it spins merrily when the stove is lit and there is a breeze on deck. Firewood for immediate use was stored in the galley itself, while most of the firewood was kept in some dry storage place or places, such as a corner of the forecastle or chain locker. During the first half of the nineteenth century, cast iron stoves replaced the brick cooking hearths of earlier centuries.[2] The utensils included pots, pans, kettles, and boilers which were often included in the initial purchase price of the stoves. These were supplemented by frying pans, pie plates, pudding bags (so-called even if made of tin), sauce pans, dippers, graters, tea and coffee pots, pepper mills, canisters, knives, cleavers, meat forks (sometimes called tormentors), ladles, skimmers, as well as possibly a coffee mill.[3]

The cook himself was often an older sailor, too old to clamber up the shrouds to take in sail, but still fit enough to go to sea and work on deck. In this case he could still be a useful man on board in addition to his duties in the galley. In many cases the cook was a friend of the captain, or someone who had served with him in previous voyages. If a cook died or left the ship in a foreign port, the captain would have to recruit one locally. "Son of a sea cook" still survives today as an exclamation of disgust and frustration, perhaps because sea cooks were once widely regarded as old and worn-out.

American cooks and crew occasionally used Dutch or German nautical terms. For example, the *Charles W. Morgan*'s stove was recorded by her master as a "camboose."[4] Spelled *kombuis* in modern Dutch, this is the time-honored term for the galley in Dutch, German, and for that matter Polish and other languages as well. Likewise, when the command "Haul aft the fore-sheet!" was given on *Akbar* in 1877, "Haul aft the fore-scoot, sir!" was answered by the men as the cook scuttled out of the galley to take in the foresheet on the formerly weather-becoming lee side.[5] "Fore-scoot" is a variation of the Dutch and German name for this line. It appears that Dutch and German linguistic influence on American English was not restricted to speech ashore, but extended to the sea as well.

The origin of the word "galley" for a shipboard hearth or kitchen is more obscure. Whether a corruption of gallery, as some have suggested, or a mysterious transposition of the name for a long, low oared vessel, galley became the accepted term for a shipboard kitchen in English after around 1750, with the Dutch-German camboose as an American alternative.

Figure 4.2. "Words with the Cook," from Gordon Grant, *Sail Ho: Windjammer Sketches Alow and Aloft* (New York: William Farquhar, 1930), 39. The irascible cook redirects the crew's complaint to Officer Country.

Cooks in Journals and Songs

The cook was often addressed as "Doctor," even in song. Here is a verse about the cook, which the crew of the ship *Akbar* sang in 1877:

> What shall we do with a drunken doctor?
> Put him in the coal locker till he gets sober.[6]

The cook was rarely addressed by name at sea. Instead, he was usually addressed by the traditional sea cook's title of "Doctor." Whether he earned this title by performing magic in converting dreary ingredients into palatable dishes, or whether his title stems from his issuing lime juice as a preventative, the name stuck, and on merchant sailing ships of the nineteenth century, the cook was usually addressed as "Doctor" by the crew. This was part of shipboard etiquette, just like addressing either mate as "Mister" and the carpenter as "Chips."[7]

Sea cooks were often interesting characters, and often reflected an even greater racial and ethnic diversity than the already diverse crew.

Hugh McCulloch Gregory, sailing around the world in the clipper ship *Sea Serpent* in 1854, stated in his journal that their cook was Chinese.[8] Frederick Pease Harlow sailed with two different cooks when he sailed from New York to Australia and Java aboard the ship *Akbar* in 1877. The first, named Brainard, was an old friend of the captain's, who had made many sea voyages before.[9] The *Akbar* replaced him with a new cook in Australia, described by Harlow as a native of New Orleans, "black as the ace of spades." The cook from New Orleans was about forty-five years old, very superstitious, and gregarious. This cook tells Harlow about his many misfortunes and travels, saying that his mother was formerly a slave and his father a white southern planter.[10] Other authors and diarists including Richard Henry Dana and Herman Melville describe African, African American, and Chinese cooks.[11]

As the cook was often an experienced sailor, he could have line-handling duties as well. Harlow gives a colorful description of Brainard shooting out of the galley at the command, "Haul aft the fore-sheet!"— a line that runs past the galley, and hauling the line hand-over-hand with a "runaway yell." According to Harlow, this was the only line the cook was to handle, but that he was expected to take responsibility for this line when setting the foresail or when the yards were braced around as the ship tacked.[12] Other writers corroborate this, including a Chinese cook the crew nicknamed "Chow," who was often soaked in performance of his duties at the foresheet while the ship was coming about.[13]

Several sailor songs also paint a portrait of the cook. A popular capstan chantey with Irish sailors is titled "Paddy, Lay Back." The task of heaving up the anchor, performed on some ships with a foredeck capstan, is a lengthy one as the ship is brought to a point over the anchor, and consequently capstan chanteys are often of great length. "Paddy, Lay Back" is a particularly lengthy capstan chantey which details the misadventures of a voyage during which the protagonist endures mishaps and misadventures galore. This song was collected by Stan Hugill (1906–1992), a British merchant sailor, author, and performer of sailor songs. The author was privileged to perform with him during the 1980s and 1990s, and he will be referenced several times in this chapter, on sailor lore and songs.

One of the verses Stan Hugill collected paints an unflattering portrait of the cook, and the rough treatment he receives at the hands of the crew:

> Oh, the cook in his galley wuz a scoundrel,
> At making sloppy hash he had a knack;
> So the flatfeet all went aft to him a-growlin',
> An' they broke the spare topmast (stuns'l boom) across his back.[14]

Over a bottle of red wine between performances at a festival in the Breton port of Douarnenez, France in 1986, Mr. Hugill related to the author a cruder version of this verse.

German chanteys and forebitters (seagoing ballads) of the hard-luck story genre also devoted a verse or two to the character assassination of the cook. In one example, originally in German and translated by Rainier M. v. Barsewisch, a verse is devoted to the cook, full of slanders against his cooking.

> The cook he was a bastard,
> He made mutton chops from sharks, adding Stockholm tar,
> His Irish Stew stank ten miles against the wind,
> And he's making a pudding from rats and seagull droppings.
> An' we all sing hurrah!
> An' we all sing hurrah!
> Such "Chow-chow" is the usual thing.[15]

This completes a well-rounded portrait of the nineteenth-century sailing "Doctor" or sea cook: a man who worked in extremely cramped quarters, making a fire in his wood stove hours before each meal, concocting palatable dishes from ingredients which had been stored in less than ideal conditions for weeks or even months.

The Steward and Food Service

The crew collected their food either individually at the galley door, or sent one of their own to collect it for the watch, much as each mess did in a warship's crew. The usual practice was for the officers to have their food brought to the cabin by a steward. The steward was another dayman, whose job it was to serve food to the "cabin" (to the officers), and to any passengers on board the vessel. The steward set the table, carried the officers' food from the galley to the officers' dining area. This area was variously called a cabin or saloon, but rarely if ever by its naval name of "wardroom." The cabin was equipped with permanently mounted tables. During the meal the steward stood by the table in an apron with a towel, and served in the capacity of a waiter ashore. Not all ships carried a steward: a sailor with genteel manners might be dragooned into doing the job, as Frederick Pease Harlow related. Harlow served the *Akbar* as a steward while the regular steward was laid up with an injury. He described his duties as washing dishes, dusting and cleaning the cabin, and standing in a white apron to serve the officers during meals. He wrote that while he enjoyed having "all night in," he was eager to return to standing watches on deck.[16]

Figure 4.3. "The Steward in Difficulties," from Gordon Grant, *Sail Ho: Windjammer Sketches* Alow and Aloft (New York: William Farquhar, 1930), 41. "There goes the skipper's dinner!"

The steward assisted in a variety of food-related tasks, from slaughtering animals for fresh meat to procuring foodstuffs ashore. He was occasionally mentioned in sailor songs as well:

> What shall we do with a drunken steward?
> Lock him in the galley till he gets sober.[17]

There was racial and ethnic diversity in stewards as well as cooks. The clipper *Intrepid*, sailing in 1859, had a Chinese steward who had known the captain since boyhood.[18]

Besides eating off ceramic dishes, there were some other distinctions between the food as served to the crew forward and the officers aft. Harlow stated that on the *Akbar* in 1877 the cabin fare shared the same entrees as the crew, but there were differences in the "sides": white bread ("soft tack") with butter instead of ship's biscuit; sugar instead of molasses in their coffee. While most of the entrees might be the same as the crew's, Harlow says the choicer cuts of meat from those dishes went aft to the cabin.[19]

The Pantry

By the nineteenth century, large oceangoing sailing vessels were equipped not only with a galley in which the cooking was done, but also a nearby pantry. Much of the food destined for the cabin passed through the pantry on its way aft, and the pantry was the steward's domain. Meals in the cabin were served on ceramic plates, which were stowed in special shelves in the pantry which held them in place as the vessel rocked, pitched, and rolled. The design of these dish shelves varied from one vessel to another. In all cases, the shelf was just barely wider and deeper than the plates, for a snug fit to prevent them jostling around. Sometimes there was a wooden plank that completely covered the front of the shelf, with a T-shaped slot. The plates were stacked no higher than a few inches below the "cross" of the "T": to remove a plate, one could take hold of the top-most plate through the vertical part of the slot, then raise it to the horizontal part of the slot, and draw it out. An alternate design had wooden extensions on each side of the shelf, which terminated a few inches from the top of the shelf. With any variation of the design, the trick is to leave plenty of space above the plates, so that they will not easily fly out the horizontal slot on their own. The plates themselves were of a standard pattern used ashore: it was the shelves designed to hold them that had a specific seagoing design.

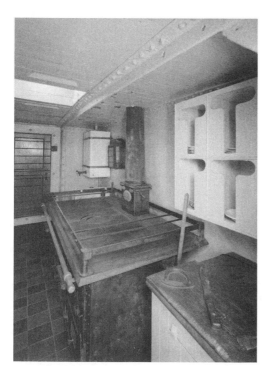

Figure 4.4. *Balclutha*'s galley, in a deckhouse. Note the T-shaped opening in the shelves for ceramic dishes. Similar racks are found in the pantry. Reproduction Number HAER CAL,38-SANFRA,200—35 in Collection: Historic American Buildings Survey/Historic American Engineering Record/Historic American Landscapes Survey. Courtesy of Library of Congress Digital Collections. http://www.loc.gov/pictures/item/ca1493.photos.033449p/.

Figure 4.5. The Steward's stores and pantry on steam schooner *Wapama*. This shows another variation on the shelf design, to keep dishes from falling out and breaking at sea. Reproduction Number: HAER CAL,21-SAUS,1—16 in Collection: Historic American Buildings Survey/Historic American Engineering Record/Historic American Landscapes Survey. Courtesy of Library of Congress Digital Collections. http://www.loc.gov/pictures/item/ca1521.photos.013124p/.

The design of the shelves for ceramic dishes can vary. These three pantry photographs are from three different vessels from the period between 1880 and 1910, each showing a different variation on the same idea: making it possible to remove dishes for use, yet not letting them remove themselves in heavy weather.

The meals in the cabin were served on a table, which was securely bolted to the floor. The cabin table was usually equipped with removable baffles sometimes called "fiddles" that could be fitted across the tables, so that dishes could only slide so far on the table. Sometimes there were additional baffles which were hinged to each edge of the table, a design feature that has lasted right up to the present day on shipboard tables.

Eating Areas

On sailing merchant vessels, the crew was much smaller than the crew of naval vessels of similar size. In place of the gun decks of the sailing warship, the merchant vessel had a large cargo hold. The crew lived in a forecastle,

Figure 4.6. Schooner *Thayer's* galley with special shelves for plate storage. This lumber and fishing schooner features an alternate design of the shelves for the dishes on which cabin meals were served. Call Number: HAER CAL,38-SANFRA,199—19 in Collection: Historic American Buildings Survey/Historic American Engineering Record/Historic American Landscapes Survey. Library of Congress Digital Collections. http://www.loc.gov/pictures/item/ca1506.photos.041956p/.

Figure 4.7. Saloon on *Balclutha* with built-in sideboard and mirror. This is where the officers and passengers ate their meals, from ceramic dishes. Reproduction Number HAER CAL,38-SANFRA,200—67 in Collection: Historic American Buildings Survey/Historic American Engineering Record/Historic American Landscapes Survey. Courtesy of Library of Congress Digital Collections. http://www.loc.gov/pictures/item/ca1493.photos.033481p/.

which could be in its traditional location forward under the foredeck, sometimes called the "topgallant forecastle" by Harlow and others. On vessels in which this deck was low, the forecastle could be a space separated from the cargo by a thwartship (side-to-side) bulkhead, set into the forward section of the vessel. In other cases, the crew was housed in a large deckhouse. The captain, mates, and any paying passengers lived aft under the quarter deck, also known as the poop deck, in greater comfort, usually with individual cabins. The cook, carpenter, and sailmaker usually slept in shared cabins located in deckhouses, though this could vary.

Meal Preparation and Schedules

Most merchant ship crews were divided into two watches, known as the first and second watch (after the first and second mates who supervised them), or sometimes as the starboard and port watch on British ships. The port watch was usually called the larboard watch on American ships, preserving an older terminology. These two watches, somewhat like the "squadrons" described by John Smith in 1627, would stand watch (i.e., work) alternate four-hour periods, which were also called watches. The most common arrangement of watches during the Age of Sail was for the crew to work "watch on and watch off" as follows:

Noon–4:00 p.m. Afternoon Watch
4:00–6:00 p.m. First Dog Watch
6:00–8:00 Second Dog Watch
8:00–12:00 p.m. Night Watch
Midnight–4:00 a.m. Middle or Mid Watch
4:00–8:00 a.m. Morning Watch
8:00 a.m.–Noon Forenoon Watch

The two shorter watches (working time periods) of two hours apiece are called dog watches because they "dog" or adjust, which of the two watches (working team of sailors) stand a given watch each day. This is important to keep harmony aboard: most people find they prefer standing watch from 8:00 p.m. to midnight, rather than being woken up at midnight to work for four hours, then trying to catch some sleep again at 4:00 a.m.

The cook usually prepared meals so as to be ready before changes of watch, so that one watch could eat before turning out to work; then the other watch could eat after being relieved. On many ships, breakfast was served to the resting watch at about 7:00 a.m.: when they relieved the working watch at 8:00 a.m., that watch had their breakfast. The cook would clean up breakfast and then commence cooking the noonday meal, usually the largest of the day. This would be served to the watch at rest at about 11:00 a.m.; then to the other watch at noon when they had been relieved from duty.

The third meal of the day was commonly prepared during the afternoon watch, and could be served to the two watches in turn around 4:00 p.m. This schedule puts all three meals rather close together, which would make the men rather hungry by breakfast time. Many ships served the evening meal later. A careful reading of Frederick Pease Harlow's account of his voyage in the *Akbar* in 1877 shows that the evening meal was served at the break of the dog watches, before and after 6:00 p.m. This would be an improvement for the men, though it lengthens the cook's day.

Ships of other nations used modifications of this watch routine. French vessels sometimes shortened the morning and forenoon watches by changing watches at 4:30 a.m., 7:30 a.m., and 9:00 a.m. German and Scandinavian vessels were known to use a system of five watches, noon to 6:30 p.m., 6:30 p.m. to midnight, midnight to 4:00 a.m., 4:00 a.m. to 8:00 a.m., and 8:00 a.m. to noon. One sailor opined that these variations in watch routine were to facilitate "continental meal times." [20]

Eating Utensils

Throughout most of the nineteenth century, merchant sailors ate from tin plates or pans, and tin cups. They generally used spoons and their sheath knives for utensils. The tin cup could serve as a tea or coffee mug, or as a bowl for soup or porridge. The men usually ate seated on their sea chests in the forecastle. The usual arrangement of bunks was two rows, upper and lower. Most sea chests (customarily the private property of each sailor) were less than three feet long, so that two men could sit on their chests set beside their bunks. By the later nineteenth century, some merchant vessels' forecastles were equipped with permanent tables. Other sailing vessels retained the table-less forecastle well into the twentieth century.

As merchant sailors often used their knives as eating utensils, these knives merit some attention.[21] Nineteenth-century sailors' sheath knives were somewhat suitable as eating utensils. They were usually broad, with parallel edges. They had a straight sharp edge, while the back was usually rounded so that the back or the knife could be tapped with a marlinspike to cut line. The end was usually blunt; either straight, curving toward the edge, or a very broad point. In either case, the entire back of the knife was blunt or even rounded, and there was not a sharp acute point. This made a sailor's sheath knife a more suitable eating utensil than a steak knife, skinning knife, or dagger.

At work, the nineteenth-century merchant sailor wore his knife in a sheath that usually enclosed not only the blade but much of the grip as well. Some sailor knives were equipped with lanyards by which they could be secured to the user's wrist or waist belt for use aloft. The lanyard prevented the knife falling to the deck if dropped from aloft, an important safety consideration. The knife in its sheath was secured to the sailor's belt, and slid to a location over the "starboard buttock" or dead center in the small of his back. In this location, it was out of the way until needed, and was less likely to catch on rigging or spars.[22]

The sheath knife was a merchant sailor's tool. Most nineteenth-century navies prohibited the wearing of sheath knives, and issued folding clasp knives which were secured to the wearer by a lanyard around the neck. The blade of the naval clasp knife was usually shaped like a smaller version of the merchant sailor's sheath knife. However, its smaller size, and the possibility of food particles finding their way into the hinge, made it a poor choice of eating utensil.

Merchant sailors could put their eating utensils to use as noisemakers or percussion instruments. When the crew of the *Akbar* crossed the equator, the crew commenced the festivities by making a racket with their eating utensils: tinware, spoons, and knives.[23]

What's on the Menu?

Hugh McCulloch Gregory, serving aboard the clipper ship *Sea Serpent* on a passage from New York to San Francisco in 1854, described the bill of fare:

Thursday, March 30, 1854
Today I made out a bill of fare a la St. Nicholas:

Sunday, Scouse—Duff—	Bread & Beef	
Monday, Mush—Spuds—	"	"
Tuesday, Scouse—Beans—	"	"
Wednesday, Scouse—Rice—	"	"
Thursday, Mush—Duff—	"	"
Friday, Scouse—Beans—	"	"
Saturday, Scouse—Cape Cod Turkey—	"	"[24]

The scouse is a libel on pig fodder, the mush is never cooked, the beans are awful and the Cape Cod turkey, or in plain English, codfish, is the meanest mess of all. The coffee and tea, which we have morning and night, is a muddy compound not fit for any civilized man to drink. However I am always so hungry I can eat what is set before me without a second bidding.[25]

Some of these dishes we have encountered in the last chapter. Duff, spuds, and "Cape Cod Turkey" are described later in this chapter. Harlow also describes certain dishes that usually fell on certain days; this seems to have been common on nineteenth-century merchant sailing ships, even if the exact choices varied from ship to ship and from voyage to voyage.

Early in a voyage, there would be more fresh ingredients in the crew's food. Harlow's first meal aboard the *Akbar* consisted of mutton stew, potatoes, boiled salt pork, soft-tack (white bread), ginger bread, and coffee sweetened with molasses. After spending the day setting the sails and getting underway, Harlow says he was "hungry as a bear and wasted no time in starting in."[26]

Meat Preserved in Brine

The basic ingredients for long voyages in nineteenth-century sailing merchant vessels were much like those described by John Smith in 1627, and in the previous chapter. Salt beef, preserved in brine containing saltpeter as well as salt, was a staple. Harlow describes *Akbar*'s salt beef as coming in three-hundred pound casks, "soaked in brine well saturated with saltpeter . . . when taken from the cask it was as red as a flannel shirt."[27]

Salt beef fresh from the cask was not only bright red, a result of the saltpeter in the brine, but was described as hard by some sailors of the era, allegedly becoming harder the longer it soaked in saltpeter. Harlow relates that it was the fatty pieces of salt beef that the steward set apart for the cabin, while it was the lean pieces which were relegated to the crew. Preferences change with the times! The salt beef was soaked for a day or two in the "harness cask" to leach out some of the salt, but it remained hard even after its long soak. Nonetheless, salt beef was a food that lasted for a very long time at sea, and so it remained a staple of the shipboard diet until replaced by tinned beef. The harness cask was made of wood, bound with polished brass, in an oval or round shape, wider at its base than its top. It had a lid, and the lid was usually equipped with a hasp so that it could be locked. Harlow speculates that the harness cask may have gotten its name by comparing the salt beef to leather horse tack.[28]

There is another possible reason for the desalinating tub being called a "harness cask" at sea. There was a legend about horsemeat being passed off as salt beef by an unscrupulous ship chandler. Because of this story, a common sailors' nickname for salt beef was "salt horse." There was even an "Ode to Salt Horse," related by Harlow. He had heard about an old sailor who tried to stab violently with his fork at a very dry piece of salt beef with little success. Finally, he held the piece of beef above his pan and recited a well-known verse:

Figure 4.8. "Harness Cask," from Gordon Grant, *Sail Ho: Windjammer Sketches Alow and Aloft* (New York: William Farquhar, 1930), 37. The cook dredges a piece of "salt horse" from the desalinating cask, also known as a steep tub.

Old horse! Old horse! What brought you here?
From Sacarap' to Portland pier
I carted stone for many a year.
I labored long and well, alack,
'Till I fell down and broke my back.
They picked me up with sore abuse
And salted me down for sailor's use.
The sailors they do me despise,
They pick me up and damn my eyes,
They eat my flesh and gnaw my bones
And throw the rest to Davy Jones.[29]

While Harlow gives a poem that could be recited, Hugill offers two versions of this "Sailor's Grace" that could be chanted or sung.[30] Salt beef was also known as "salt junk" or just "junk." One verse of the halyard chantey "Lowlands Low" says of the captain,

He gives us bread as hard as brass,
Our junk's as salt as Balaam's ass.[31]

In performance, Mr. Hugill usually sang something slightly racier for this verse. He often altered his songs for publication.

Salt beef was alternated with salt pork, which could also be stored in casks of brine. Alternatively, the salt pork could be stored dry, as was the salt pork issued to nineteenth-century soldiers. Harlow relates that salt beef was hard and dry, but that on *Akbar* they had salt pork with their beef three times a week, and this made the beef more palatable. He suggests that prolonged exposure to salt beef would toughen one's mouth, much as hauling on lines would toughen one's hands; and "the sailor can digest anything he can swallow."[32]

The brine from salt beef and salt pork was said to have medicinal properties. In this case the cook could live up to his traditional title of "Doctor." On the first day of the *Akbar*'s voyage, the foresheet slipped through Harlow's hands, and the rope tore the skin of both his palms. The cook prescribes a traditional remedy, soaking the injured hands in beef or pork brine. The salt and saltpeter made Harlow jump around the deck in pain, but in the end he wore a handkerchief soaked in brine on his hands for the rest of the watch, according to the "Doctor's" prescription.[33]

Fish Preserved in Salt

Salt cod is a commodity of great antiquity, which we have met in earlier chapters. During the modern period, Atlantic cod filets packed dry in salt replaced stockfish as the preferred form of long-lasting fish. At the height of the West Indian sugar trade, the enslaved population was fed mostly imported food, so that as much land as possible could be devoted to sugar production. Salt cod, also known by its Portuguese name of *bacalhao*, was exported from New England to Jamaica and other sugar-growing islands. Imported salt cod is still a staple in Jamaica. After soaking it to reduce its saltiness, Jamaicans combine salt cod with greens in the traditional dish *cullaloo*. Sailors often called salt cod "Cape Cod Turkey." This is evident in the bill of fare from the *Sea Serpent* and in Harlow's writing: "Our Christmas dinner consisted of plain duff and turkey (Cape Cod) which of course brought a big growl from the forecastle, with many comparisons with the Astor House." [34]

Fresh Meat: Pigs and Chickens

Just as navies purchased livestock to slaughter and feed to their crews, it was a common practice on nineteenth-century merchant ships on long voyages to carry one or more pigs on board, usually in a pen on deck, which could be fed on leftovers and then slaughtered at sea to provide fresh meat for the crew, well into the voyage. This could provide a welcome change in diet during long voyages when supplies of fresh ingredients were running low—"The cook killed two pigs for a fresh mess tomorrow."[35] There would be great health benefits from the dose of fresh meat everyone on board received for some days after the slaughter of a pig. The pig or pigs were fed on leftovers from the galley and from the cabin, converting these scraps into fresh meat that could be consumed just when it was needed most. Fresh meat was often used quickly on board ship—"Now let me see, we have 3 pigs left of the 12 we started with, so I guess we will procure some more at the first opportunity."[36]

The most colorful account of a pig slaughtering at sea must be from the 1877 voyage of the ship *Akbar*. In cold weather on the way to Australia, Captain Lamson wanted a change of diet and decided it was time to slaughter one of four pigs they carried on board. The steward said that he knew how to kill a pig; so the captain planned the execution of the pig for Saturday, so as to have fresh meat for Sunday dinner.[37]

In the end, the pig slaughtering aboard the *Akbar* did not go well. Like condemned pigs everywhere, the pig seemed to sense exactly what was in

Figure 4.9. View of *Balclutha*'s main deck, taken from abaft the forecastle bulkhead, facing aft. Note the ship's pig pen. Reproduction Number: HAER CAL,38-SANFRA,200—33 in Collection: Historic American Buildings Survey/Historic American Engineering Record/Historic American Landscapes Survey. Courtesy of Library of Congress Digital Collections. http://www.loc.gov/pictures/item/ca1493 .photos.033447p/.

store for him, and he put up a good fight. The pig was held down on the deck and the steward stabbed him in the neck. Thinking he had cut the pig's windpipe, the steward ordered the sailors holding the pig to let him go. The wound missed his windpipe; so the bleeding pig fled his pursuers to the cabin, where he bled everywhere until hauled back on deck and finally dispatched with multiple wounds to the neck. Harlow suggests that the pig had not been slaughtered so much as "murdered," with multiple stab wounds that in some cases went past the pig into the deck planks.[38] After this gruesome incident, the mate commiserated with the captain on the terrible mess the steward has made of butchering the pig, and then offered up a story of his own. His previous vessel, the *Oliver Cromwell*, had stern windows. The men stuck the pig and then let go of him; this pig, like the *Akbar*'s, was wounded somewhat less than mortally. The pig made a run for the cabin, and did not stop until he had jumped through the window into the sea. Whether the window was opened to air the cabin, or the pig smashed the glass panes in his break for freedom, the mate did not say. As (bad) luck would have it, a shark had been following the *Oliver Cromwell* for days. The pig had scarcely hit the water before the shark gobbled him up "like a piece of cheese."[39] The captain was so angry at the loss of the pig that he knocked the steward down and jumped

Figure 4.10. "Christmas Dinner," from Gordon Grant, *Sail Ho: Windjammer Sketches Alow and Aloft* (New York: William Farquhar, 1930), 108. A pig-slaughtering scene, much like the gruesome tales from the *Akbar* and *Oliver Cromwell*.

on him. No doubt the loss of the *Oliver Cromwell's* pig to the shark must have been a deep disappointment to the crew; yet it must have been an easier, quicker death for the pig than the prolonged struggle and death by multiple stab wounds suffered by the pig aboard the *Akbar*.[40]

Some ships carried poultry as well as pigs. Two chickens, out of a dozen or so that were kept for cabin fare, were lost overboard from the *Akbar* while coming about.[41] When a young passenger aboard the clipper *Sea Serpent* celebrated his birthday, a turkey was slaughtered and eaten. On December 8, 1854, Gregory describes how a turkey from Shanghai was slaughtered and cake was also prepared for the birthday. Gregory reports that it was an especially good day because "We forward had apple sauce!! for our duff instead of molasses, in honor of the occasion."[42]

Bread

Ship's biscuit or hard bread would last much longer than soft bread, but like the hard tack issued to nineteenth-century soldiers, it lost its luster with the passage of time. On some vessels, a tray or "barge" of ship's biscuit was a fixture of the forecastle, so that the crew could help themselves to biscuit any time they chose. This was the case in a coastwise trip in the schooner *David G. Floyd*, undertaken by Harlow before his long voyage on the *Akbar*. He describes a "bread barge" as a box twelve by eighteen inches long, stocked with "sea-biscuit, i.e. pilot bread."[43] This quote is interesting because it shows that for Harlow at least, sea-biscuit and pilot bread were one and the same. With a bread barge in the forecastle constantly stocked with ship's biscuit, there was no need for anyone to go hungry, as occurred on other vessels and voyages.

Beans, Rice, and Potatoes

Beans could be kept a long time in their dry state, and were regular fare on nineteenth-century merchant sailing vessels. In this journal entry from March 10, 1854, one sailor took a practical approach to beans on the menu—"Beans for dinner! Much as I dislike them I was hungry enough to eat them."[44] However, many sailors liked beans and appreciated it when beans and bean soup appeared on the shipboard bill of fare. Beans got star billing in the food-related verse of a well-known nineteenth-century English sailor song, "Rolling Home." This time-honored English forebitter and sometime capstan chantey was also adapted and sung by sailors from America and Germany. One of the verses, published and sung by British merchant sailor, chantey singer, and author, Stan Hugill, goes as follows:

> Eighteen months away from England,
> Now a hundred days or more,
> On salt-horse and cracker-hash, boys,
> Boston beans that made us sore.[45]

Like beans, rice will keep a very long time if kept dry. American sailor Charles A. Abbey commented on the use of rice on ships. Abbey sailed in some of the most famous clipper ships that went to San Francisco, the Far East, and the Hawaiian Islands between 1856 and 1860. Aboard the clippers *Surprise*, *Charmer*, *Telegraph*, and *Intrepid*, he kept journals on his voyages. While rather terse, his journals offer fascinating glimpses of life aboard the clipper ships of that age. The following Charles Abbey entry referring to rice suggests that it was served up sweetened with molasses, something like duff. On the clipper ships of the 1850s, rice was served often, not always to the delight of the crew:

> Tomorrow is Wednesday, Rice, it would be good but that blasted steward is so afraid of his molasses that it is never sweet enough. So tomorrow "brings no comfort."[46]

Rice was often carried as a long-keeping food on clipper ships, but there is more than one account of it being unpopular, like this one from *Sea Serpent* on March 22, 1854:

> Made quite a bargain today. Promised my allowance of mush and rice for George's allowance of "duff." Our rice is poor stuff, being very wormy, and our mush is never cooked enough, so that all things considered I have driven a Yankee bargain.[47]

Potatoes were carried on board, but usually spoiled after some time at sea. Potatoes were served frequently in the first weeks after leaving port, but then disappeared from the bill of fare after many weeks at sea. This journal entry was made early in the voyage of *Sea Serpent* on March 13, 1854: "Had 'spuds' for dinner, which is potatoes and pork, and a grand feast I did have, for "spuds" come but once a week."[48] Later on in a voyage, potatoes might not be so well received. Harlow writes about how potatoes began to "feel the effects of the damp, chilly weather" and began to rot and give off so strong an odor that the sailors could not eat them.[49] Harlow goes on to relate that the men "went in a body to the cook and told him if any more sour spuds were cooked for the fo'c'sle they would send them back."[50]

Methods of Preparation:
Lobscouse, Crackerhash, and Duff

These ingredients were combined in a number of traditional recipes. Lobscouse has been discussed in the previous chapter. A question sometimes debated among maritime historians is what distinction, if any, existed between lobscouse and crackerhash. Nineteenth-century merchant sailors appear to have used the terms interchangeably. Crackerhash was a baked combination of broken pieces of softened hard tack and chopped up salt beef, pork, and onions. Harlow relates that "this crackerhash or 'lobscouse' was usually more than Alonzo could stand, but I was very fond of it when it was baked with a crisp top."[51] Descriptions of lobscouse for the cabin (i.e., for the officers) mention vegetables in the mix of onions and potatoes.[52] Some authors describe putting the biscuits in a bag, breaking them with a hammer, and soaking them overnight before using them to cook lobscouse.[53] Black pepper is often mentioned as the principal seasoning for lobscouse, which is also a feature of the traditional lobscouse recipes ashore in Denmark, Sweden, and Finland, the possible home-place of the dish and its name.[54]

There were other baked dishes that allegedly comprised layers of salt beef and biscuit—two names so identified by one sailor-author are "skillagalee" and "dandyfunk." [55] Skillagalee was sometimes a name for oatmeal porridge in British naval usage, an alternate name for "Burgoo."[56] While is possible that for some sailors "dandyfunk" was just an alternate name for lobscouse, other sailors clearly identified dandyfunk as a dessert made from crumbled biscuit and molasses, much like duff, but baked in a pan not boiled in a bag.[57] With some of these names for shipboard cuisine, it may be as with so many things at sea—"different ships, different long-splices."

Duff, a sort of bread pudding boiled in a bag, has been described in chapter 3. Thankfully, it appears to have lost its lurid nicknames by the middle of the nineteenth century. Usually boiled in a cloth bag, duff was a staple of merchant ships as well as warships. In its simplest version, "plain duff" could be little more than a basic bread pudding.[58] When dried raisins or fruit and some spices were added, it could merit the name of "plum duff," being "plumb full" of good ingredients, and could be quite tasty. Harlow ate his first plum duff aboard the schooner *David G. Floyd*, and since he liked it very much, describes it in some detail. In this case, the cook had steamed it in a tin mold rather than boiling it in a bag, and had seasoned it with spice. Harlow says this plum duff was like a cross between cake and pudding, served with hard sauce, and was "the color of spice cake, almost as dark as gingerbread."[59]

The contents, seasoning, and sauce of the duff could vary according to whether it was intended for the cabin or the forecastle. Harlow relates that aboard the *Akbar*, soft-tack (normal bread) and duff were served on Wednesdays and Saturdays. The crew's duff was steamed in a cloth sack, seasoned with salt and dried apples, and was served up with molasses as sauce. The cabin duff was more elaborate; seasoned with spice, raisins or plums, and served with lemon or wine sauce.[60]

But enough could be enough, where duff was concerned. After *Akbar* had been sailing for months, the cook had been cutting corners by throwing flour in a sack and boiling duff instead of baking soft bread for the crew, and so they came to the galley in a group to protest. The protest was successful, and the crew was given fresh-baked bread with their next meal.[61]

Fishing

Changes in the rigging of sailing ships during the nineteenth century resulted in improvements in sailor's diet. The chain of causation is indirect but unambiguous. During the mid-century, sailing vessels, especially those built for speed such as the China and California clipper ships, carried numerous additional sails that could be set outboard of the principal square sails, called "studding-sails," pronounced "stunsails." These sails provided additional drive in light-to-medium winds, but at a cost of great additional labor for the crew. Crewmen would have to go aloft, walk out on the footropes of the yards, and slide "stunsail-booms" along the yards, then hoist the stunsails up into position, and adjust the lines that controlled them. If the wind increased significantly, the stunsails would have to be struck, and the stunsail booms had to be slid back over the yard by sailors aloft.

Journals kept by sailors aboard clipper ships in the 1850s mention stunsails constantly, as the crew was constantly setting or striking them. The crew was given little time for leisure, with a cry of "All Hands!" constantly calling the watch below back on deck; and when not working, the crew was often too tired to fish. Charles Abbey sailed on the clipper ships *Surprise* and *Charmer* with stunsails: when he subsequently shipped in the clipper *Intrepid*, which lacked stunsails, he writes more about catching fresh fish during his off watches. Frederick Pease Harlow, sailing on the *Akbar* without stunsails in 1877, had enough leisure time to catch enough fish from the *Akbar*'s jibboom to feed the entire crew several meals.

Charles Abbey, sailing in the clipper *Intrepid* without stunsails, suggests that in the end, a vessel without stunsails may actually make better time:

"Oh these stunsail ships—that's where we get to windward of them all, while they are lumbered & bothered taking them in, we merely stand by the braces, swing our yards, & dip our ensign to them as we pass."[62]

The *Intrepid* was built with a deeper hull so that she could carry more of her sails in a stiff wind, and this ability to carry more of her sails in conditions which would compel other clippers to take in their upper sails, combined with savings of time by dispensing with stunsails, made her at least as fast as contemporary clippers that flew stunsails.

Most square-rigged vessels had dispensed with stunsails and stunsail booms by the 1870s, and this gave the crew more time to take advantage of the opportunity to fish when passing through the waters where albacore, bonito, and mahi-mahi—which nineteenth-century sailors called dolphin—were abundant. Several days of eating fresh fish must have been very good for the health of everyone aboard, staving off maladies caused by dietary deficiency.

The practice of sailing ships outbound from North America or Europe supplementing their diets with fresh fish as they passed through waters where edible fish were plentiful and where they swam near enough the surface to be hooked or speared from the bowsprit of a moving vessel must have begun quite early. John Smith in 1627 described the same equipment to catch the same species of fish as Frederick Pease Harlow did on his voyage exactly 250 years later.

Hugh McCulloch Gregory, aboard *Sea Serpent* in 1854, did some fishing, and liked the change in diet. On May, 23, 1854, a hot day with little wind, he caught three large bonitos on his fishing line, although he lost two larger fish and all of his fishing hooks in the excitement of trying to haul them in as they were "about a foot and a half long and pulled very hard."[63] Gregory was amazed by the variety of fish in the region and relished the change from ship's rations to fresh fish. "They were in pursuit of flying fish, which I saw for the first time in the Pacific . . . For supper we had fried bonito and to me it was a most agreeable change."[64]

Aboard the *Intrepid*, Charles Abbey and his shipmates also had time to do some fishing. On August 12, 1859, they tried, unsuccessfully, to catch some "dolphin," but like Gregory, did catch several "Bonita" [*sic*] and had them for supper.[65] The reference to catching dolphin requires some explanation. The dolphin described by authors of previous centuries is not to be confused with the sea mammal of the same name, which was usually called "porpoise" in historical accounts. Rather, it is *Coryphaena hippurus*, the fish usually known today either by its Spanish name of *dorado* or by its Hawaiian name, *mahi-mahi*.

Fishing Technique

Harlow described his fishing gear and technique in fascinating detail. He made a trolling line from cod line, and baited his hook with a lure he made from a bit of white cloth, resembling a flying fish in size. On his off day watches, he would look to see if any fish were swimming around the cutwater, that is the *Akbar*'s stem. Carrying his line out to the end of the jib-boom, he would straddle the jib-boom facing back toward the *Akbar*, leaning against one of the stays. Then he would let his lure skip around the water in front of the cutwater, until he had a fish on his line. On successfully hooking a fish, Harlow pulled his line "short," hitched his line to one of the stays, hugged the fish, and called for help from the deck—"On deck! On deck! Bring out a gunny sack. I've caught a dolphin."[66] One of his shipmates would come out to the end of the jib-boom with a gunny sack, and together they would wrestle the hooked fish into the sack, and come back aboard. With this technique, Harlow and his shipmates fed the whole crew on fresh fish for several days.[67]

Figure 4.11. Captain Firewood Hansen, age 84, catching a bonito from the jibboom, no date. Schooner *Muriel* (built 1895). This shows the position and technique used by Charles Abbey and Frederick Pease Harlow to catch fish from the jibbooms of their respective vessels while at sea. Courtesy of San Francisco Maritime NHP, Image J09.20965n (SAFR 21374).

Harlow observed that the bonito, albacore, and dolphin (mahi-mahi) did not mix together but always swam with their own.[68] This last observation derives from these fish traveling in schools, something which may not have been obvious to a sailor on the deck. There is a daredevil aspect to fishing off the end of the jib-boom; it is at the very forward-most point of the vessel. Had Fred Harlow fallen off his precarious perch, the ship would have run over him before it could have been turned or slowed. In spite of these dangers, Harlow comments on the beauty of the dolphin leaping out of a wave into the sunlight, and famous phenomenon of the fish changing color several times in its death throes. As he put it, "Blue-fishing and salmon-trolling is tame sport compared with trolling from the jib-boom-end."[69]

Both Hugh McCulloch Gregory and Frederick Pease Harlow lost hooks by their fish biting through the line. Harlow remedied this problem by "ganging" the hook with a copper wire, so the fish could not bite through the line if it swallowed the hook.[70] As stated in chapter 2, John Smith in 1627 advised commanders at sea to carry a "harping iron and a fisgig" or harpoon and *fisga* (small trident) for fishing.[71] Keeping a grains-iron or gig aboard for spearing fish was still standard practice in the nineteenth century. After Harlow lost a dolphin (mahi-mahi) off his line, the *Akbar*'s second mate hitched some "ratline stuff" to a "grains-iron" on a pole.[72] Standing on the martingale shrouds just forward of the cutwater, the mate harpooned two fish. One of these tore out of the iron, fell back into the sea, and was instantly devoured by his fellows; but the second was a successful catch. [73]

There can be no doubt that eating fresh fish when they were available must have been very healthy, and probably did a great deal to stave off the lurking health dangers of a steady diet of vitamin-poor food. However, the cook could get tired of frying up all these fish caught by the crew. After several days of successful fishing, the *Akbar*'s cook Brainard threatened to throw Harlow's catch overboard, if he brought him any more fish to be fried.[74]

Coffee and Tea

From food we now turn to drink. On nineteenth-century American merchant ships it was a common practice to serve coffee with breakfast, and tea with supper.[75] Coffee was often served to the crew well before breakfast, shortly after those working the 4:00 to 8:00 morning watch had just turned out. This was described during a coastal trip on the schooner *David G. Floyd*:

> I heard the cook's alarm clock at one bell (4:30 a.m.) and he was soon stirring around building a fire. At two bells (5:00 a.m.) he called us for coffee. It is a custom aboard sailing vessels to serve a pot of coffee before the men go to

work. Some vessels serve it a half-hour before turning to. On coasters, the coffee is served with sugar, but on deep-water vessels, black strap, or molasses, is boiled in the coffee and it is surprising how one learns to like it and if the cook is not as generous some mornings as others, old Jack is there with a kick just the same.[76]

It appears that the serving of coffee at 5:00 a.m. was not restricted to this one schooner or to coasting vessels generally. Another American merchant sailor and later captain, Isaac Hibberd, commented on the importance of that early morning cup of coffee: "it is hard to make a landsman understand what a cup of coffee means to a sailor at five o'clock on a cold, stormy morning."[77] Later on, Harlow, now on a long voyage aboard the ship *Akbar*, commented on the deterioration of the coffee's quality, as the contents of the fresh water tank ran low: "The coffee, sweetened with sorghum molasses, now began to taste strong as the water was drawn from an iron tank and no doubt was quite rusty."[78]

Further along in Harlow's voyage in *Akbar*, the molasses ran out, and the captain instructed the cook to give the men some of the cabin syrup/treacle in their coffee. "There was a growl that the coffee didn't taste natural and the day following it was worse and they were not slow in calling the syrup 'Baby-food,' 'Angel Dressing,' etc., and not fit to feed sailors, for it was a poor substitute for molasses to sweeten coffee."[79] One cannot help but pity the captain, who was hundreds of miles from the nearest source of molasses.

Something similar happened to Captain Hibberd aboard the three-skysail-yard ship *Cyrus Wakefield* in 1888. On their way out of Seattle, Captain Hibberd heard a fracas outside the galley door, and on investigating, found that the cook had used some of the captain's pumpkins to make the men in the forecastle some pumpkin pies. The men rejected them, saying they would not eat "vegetable pies." Hibberd observed that "some of our Down East friends . . . would say that these sailors didn't know a good thing when they saw it."[80]

Aboard the whaler *Charles W. Morgan* in 1841, coffee is specified for breakfast, and tea for supper. No beverage is specified for mid-day dinner, which suggests that water was probably served with this meal.[81]

While tea is hardly mentioned by some diarists who served before the mast, it seems to have been common enough in the cabin. Some ship's crews were quite fond of tea. Isaac Hibberd remembers that very strong tea, brewed for two to four hours, was a favorite of the crew aboard *Jane Fish* in 1881.[82]

Spirits

Nineteenth-century sailors in the world's navies received alcoholic beverages on a daily basis. For contemporary merchant sailors, intoxicating drinks were a special treat or (more often) a reward offered for arduous and danger-ous work. Harlow describes the scene when the crew is sent aloft to take in sail in heavy weather:

> When the weather was unusually thick and disagreeable the second mate lightened our hearts with a cheerful word while clewing up: "Hurry aloft, boys! You're all entitled to 'splice the main brace' when you get down again." At once there would be a scramble up the rigging to see who would be first out on the weather yardarm.[83]

Clipper ship diaries such as Charles Abbey's and Hugh McCulloch Grego-ry's also make reference to the promise of a tot of liquor after crewmen have been aloft to shorten sail in heavy weather. The promise in all cases is made when the men are sent aloft to furl the sails; then the promise is fulfilled after the work is done and the men are back on deck. This was surely the safest course. Returning to the *Akbar* in 1877:

> While under topgallant sails, the outer jib stay was carried away and we clewed up and furled the fore- and mizzen-topgallant sails and later the main-top-gallant sail came in. The upper fore and mizzen topsails were furled and the mainsail reefed, after which we were called aft to "Splice the main brace" and the . . . steward . . . trotted out another black bottle and joined in with the rest, not forgetting the man at the wheel and again drinking to his success.[84]

This was a great deal of hard and dangerous work, well meriting the re-ward the men received.

The origins of "splice the main brace" are obscure, and the subject of some disagreement. The main brace is an important and ancient part of a square-rigged vessel's standing rigging, extending from the main top to the foremast where it meets the deck. It is usually eye-spliced around the foremast. It has been suggested that the infrequency of rigging a new main brace is the origin of the expression.[85] Alternatively it could be that as a fundamental operation of setting up the vessel's rigging, it was seen as a metaphor for the fortifying of the crews spirits with ardent spirits. The exact derivation of the term, in common usage by the mid-nineteenth century, remains elusive.

Somewhat less mysterious is the origin of the phrase "three sheets to the wind" for extreme drunkenness. A sheet is a line attached to the clew, or lower corner, of a sail, with which a sail is controlled; a line is "to the wind" when it has come un-rove and is flying in the wind. "Three sheets to the wind" thus denotes being out of control, with two or more sails uncontrollable.

Water

Water was kept either in wooden barrels or in steel tanks, and sailors frequently complained of old water developing a rusty taste. Fresh water was often taken aboard when visiting distant ports. If taken from rivers, it usually improved after the silt and other material had settled to the bottom of the tank or cask. In southern latitudes, sailing vessels could travel great distances without obtaining fresh water ashore, and would collect rainwater to top up the ship's supply of fresh water. This practice dates back at least to the Portuguese *Carreira da India* of the sixteenth century. The procedure is described by Harlow and other nineteenth-century diarists, in which rainwater running off one of the courses (lower sails) is funneled into a cask.

Whaling Ships and Eating Whale as Food

Whalers and commercial fishermen were non-military sailors of specialized types, and the cooking and dining arrangements of their vessels varied from those of their cargo-carrying sailor brethren. One of Herman Melville's characters, Second Mate Stubb of the *Pequod*, eats a steak cut from the "small" (the narrowing of the tail ahead of the fluke) of sperm whale meat in chapter 64 of *Moby Dick*. Melville comments on how unusual this is, and writes that on this occasion, some sharks are Stubb's only fellow diners. Whalers as a general rule discarded the meat from the whales they caught, preferring salt beef and pork that had lain in casks of brine over fresh meat from a strange and (at that time) mysterious creature.[86] Whale meat is a rich red meat much like very lean beef, as most of the whale's fat is carried in its blubber. It is tougher than beef: in Iceland, where the meat of minke whales is sometimes eaten, chunks of whale meat are pounded with a hammer or mallet before cooking, as is often necessary with venison and other game meats. Whale meat, sufficiently tenderized by pounding and then minced and cooked in a lobscouse, would have been a healthy fresh change of pace from salt beef that had lain in brine for months. Nonetheless it appears that prejudice against eating an alien meat, regarded by some whalers as a type of fish rather than a mammal, constrained the vast majority of whalers from utilizing the meat from the creatures they hunted.

On some whalers, the galley and the cook moved aft, with the galley on deck in the stern and the cook's bunk near "officer country." This was the case with *Charles W. Morgan*, and may well have been true of other American whaling vessels as well.[87] The complicated, arduous process of cutting in a whale, cutting up the blubber into small pieces, and then boiling the blubber into oil in the massive try-pots could take up all of the available deck space amidships between the main and fore masts. Moving the galley into the stern, or at least abaft the mainmast, would keep the preparation of meals out of the way of this essential work.

Commercial Fishing

Fishermen in small boats expecting to return in the evening would often bring food with them which required no preparation. Scottish fishermen within living memory brought their "piece" with them, which could be a pasty, sandwich, or other handy precooked meal wrapped in wax paper. Fishing craft designed to stay offshore for longer periods were equipped with galleys like cargo-carrying sailing vessels; in the case of fishing schooners from New England and the Maritime Provinces of Canada, the galley was often contiguous with the forecastle. The forecastle was usually fitted with tables, and it was common for the officers and crew to eat at these together. The quality of the food in New England fishing schooners was reputedly much superior to that in long-haul merchant sailing ships.[88]

Merchant Shipping Legislation

Throughout the nineteenth Century, the American and British governments repeatedly passed legislation mandating sufficient food for sailors; in some cases authorizing the men to seek compensation if they were not sufficiently fed. These laws were virtually unenforceable. The British Merchant Shipping Act of 1894 inspired a waggish song, which speaks to the crew's rations:

> Now when you join a merchant ship ye'll have your articles read,
> They'll tell ye of yer beef an' pork, yer butter an' yer bread,
> Yer sugar, tea, an' coffee, boys, an' peas an' beans exact,
> Yer limejuice an' vinegar, boys, according to the Act.[89]

The song goes on to specify that "Ten days out we all lay aft to get our limejuice whack."

Food Ashore in Distant Ports

In foreign ports, it was a common practice for sailors to purchase fresh fruit, and to hire locals to cook fresh food for them. This was particularly common on the China Coast. While their ship was anchored in Whampoa, Charles Abbey and a shipmate hired a Chinese bumboatman to take them to sightsee in Canton, and to cook for them. Abbey describes one of the meals they had aboard their host's sampan:

Our meal . . . was a nice one, better than we had seen since leaving our own country. First came some vegetable soup, then some fish; next he brought on some roast beef, Macao potatoes, beets, turnips &c., and then a roast chicken, after which came a pudding, some walnuts, nankin dates & Lychees [sic] (a fruit tasting like a raisin). We filled up with everything but the chicken; he was roasted, claws, head, comb and all and we didn't like the looks of him.[90]

This custom of Chinese cooking for sailors in port is mentioned in a sailors' song, which appears to be based on a hawking song, or at least hawking cries, from Chinese "bumboatmen" or "bumboatwomen." The song, in Cantonese Pidgin-English, offers among other available services, translation, meal preparation, and obtaining local liquor:

Homeside have got pidgin,
Me savvy, me can tell,
Bring me master chicken,
Chi-da velly well.
Suppose he likee Sam-shu,
It all the same can do,
Chop-chop me fetch him,
Big-big Da-bing-yu.[91]

Late Nineteenth-Century Changes

After the completion of the Suez Canal in 1869, more and more of the Asian trade in passengers, tea, and other high-value commodities was taken over by steamers. Sailing vessels were competitive with steamers in the carriage of bulk cargoes of lesser value, such as grain and wool. Sailing vessels continued to carry nitrates from western South America to Europe and North America, where they were used in the production of fertilizer and explosives, into the early twentieth century.

During the late nineteenth century and the early twentieth century, British sailing ships experienced a kind of decline. British shipbuilding remained superb, with the result that most of the iron and steel sailing ships that survive from this era are British. It was in this era that British established leadership in the design, building, and operation of steamships, and British steam vessels fed their crews well. However, parsimony in the operation of British sailing vessels produced dangerous and uncomfortable conditions for their crews. Long open decks allowed waves to sweep men off their feet into the scuppers or overboard, while single topgallant-sails and other large square sails made sail handling aloft difficult and hazardous. During this period the food on British merchant sailing ships was small in quantity and low in quality, lagging behind the crew's food in ships of other sailing nations.[92]

During the same period, German sailing ships improved. F. Laisz lines built a fleet of "Flying P Liners" (P stood for *Peking*, *Padua*, *Pommern*, etc.); large steel-hulled sailing vessels that were efficient and profitable in the nitrate/guano trade with western South America. These German "nitrate clippers" incorporated numerous innovations to improve crew comfort and safety.[93] Not only the topsails but the topgallant sails were divided into more manageable upper and lower sails. "Liverpool Houses" amidships interrupted the flow of water over the deck, increasing crew safety. Halyard and brace winches made the handling of sails easier and safer. The brace winches were an ingenious invention of Scottish Captain John Jarvis (1857–1935). Captain Jarvis was unsuccessful in interesting British shippers in his brace winches, but German shipping embraced his labor-saving invention, though without paying him. The nitrates that were used in German munitions during World War I were carried from South America in sailing ships which turned a profit and which treated and fed their crews well.[94]

Late nineteenth- and early twentieth-century French sailing vessels enjoyed government subsidies, and they too offered better conditions and food to their crews. American sailing vessels of this period also enjoyed a reputation for feeding their crews better than their British counterparts. In North America, sailing vessels continued to operate in important "niche markets," such as the floating canneries of the Alaska Packers. American sailing vessels for local trades on both coasts were increasingly built as schooners and barkentines, rigging configurations that required fewer men; but they did not cut corners by starving their crews as British nitrate clippers reputedly did.

A sailor song makes a good conclusion for this chapter, bidding farewell to shipboard cuisine and sartorial style. "Soul and body lashings" in the song were lashings of marline or other twine over a sailor's oilskin clothes. Tied around a sailor's knees, wrists and elsewhere, they would keep "soul and body" together in the torrential rain and high winds of a serious sea gale.

No more I'll stand by the royal halyards,
Nor eat their crackerhash;
No soul an' body lashin's tie,
Nor in saltwater wash.[95]

FIVE

Immigrant and Slave Ships

This chapter tells the story of immigrants who have crossed the oceans in search of a new life, and of the culinary experiences of their passages. Many immigrants have been driven by some degree of desperation or need, and therefore booked the least expensive possible transportation from their old homes, or a nearby embarkation point, to their new homes. In some cases the vessel's operators provided food for immigrants on their journey; but in many cases, during the Age of Sail, immigrants were expected to bring their own food with them. During most of the nineteenth century, immigrants were given access to limited cooking facilities and were expected to cook for themselves.

Before considering the food aboard ships for voluntary immigrants, let us consider the ships that carried the most miserably treated passengers of all: slaves in the Middle Passage across the Atlantic.

Slave Ships

Beginning in the seventeenth century, Portuguese, Spanish, Dutch, French, Danish, and English ships transported slaves from the Guinea Coast of Africa across the Atlantic, in what was called "The Middle Passage." Conditions for the human cargo in these voyages are notorious and need little reiteration; naked adults and children jammed into fetid holds, usually shackled to one another, with high mortality on the trip. The feeding of the slaves varied from ship to ship, as well as the circumstances. Some ships fed the slaves when they were on deck getting air and exercise: while others apparently brought the food into the hold. The Dutch are alleged to have fed their slaves three times a day, the French and English just twice.[1] The French are said to have sometimes prepared a stew of oats, dried turtle meat (plentiful in the West Indies), and dried vegetables; this implies that they may have let the slaves use wooden bowls to eat it. Some slave ships served rice to the slaves they carried, a food which may have obviated the issue of bowls or plates. Some slaves attempted to commit suicide by starving themselves, and some slavers carried mechanical devices to force their mouths open to force-feed them.[2]

An early account that mentions a specific dish for slaves is found in the instructions left by slaving captain William Snelgrave for his chief mate in 1727. Snelgrave enjoins his mate to boil well the "dab-a-dab," a mash of fava beans, rice, and corn (British maize) in order to keep the slaves healthy; and to give them water three times a day.[3] John Newton, the slaving captain best known for his authorship of the text of "Amazing Grace," purchased large quantities of rice on the Guinea Coast to feed his slaves on the Middle Passage. His policy was to feed the slaves he carried twice a day, on a blend of fava beans, rice, and peas with a little salt meat added.[4]

Mealtimes usually began by bringing the slaves up on deck; in many cases they were handed their food in eating bowls called "crews" in the slave trade, and were issued spoons. The food was sometimes chosen to suit the region of origin of most of the slaves: rice for those from Senegambia and the Windward Coast, yams for slaves from the Bight of Benin and Biafra; and corn for slaves from the Gold Coast. Water was usually given to the slaves as well, and then the "crews" and spoons collected and washed.[5] In a few cases, enslaved women were employed as cooks, "paid" for their service with extra food, tobacco, or brandy.[6]

Outcry over conditions in the Middle Passage moved Great Britain (in 1807) and the United States (in 1808) to outlaw the importation of slaves from abroad into their countries and dominions. From this time on, the British and American navies patrolled the waters off the west coast of Africa, intercepting any vessels suspected of carrying slaves. When slavers were apprehended, the vessels were confiscated and the human cargo returned to Africa. Most slavers sailed under the flags of Spain or Portugal, states which had not yet outlawed the slave trade.

Conditions aboard slavers were worse after 1808, when the trade became clandestine, and speed was essential. Vessels for the slave trade, many of them built in Havana, had small streamlined hulls based on the privateering "Baltimore Clipper" topsail schooners built during the War of 1812. The rig was usually a topsail schooner, brigantine, or brig; in every case with a large sail area for maximum speed while making the dash across the ocean with their illicit cargo.[7] These vessels had very small capacity, yet somehow they managed to hold enormous numbers of slaves. The *Feloz*, a Portuguese slaver apprehended in 1829, was carrying 564 slaves at the time, though her crew had already thrown overboard the bodies of an additional fifty-five. All were branded with ownership marks, like cattle.[8]

Before 1808, some slaving captains believed in "loose packing" their cargo, and feeding them regularly, so that most if not all of the slaves they carried would be alive and reasonably healthy on arrival in the West Indies. Others subscribed to "tight packing" their slaves and were more cavalier about feeding them, accepting the death of many of their cargo as an operating expense.

After 1808, tight packing was the rule. Slavers who thought they were about to be boarded and searched would sometimes throw their slaves overboard, in chains, to drown and thus to destroy the evidence of their mission.

Aboard the *Feloz* at the time of her capture: "The first object that struck us was an enormous gun, turning on a swivel, on deck . . . and the next were large kettles for cooking, on the bows—the usual apparatus of a slaver."[9] From this account, it would appear that aboard *Feloz*, the cooking for the slaves, and possibly for the crew as well, was done above decks. A slaving brig, the *Diligente*, had her lines, deck plan, and spar dimensions recorded in 1839. As Howard Chapelle wrote of these data, "No galley is shown, but it was probably on deck, West Indian fashion."[10] Situating the cooking stove on deck was a common West Indian practice, and not confined to slave smugglers. It seems a sensible design for vessels whose operations were entirely in the Tropics.

Transporting slaves across the Atlantic after 1808 was a furtive business, making it difficult to ascertain many details of what sort of food, and in what quantity, was allowed the most unfortunate of all passengers in the history of sea navigation.

Immigrants to North America: Early Arrivals

During the seventeenth and eighteenth centuries, emigrants from the British Isles and Germany took passage to American ports, most commonly Philadelphia. Many of these had indentured themselves; which is to say, they had agreed to serve a sponsor for a certain period in exchange for their transportation, as well as food, clothing, and lodging during their service. Indentured servants were limited in their choices. For example, most indentured servants could not marry without their master's consent, which was rarely given. William Moraley, an indentured servant sailing to Philadelphia in 1743, described the food he received during the voyage:

> Three Biscuits were given to each Man for the Day, and a small Piece of Salt Beef, no bigger than a Penny Chop of Mutton. Some Days we had Stockfish, when every Man was obliged to beat his Share with a Maul to make it tender, with a little stinking Butter for Sauce. Every Morning and Evening the Captain called every one of us to the Cabbin Door, where we received a Thimble full of bad Brandy. . . . We attempted to drink the Salt Water, but it increased our Thirst. Sometimes, but rarely, it rained, when we set our Hats upon Deck to catch the Water; but it sliding down the Sails, gave it the Taste of Tarr.[11]

Moraley's clothing was issued to him, as was the food; though he complained of the quality of the food, it may have been the same food issued to the crew. The reference to water is strange. Perhaps he and his fellow indentured men were not given the access to the scuttlebutt, as presumably the crew were.

The Highland Clearances

In this same period and through the early nineteenth century, the Highland Clearances produced a flood of Scottish immigrants to Canada and the United States. Tenants were evicted from the lands they had worked since time out of memory, and many areas of the Highlands were converted to sheep pasture. This was hailed as economic improvement by some; however the human cost was immeasurable.

An early Scottish immigrant voyage was that of the *Batchelor*, sailing from Thurso under the command of Captain Alex Ramage in September 1773. James Hog, the organizer or the voyage, promised to provide each immigrant with four pounds of meal, five pounds of biscuit, two pounds of beef, two pounds barley and peas, and one pound molasses, with six gallons of water weekly. Children under eight years old were to receive half rations. The vessel was crammed with 280 people on board, and experienced a series of mishaps which drove them back first to Stromness, then a second time to the Shetlands. By this time the provisions were running low, and Shetlanders donated potatoes and oatmeal to help the suffering passengers. In the end, the *Batchelor* never made it to North Carolina, her intended destination. The passengers, shipowner, and the organizer of the voyage wound up in litigation.[12]

Another 1773 voyage that did not go well was that of the *Nancy* of Sutherland, which sailed to New York from Leith, Scotland with passengers variously estimated at 188, 250, or 300. The journey ended badly, as the captain, George Smith, had not adequately supplied food for a voyage that ended up taking twelve weeks. The passengers' provisions consisted of oatmeal, peasemeal, biscuits, cheese, and whole pease. The hatches were kept closed because of bad weather. On this voyage, more than fifty young children died. Seven women who gave birth while on board died, as did their newborn infants. When the *Nancy* at last arrived in New York, the starved and sickly passengers became the recipients of local charity.[13]

Conditions improved slightly in the early nineteenth century, mostly because the ships were usually somewhat larger and not quite as crowded. After the establishment of regular departures by the Black Ball Line and its imitators, ships left port on a schedule. At 10:00 a.m. on January 5, 1818, the packet *James Monroe* left New York as part of a regularly scheduled service between New York and Liverpool by four sailing packets operated by the Black Ball Line.[14] Prior to that, transatlantic packets left at the whim of the owner and the captain, when they had a full cargo and the weather was right. Immigrants could use up much of their precious money and food waiting for their ships to depart, usually in a seaport miles from the homes they had left.

Regular scheduled departures improved conditions for immigrants before beginning their trips, but of course the timing of arrivals could vary a great deal. This was especially true for the westward passage, when ships were likely to encounter contrary winds, and were crowded with emigrants from the Old World to the New.

William Shand immigrated to Canada in 1834, and on arrival, he wrote of his voyage to his brother in Dufftown, Banffshire. Here is an excerpt from Shand's account of his passage aboard the *Hercules*, under command of Captain Walker: "the water that we had the first 4 weeks being in cours (coarse) molashes casks became so bad in a short time that it was impossible to disgese the teast of it with any thing whatever—and I was many times that I would a gladly given a shilling for one Bottle of Small Beer."[15]

Shand then describes the scene in the hold, with several parties of the steerage passengers, some whole families and some single men from various parts of Scotland. He describes them playing cards and "dams" (draughts or checkers), smoking, fiddling and dancing on deck, debating on the ship's progress, "then other 2 or 3 singing songs, with some pairs here and there carrying on something in the way of courtship—then round the fire (which is nearly in the center) 6 or 8 of the wives, some with there children squaling, others fighting who should have on her pot first."[16]

Shand described the hold and the hatch of his ship as a beehive, with passengers constantly going in and out all the time like bees. Shand's account of the six or eight wives, accompanied by squalling children, fighting over access to the stove, illustrates the problem with providing immigrants with a stove, and expecting each family to prepare its own food. The women are left to battle each other over cooking space. Providing cooked food for 100 to 250 people at a time is the kind of challenge that is best solved by centralizing the preparation of food, cooking big cauldrons of the basic staples. Making the individual families prepare their food separately was inefficient, and flew in the face of progress. By the mid-nineteenth century the preservation and preparation of food for the crews of merchant and naval vessels had evolved into an efficient routine. Making the passengers jostle one another over limited cooking space was, in a sense, plunging them into the relative anarchy of the cooking hearth in a sixteenth-century Portuguese carrack.

The conditions of immigrant passengers improved with the passage of time, but the conditions remained crowded and uncomfortable. A challenge for those in charge was to provide adequately for all the people jammed into a ship, not knowing how long the passage would require. This was particularly true of the westward transatlantic passage, where the prevailing winds tended to be contrary. A passage planned to last five or six weeks could, and often did, take twelve weeks instead. This could be disastrous in a vessel packed to the gunwales with immigrants, and with provisions running low.

Starvation was just one of the dangers of a passage in a crowded immigrant ship. In 1822, the *Albion*, near the end of an uneventful eastward crossing, was driven ashore by squalls near the Old Head of Kinsale in Ireland, and wrecked with the loss of forty-five lives.[17] The *William Brown*, westbound in 1841, struck an iceberg and quickly sank. At least forty-six passengers perished: some were left behind in the sinking vessel, and some tossed out of one of the ship's boats by the mate, who was subsequently convicted of manslaughter in Philadelphia.[18] In 1848, the packet *Ocean Monarch*, westbound with 322 steerage passengers aboard, caught fire shortly after departing Liverpool. The ship burned quickly, and 178 people, mostly steerage passengers, lost their lives.[19]

Charles Dickens's Sailing Trip across the Atlantic

Having experienced the wonders of a transatlantic passage in a Cunard steamer in January 1842, the famous British author determined to return by the sailing packet *George Washington* in June. This made sense: the winter passage was against the prevailing winds (unluckily they were of gale force for Dickens's passage). On the eastward passage he was likely to experience favoring winds and nice weather, as indeed he did. Dickens was a cabin passenger, and so he dined with the captain, officers, and fellow cabin passengers in the cabin or saloon, not with the immigrants in the hold or on deck. Here is Dickens's own account:

We breakfasted at eight, lunched at twelve, dined at three, and took our tea at half-past seven. We had abundance of amusements, and dinner was not the least among them: firstly, for its own sake; secondly, because of its extraordinary length: its duration, inclusive of all the long pauses between the courses, being seldom less than two hours and a half; which was a subject of never-failing amusement.[20]

Dickens described their server as "a black steward, who lived for three weeks in a broad grin."[21] Between meals there were whist, cribbage, books, backgammon, shovelboard (probably the game we know today as "Shove Ha'penny" or "Shove-Groat"), watching dolphin-fish and porpoises, and walks on deck. Dickens describes the unmusical effect of passengers practicing the accordion, violin, and key-bugle (this last instrument usually commencing at 6:00 a.m.) at the same time in different corners of the vessel.[22] It is clear that the author enjoyed his eastward passage in June under sail very much more than his westward crossing in January under steam.

Dickens was acutely aware that there were fellow travelers who dined in more modest state than he:

We carried in the steerage nearly a hundred passengers: a little world of poverty . . . from looking down upon the deck where they took the air in the daytime, and cooked their food, and very often ate it too, we became curious to know their histories.[23]

The George Washington had its passenger stove up on deck, as did many other immigrant packets of the era, and not in the hold. The following passage implies that this was one of the vessels in which passengers, usually returning after an unsuccessful attempt to make a better life in the New World, were required to supply their own food:

Some of them had been in America but three days, some but three months, and some had gone out in the last voyage of that very ship in which they were now returning home. Others had sold their clothes to raise the passage-money, and had hardly rags to cover them; others had no food, and lived upon the charity of the rest . . . one man . . . had no sustenance whatever but the bones and scraps of fat he took from the plates used in the after-cabin dinner, when they were put out to be washed."[24]

Dickens argued articulately against the evils of the sailing immigrant packets. He pointed out that while the law forbade "at least upon the English side" the overcrowding of packet ships, this occurred anyhow on both sides. Insufficient medical care for the immigrants resulted in needless deaths at sea; and most importantly, nothing prevented immigrants from booking passage with insufficient food for the trip.[25]

The Potato Famine

Just a few years after Dickens's passage on the *George Washington*, an agricultural catastrophe produced a new wave of immigration. A potato blight, *Pytophthora infestans*, afflicted the Irish potato crop between 1845 and 1851. During the previous century and a half, more and more Irish land had been given over to beef cattle pasture, with tenant farmers growing their own subsistence crops, increasingly potatoes of one type, the "Irish lumper," in little plots at the edges of the arable land.

> The Celtic grazing lands of . . . Ireland had been used to pasture cows for centuries. The British colonised . . . the Irish, transforming much of their countryside into an extended grazing land to raise cattle for a hungry consumer market at home . . . The British taste for beef had a devastating impact on the impoverished and disenfranchised people of . . . Ireland . . . Pushed off the best pasture land and forced to farm smaller plots of marginal land, the Irish turned to the potato, a crop that could be grown abundantly in less favorable soil. Eventually, cows took over much of Ireland, leaving the native population virtually dependent on the potato for survival.[26]

The potato blight destroyed an estimated 33–50 percent of the Irish potato crop in 1845, and 75 percent of the potato crop in 1846. While Irish beef and grain were still exported to England, an estimated 1,000,000–1,500,000 Irish people starved to death or died of starvation-related disease, and another million emigrated to the United States, Canada, and Australia. The potato crop of Scotland and other European nations was affected, but greater variety of potato species and more diversified subsistence crops made the potato blight less devastating there. Relief came from unexpected sources: the Ottoman sultan Abdulmecid is believed to have sent money and two to three ships full of food; Tsar Nicholas of Russia also made a large contribution. The Choctaw Nation, who had experienced the Trail of Tears only sixteen years before, sent money to relieve the suffering of starving Irish.[27]

A flood of Irish refugees filled the holds of transatlantic packet ships, big boxy sailing ships that preceded the sharper-lined clippers. The trade in Irish immigrants inspired a number of songs. In one, an Irish immigrant girl, conversing with Tapscott, a well-known shipowner, inquires if he has a "packet ship bound for Amerikee." He replies:

> Oh, yes, I have a packet ship, I have got one or two
> I've got the *Jinny Walker* and I've got the *Kangaroo*.
>
> I've got the *Jinny Walker* and today she does set sail,
> With five an' fifty emigrants an' a thousand bags 'o meal.

Later on the immigrant girl sings,

> 'Twas at the Castle Gardens, oh, they landed me ashore,
> An' if I marry a Yankee boy, I'll cross the seas no more.[28]

Castle Garden was New York's immigrant station, a former fortress, at the southern end of Manhattan. Its function was taken over by a larger facility at Ellis Island in 1892. Some versions of this song have the packet encountering a northwest wind that "blows them back again," a common experience for ships westbound across the Atlantic. In one version where the immigrant is male, the song ends with the following:

> Now that I am in Amerikee, a-working on a canal,
> I'll niver go home in a packet ship, I know I niver shall,
> But I'll ship in a darn big National boat, that carries both steam an' sail,
> With lashin's o' beef, an' plenty to eat, an' none of yer yellow meal.[29]

Ironically, the Irish protagonist had good prospects for a pleasant sail on the eastward passage, as Charles Dickens did; but the experience of an extended westward passage under sail had made him wary of all crossings under sail alone. Yellow meal was corn (British maize) meal, something the United States produced in affordable abundance. Judging by the songs, it must have been customary on the packet ships of this era to lay in a good supply of this cheap food, so that if the passage took unusually long and passengers ran out of their own food supplies, there was a food supply to fall back on. Corn meal can be boiled into corn mush (served to Civil War soldiers on occasion), or baked into bread, though the latter usually requires some wheat flour as well.

Herman Melville's Redburn

Herman Melville wrote about conditions on immigrant ships in his 1849 novel *Redburn*. He describes the steerage or tween decks as occupied by four rows of triple bunks, squeezed in between water barrels and the bunks "rapidly knocked together with coarse planks."[30]

They looked more like dog-kennels than any thing else; especially as the place was so gloomy and dark; no light coming down except through the fore and after hatchways, both of which were covered with little houses called "booby-hatches."[31]

Melville went on to describe the immigrants' cooking facility, which like the *George Washington* described by Dickens, consisted of a stove lashed down on the open deck.

Upon the main-hatches, which were well calked [*sic*] and covered over with heavy tarpaulins, the "passengers'-galley" was solidly lashed down. This galley was a large open stove, or iron range—made expressly for emigrant ships, wholly unprotected from the weather, and where alone the emigrants are permitted to cook their food while at sea.[32]

Melville pointed out that this open-air stove might be sufficient for the steerage passengers traveling from the New World to the Old; but it was insufficient for the needs of the more numerous westward-bound immigrants. As the stove was only allowed to be lit during certain hours, quarrels ensued. "And no sooner would the fire by fairly made, then up came the old women, and men, and children; each armed with an iron pot or saucepan; and invariably a great tumult ensued, as to whose turn to cook came next; sometimes the more quarrelsome would fight, and upset each other's pots and pans."[33] The hours during which the immigrants' stove could be used were limited, and were not sufficient for all to cook their food if the ship was crowded. Melville wrote about a scene when a sailor has to douse the cooking fire under the eyes of passengers who are still waiting to cook: "every evening in the second dog-watch (i.e., between 6:00 and 8:00 p.m.), at the mate's command I would march up to the fire, and giving notice to the assembled crowd, that the time was come to extinguish it, would dash it out with my bucket of salt water; though many, who had long waited for a chance to cook, had now to go away disappointed."[34]

Melville published *Redburn* in 1849, early in the tidal wave of Irish immigration that followed the Great Famine. He describes the staple food of the Irish immigrants as "oatmeal and water, boiled into what is sometimes called *mush*; by the Dutch is known as *supaan*; by sailors *burgoo*; by the New Englanders *hasty-pudding*."[35] It would appear that as the wave became a flood, "yellow meal" provided by the ship-owners began to supplement the oatmeal which early immigrants provided for themselves. It is likely that the cooking method, boiling the meal with water into mush, remained the same.

Like Dickens, Melville informed his readers that laws passed by both the British and American governments restricting the number of immigrants that could be carried, and requiring captains to ascertain that there was sufficient food for all aboard, were unenforceable, and were widely ignored.[36] The stove lashed to the deck was the usual cooking facility for steerage passengers on sailing packets of this era. Meanwhile, the food for the crew, officers, and cabin passengers was prepared in a permanently installed galley in one of the deckhouses.

Conditions on German immigrant sailing ships, mostly sailing from Hamburg, were similar to those that carried Scottish and Irish immigrants. The lot of steerage passengers improved with the transition from sail to steam. With the change in propulsion came more predictable passage times. The sailing packets customarily obliged the passengers to provide part or all of their food themselves; and to prepare it, piecemeal, for themselves. Steamships customarily provided and cooked food for their steerage passengers, which made the entire process safer, surer, and more comfortable for all concerned.

From a modern perspective, it is baffling that the operators of sailing immigrant ships expected their passengers to cook for themselves, in stoves that were simply lashed to the deck or the main hatch. It is understandable in the case of some of the early immigration ships and, a few years later, vessels such as the clipper *Sea Serpent* which carried passengers on a temporary basis. For these, nailed-together bunks and a separate, lashed-on-deck "passenger galley" was reasonable, as they were dismantled when the vessel returned to her normal business of carrying cargo. However, vessels such as *George Washington*, and other transatlantic sailing packets of the 1840s, were carrying passengers on a regular basis, even if they carried larger numbers westward than eastward. The navies of the world had been feeding similar numbers of people on vessels of similar size for centuries before evictions, famine, and poverty motivated huddled masses to forsake the Old World for the New. A large Brodie stove, suitable in size for a naval vessel with a like number of souls aboard, would have served the needs of crew and passengers alike aboard the packet *George Washington*.

By the 1880s, steamships provided permanent berth arrangements, spartan at first, for steerage passengers to sleep in, with tables at which to eat, and permanent galleys in which their food was prepared by paid cooks. Not surprisingly, once the prices for steerage in steamers became competitive with sailing vessels, the steerage passenger trade flocked to the steamers. The faster, more consistent passage times are usually assumed to be the cause of the immigrant business leaving sail for steam; but the accounts of immigrants unable to cook their food on exposed stoves on deck suggest a more compelling reason. The better food arrangements on the steamers must have substantially motivated the change.

Chinese Immigration and the Poetry
on the Walls of Angel Island

Chinese arrived in large numbers in California after gold was discovered there in 1848. They endured prejudice and even persecution there; but many Chinese did well, either returning to China with some wealth, or staying in California and starting businesses. Probably because of the Gold Rush associations, California was known to the Chinese as "The Gold Mountain."[37] The United States was known as "The Land of the Flowery Flag," often abbreviated to "Flowery Flag."[38]

Accounts of Chinese steerage passengers in the era of the California and Australia Gold Rushes are rare, but they exist. The clipper ship *Sea Serpent* sailed from San Francisco to Hong Kong in 1854 with sixty Chinese steerage passengers, probably returning gold miners. Hugh McCulloch Gregory, sailing before the mast in the larboard watch, kept notes on various incidents with their passengers returning from Gold Mountain:

> Monday, July 3—At 6:00 a.m. the steamer *Hercules* took us in tow and proceeded down the harbor. . . . We have three cabin passengers . . . and sixty Chinese in the steerage.
>
> Friday, July 7—All night long we . . . had a concert . . . the hen coop being front of our quarters, we . . . had a full share of rooster, hen, goose, and duck melody; added to this the Chinese brought a grizzly bear (a cub) which one of them owned and sat his cage by the hen coop, and such a outrageous racket as he raised was a caution . . .
>
> Monday, July 10—I never saw such a filthy, loathsome set of creatures as the Chinamen we have on board are. And such a chattering as they keep up night and day is enough to make one cut his throat in despair.
>
> Friday, August 18—while washing down decks we had a row with the Chinamen, Harry knocking one of them over the head with a bucket. Soon after a whole crowd of them got ready for a rush on him, which was prevented by the rest of the watch making their appearance on the scene of action, each armed with a handspike. Stacking arms, the mate held a parley with them, which ended in his telling them "to go to the D----l" and the crew shaking their handspikes, when John Chinaman, believing with Shakespeare that "discretion is the better part of valor" beat a hasty retreat.
>
> Tuesday, August 22 (anchored in Hong Kong)—Busy clearing up after the Chinamen, who all left early in the morning. Sampans were alongside all day with fruit, comprising bananas, pineapples and apples, which were eagerly bought up by all hands.[39]

Gregory does not say what or how the Chinese steerage passengers were fed, but their food was probably cooked by their own cooks, either in the

Sea Serpent's galley or on a separate stove somewhere. It is likely that the Chinese passengers' food was similar to the camp food served in the gold fields, described by one modern author as "the customary rice, vegetables, meat, and fish."[40] The grizzly bear cub is noteworthy: it was probably a specimen of the now-extinct California Grizzly Bear, the state's official animal.

Charles Abbey, sailing to Australia a few years later, heard tales of encounters with Chinese miners there:

> Friday Aug 12th 1859: Oh these old sailors . . . there they sit, sewing, & talking about Australia (they have been in the mines) & burning Chinese gambling houses, & driving the Celestials out of the diggings.[41]

Anti-Chinese prejudice was rife in Australia as well as in the United States, and Abbey's shipmates who had dug gold there were apparently as bitterly prejudiced as their American brethren.

In the late 1860s, there was another boom of Chinese workers coming to California, to work on the construction of the Central Pacific Railway, planting explosives in rock faces while suspended in baskets, and hewing roadbeds through the mountains of the Sierra Nevada. Workers were recruited in the Sinning and Sinhwui districts, and credit brokers in Hong Kong could advance the fare for a worker, with the worker's family guaranteeing repayment. The fee in a sailing vessel ran $25 for a two to three month passage; in a steamer, the trip could be made in a month, and cost around $40.[42] A description of Central Pacific camp food probably resembles the food aboard the ships in which the Chinese laborers arrived: rice with dried and rehydrated shellfish, vegetables, and seaweed, served with quantities of tea. Every construction crew included a tea carrier, toting a pair of small barrels hanging from a shoulder pole. It may be that the Chinese diet was better balanced than the Caucasian workers' diet of beef, beans, bread, butter, and potatoes. Drinking regular doses of water which had been boiled probably contributed to the health and vigor of the Chinese railroad workers.[43]

Some Chinese miners and railroad workers returned to China; others settled in Gold Mountain. By the 1850s, some Chinese had built a pioneer fishing village at Rincon Point in San Francisco, which supplied fish and shellfish to the early San Franciscans.[44]

Camp-style food, prepared by non-professional Chinese cooks in mining camps, railroad construction camps, and aboard ships, often using Western ingredients along with more traditional ones, eventually found its way into American culture. Camp-style improvisations such as Chop Suey and Chow

Mein became American staples in the twentieth century. Many Americans did not realize, and may not know today, that these dishes originated not in China, but in the work camp and sailing ship kitchens of Chinese laborers and immigrants working in and traveling to and from the Land of the Flowery Flag.

Chinese immigrants continued to influence American culinary traditions. In Florida, Lue Gim Gong developed the hardy Lue Gim Gong Mediterranean Valencia Orange. In Oregon, Ah Bing and his employer developed the Bing Cherry.[45]

"Island": Angel Island Immigration Station

From 1910 to 1940, immigrants arriving in San Francisco were processed at a facility on Angel Island, on the northern part of San Francisco Bay.[46] Prejudice against the Chinese made the screening for Chinese immigrants more extensive and detailed than it was for European, and for that matter, Japanese immigrants. Many were kept on Angel Island (which the Chinese called simply "Island") for months, waiting to be admitted to the United States, or in some cases, to be sent back to China. Some Chinese immigrants remembered the food on their voyages to the United States, usually in American or Japanese steamships. Mrs. Jew, age thirty-three, remembered her difficult experience in 1922:

> Aboard ship, we stayed in a room with two sets of bunks. Confined there, it was difficult to eat. For breakfast, I'd have two eggs. I didn't eat lunch. For dinner, I had a little vegetable with rice. The woman I shared the room with didn't eat anything the whole time. She was seasick.[47]

Some of the Chinese detainees wrote about their journeys in the poems they wrote on the walls of their temporary prison. Sadly, all the women's poems were lost when their barracks building burned in 1940. Many of the men's poems were recorded before being painted over: other poems are still there, carved into the wooden walls.

It was on the day that the Weaver Maiden met the Cowherd
That I took passage on the *President Lincoln*.
I ate wind and tasted waves for more than twenty days.
Fortunately, I arrived safely on the American continent.
I thought I could land in a few days.
How was I to know I would become a prisoner suffering in the wooden building?[48]

Here is a translation of a poem from the walls of Angel Island, evidently written by a male immigrant who is going to be sent back to China:

> For one month I was imprisoned; my slippers never moved forward.
> I came on the *Manchuria* and will return on the *Mongolia*.
> But if I could make the trip to Nanyang, I would.
> Why should America be the only place to seek a living.[49]

The *Manchuria* and the *Mongolia* were both steamers in the Pacific Mail Steamship Line, founded in 1848 and one of the major American lines in the Pacific. Nanyang is Southeast Asia. A rejected immigrant would return on a vessel owned by the same company, as the shipping line which brought him was legally responsible for bringing him back. For this reason, immigrant ships from Asia and Europe provided some degree of coaching for their passengers, offering tips on gaining admittance through the immigration authorities.

Japanese immigrants also passed through Angel Island, although they were rarely held for months as were the Chinese. From the following passage, it appears the Japanese steamers booked more passengers than they had bunks. Chojiro Kubo remembered the crowded conditions and poor conditions:

> In August 1897 I went to the U.S by cargo boat, *Yamaguchi Maru* from Kobe. I was then 16. The third class accommodations were crowded with more than 160 passengers and there wasn't any bunk in which to rest. I slept spreading my own mat and blanket on the wooden floor in the front hatch where there were no windows and no lights . . . The hatch was tightly closed and there was no circulation of air, so we were all tortured by the bad odor . . . the food was second class Nankin rice and salted-kelp, with dirty clams preserved by boiling in soy sauce . . . I shivered, thinking that I would probably go back to Japan some years later in just such a boat.[50]

Beginning in the early 1950s, the United States began screening applicants at their consular offices overseas, so that immigrants were no longer waiting for months on end, only for some of them to be sent back.

Departure

This chapter closes with a poem by an extraordinary nineteenth-century author and humanist. Helen Hunt Jackson's poem "Emagravit" sets the scene of an immigrant ship's departure, then makes a metaphor for the "immigration" at the end of life's journey.

With sails full set, the ship her anchor weighs,
Strange names shine out beneath her figure-head.
What glad farewells with eager eyes are said!
What cheer for him who goes, and him who stays!
Fair skies, rich lands, new homes, and untried days
Some go to seek: the rest but wait instead,
Watching the way wherein their comrades led,
Until the next staunch ship her flag doth raise.
Who knows what myriad colonies there are
Of fairest fields, and rich, undreamed-of gains
Thick planted in the distant shining plains
Which we call sky because they lie so far?
Oh, write of me, not "Died in bitter pains,"
But "Emigrated to another star!"[51]

SIX

Steam Power and
Canned Food

During the nineteenth century, the nature of sea travel was transformed by the application of steam power to oceanic travel. At roughly the same time, the development and application of canning changed the way people ate while traveling on the sea. Both processes were gradual and partial: the adoption of both steam power and canned food was accompanied by challenges and misadventures. In 1800, oceanic passenger travel was entirely powered by the wind; by the end of the century, passenger travel was almost entirely powered by steam. In 1800, the navies of the world were wooden-hulled, wind-powered, and carried their guns in long rows in broadside; by 1900, the world's warships were steam-powered, steel-hulled, and carried their biggest guns in armored revolving turrets. During the same period, techniques of canning food made it possible to keep food for much longer periods. Both the introduction of steam power and the canning of food changed the way people ate at sea.

Steam Power Comes to the Oceans

The earliest steam-powered vessels were designed for protected waters. Paddle wheels quickly became established as the most convenient way to use steam power to propel a vessel through the water, and paddle steamboats proliferated in the bays, lakes, and rivers of the world during the first decades of the nineteenth century. It is not surprising that the adoption of steam power was more gradual for sea-going vessels than for those in protected waters. The keelboats and flatboats that preceded steamboats on rivers had great difficulties when navigating against the current. Sails could be useful if the wind was blowing in the right direction, but as there is limited maneuvering space on a river, the wind was only useful if astern to one's direction of travel. Flatboats were navigated against the current by rowing, poling, and all too often "cordelling." When cordelling a flatboat, the crew went ashore and pulled the boat upstream, like the mules on a towpath (but lacking a towpath along the banks of a river), marching or struggling along with a towrope or "cordelle." It is hardly surprising that steam power, driving side- or stern-mounted revolving paddles, was quickly applied to river and inland water transport. In North America, most steam-powered riverboats were designed to use wood rather than coal for fuel. The hinterlands around the Mississippi, Missouri, and Ohio rivers have yet to recover from the deforestation of the nineteenth century, to fuel the steamboats that plied their waters.

The adoption of steam for oceanic travel took longer. The seagoing sailing vessel had been evolving for centuries, and wind power was harnessed efficiently by vessels in a wide range of sizes and designs. Early ocean-going steamboats used paddlewheels, which were easily damaged by powerful waves. The action of the waves could leave the paddles on one side or the other momentarily out of the water: it was customary to set a couple of sails on paddlewheel steamships just to stabilize the vessel, and thus to keep both paddlewheels in the water.

Another problem hindering the application of steam power to ocean transport was the inefficiency of the engines themselves. Until the development of the triple-expansion engine in the second half of the nineteenth century, steam engines lost a great deal of energy in operation, and required enormous supplies of coal to keep running. It is a common misconception that the mast and sails that grace early ocean-going steamers were decorative anachronisms. In fact, most ocean-going steamers of the mid-nineteenth century relied on the power of the wind in their sails to stretch their coal supplies. Charles Dickens, writing from the United States to his friend John Forster in 1842, observed that the steamer *Britannia*, weighing 1,200 tons (she is recorded as weighing 1,150 gross tons) had to carry a staggering 700 tons of coal for a transatlantic passage: thus she would "ride heavy" when she left port, and "ride light" on arrival.

The first ocean passage using steam was made by the American vessel *Savannah*. Moses Rogers fitted a steam engine with collapsible paddle wheels on an existing sailing packet hull. The resulting vessel, which could be described as a sailing ship with auxiliary steam power, crossed the Atlantic west to east in 1819 under the command of Moses Rogers. Most of the trip was made under sail power, but steam propulsion was used for parts of the trip.[1]

In 1838 two British side-wheel steamers crossed the Atlantic under steam power alone. One of these was *Great Western*, the brainchild of Isambard Brunel; the other was *Sirius*, a Cork-London mail steamer. The *Sirius* arrived in New York ahead of *Great Western*, though she had a head start of four days. Designed for much shorter runs, the *Sirius* was loaded with extra coal; when even this ran short, the crew ended up burning cabin furniture, spare yards and even one of her two masts. This inspired Jules Verne to include a similar event in his novel *Around the World in Eighty Days*.

It was during those final years of the 1830s that Samuel Cunard of Halifax, Nova Scotia won a contract from the British Admiralty for carrying the mails between Liverpool and North America. The first of Cunard's steamers, RMS (Royal Mail Steamer) *Britannia*, entered service in July 1840, making regular sailings between Liverpool, Halifax, and Boston. The carrying of mail guaranteed Cunard a fixed income in return for making the transatlantic run on a schedule. Initially incorporated as "The British and North American Royal Mail Steam-Packet Company," Cunard Company was one of several early steamship companies which secured government postal contracts to support the initial high costs. The *Britannia* was soon joined by her sisters *Acadia*, *Columbia*, and *Caledonia*; then the slightly larger *Hibernia* and *Cambria*, so that Cunard could offer regular sailings in both directions twice a month.[2]

The concept of regular sailings had been pioneered earlier in 1818, by an American company called the Black Ball Line. As described in chapter 5, the Blackballers and their imitators promised to leave port (Liverpool and New York) on a regular schedule. This of course did not guarantee their arrival times, especially sailing east to west where prevailing winds were often against them. The implementation of steam power made not only regularly scheduled departures, but reasonably regular arrivals, an achievable goal.

Cunard Company: "Speed, Comfort, and Safety"

The early years of Cunard's transatlantic service reflected a kind of no-frills efficiency. He instructed his builders, "I want a plain and comfortable boat, not the least unnecessary expense for show." The Cunard steamers were modest in size, smaller than Brunel's *Great Britain*, and they were efficiently run. The company motto was "Speed, Comfort, and Safety," and Samuel Cunard instructed his captains to avoid the three taboo R's: racing, rivalry, and risk-taking. In his own words, "Your ship is loaded, take her; speed is nothing, follow your own road, deliver her safe, bring her back safe—safety is all that is required."[3]

While Cunard's steamers may have been built without frills and operated with caution, they represented a technological marvel of their day, an age that was giddy with technological marvels. Crossing the Atlantic aboard *Britannia* and her sisters was an experience comparable to crossing the Atlantic aboard the supersonic transport *Concorde* in the 1970s. The accommodations, while not flamboyantly luxurious, were elegant and relatively comfortable. Passengers enjoyed a degree of comfort in accommodation and food that was comparable to cabin passengers in sailing vessels. No passengers on Cunard steamers endured anything like the conditions aboard immigrant ships, subsisting on food they had to bring and prepare themselves. Instead, passengers aboard *Britannia* could expect staterooms that resembled a more cramped version of a hotel room ashore, and food that resembled contemporary hotel fare.[4]

Charles Dickens Takes Passage to North America

In January 1842 Charles Dickens was a passenger on the first Cunard steamer *Britannia*, which had only been making transatlantic passages for eighteen months at the time. Dickens was possibly one of Cunard's most famous passengers of all time. It is fortunate for posterity that he wrote about his experience on one of the first transatlantic steamers. We have heard already about his return trip on a sailing immigrant packet in June.

Dickens's choices of adjectives and adverbs suggest that he disapproved of the steamer; or possibly that he felt the experience did not live up to its promises. Perhaps Dickens felt compelled to tell his readers that this new wonder of technology was not all it was cracked up to be.

Whatever his reasons, Dickens chose language that clearly indicates his preference for sail over steam. The reader should bear in mind that he crossed from east to west, against the prevailing winds; and in January, when the Atlantic weather is especially stormy. His passage was made in just eighteen days—Liverpool to Halifax to Boston. This time, in that direction at that time of year, is an achievement of which Cunard had every right to feel proud. Dickens's return voyage in sail was made in June, when the weather tends to be much more pleasant; and with, not against, the prevailing winds.

> Before descending into the bowels of the ship, we had passed from the deck into a long narrow apartment, not unlike a gigantic hearse with windows at the sides; having at the upper end a melancholy stove, at which three or four chilly stewards were warming their hands; while on either side, extending down its

Figure 6.1. The Cunard Steamship RMS *Europa* before 1866. This ship represents the next generation of Cunard steamers after the *Britannia*. While slightly larger that *Britannia*, its appearance is very similar. Source: unknown. Courtesy of Wikipedia. Public domain. https://en.wikipedia.org/wiki/File:RMS_Europa.jpg.

whole dreary length, was a long, long table, over each of which a rack, fixed to the low roof, and stuck full of drinking-glasses and cruet-stands, hinted dismally at rolling seas and heavy weather . . . He (the booking agent) had spoken of the saloon. . . . To form a just conception of it, it would be necessary to multiply the size and furniture of an ordinary drawing-room by seven.[5]

This saloon was a long space, resembling a hearse in that it had windows which were above the level of the deck. It functioned like a larger version of the "cabin" in a contemporary sailing vessel. Dickens's description gives us a sense of this communal dining and lounging space: that it had two long tables along its length, each with a hanging rack for glasses and cruets. Here the passengers ate their meals, played card games such as whist, read books, and passed the time.

Dickens offers a description of the loading of the provisions aboard *Britannia*:

one party of men were "taking in the milk," or in other words, getting the cow on board; and another were filling the icehouses to the very throat with fresh provisions; with butchers'-meat and garden-stuff, pale sucking-pigs, calves' heads in scores, beef, veal, and pork, and poultry out of all proportion.[6]

Here Dickens refers to an intriguing detail of the food service aboard early Cunard steamers, as aboard some contemporary sailing packets. A live cow was carried in a padded stall, which was milked during the passage so that the passengers could enjoy fresh milk throughout their time aboard *Britannia*. Dickens may have been surprised at the quantity of provisions that were laid in for him and his fellow passengers, and we get a glimpse of the sort of ingredients that made up the fare for early Cunard passengers. Icehouses held meats and other perishables: as the passage was unlikely to require more than three weeks, the ice only had to last that long.

Dickens describes a midday meal aboard *Britannia*, after most of the passengers have overcome their seasickness.

> At one, a bell rings, and the stewardess comes down with a steaming dish of baked potatoes, and another of roasted apples; and plates of pig's face, cold ham, salt beef; or perhaps a smoking mess of rare hot collops. We fall upon these dainties; eat as much as we can (we have great appetites now); and are as long as possible about it.[7]

Britannia carried several male stewards and at least one female stewardess, an innovation in passenger service for that era. The collops were slices of meat, lightly breaded and usually served with a sauce. The name may be a Scottish variation of the French "escalope," and the Scottish recipes resemble veal scaloppini. The timing of the meal is interesting, an hour later than the customary time for the crew's midday meal. It may be that the crew was served their meal at noon, the traditional time; then the cooks prepared the food for the passengers. Though Dickens seems to have favored wine and brandy-water as beverages, he mentions "dozens of bottled porter" as well.[8]

A few hours later, the evening meal was served.

> At five, another bell rings, and the stewardess reappears with another dish of potatoes—boiled, this time—and store of hot meat of various kinds. . . . We sit down at table again (rather more cheerfully than before); prolong the meal with a rather mouldy dessert of apples, grapes, and oranges; and drink our wine and brandy-water . . . we make a party of whist . . . At whist we remain with exemplary gravity (deducting a short time for tea and toast) until eleven o'clock, or thereabouts; when the captain comes down again, in a sou'wester hat tied under his chin, and a pilot-coat: making the ground wet where he stands. By this time the card-playing is over, and the bottles and glasses are again upon the table.[9]

The timing of this meal is interesting also: crew meals were usually served at 4:00 p.m. or more conveniently for them, at 6:00 p.m. It appears that cooked meals for passengers were offset by an hour from the crew meals. Dickens refers to brandy-water several times in his description of his passage in *Britannia*, it must have been a favorite of his, and probably of other passengers who were feeling somewhat bilious as *Britannia* pounded her way into the adverse westerly gales of the Atlantic in January. The evening tea and toast was an excellent choice for passengers, who like Dickens, were experiencing the torpor and queasiness of mild seasickness. Dickens's passage was particularly rough: heavy weather stove in one of *Britannia*'s boats and carried away some of the planking on her starboard paddle box.

The regular appearance of the captain in the passengers' saloon is also interesting, as it presages the institution of "the captain's table" in later transatlantic liners. Clearly the captain wanted to make himself available to the passengers, and to visibly demonstrate his fellowship with them.

Dickens writes of how events in the closed community of a ship at sea can take on an accentuated interest, as he shares some shipboard gossip:

> The ship's cook, secretly swigging damaged whiskey, has been found drunk; and has been played upon by the fire-engine until quite sober. All the stewards have fallen down-stairs at various dinner-times, and go about with plasters in various places. The baker is ill, and so is the pastry-cook. A new man, horribly indisposed, has been required to fill the place of the latter officer; and has been propped and jammed up with empty casks in a little house upon deck, and commanded to roll out pie-crust, which he protests (being highly bilious) it is death to him to look at. News! A dozen murders on shore would lack the interest of these slight incidents at sea.[10]

The "fire engine" turned on the cook would have been a hand-pumped hose; a very sensible precaution for a steamer in 1842. Dickens certainly paints an amusing portrait of food service on his passage, with bandaged stewards, a sobering-up cook, an ill baker, and a replacement pastry chef on the verge of nausea.

Dickens and his wife had a stateroom off of the saloon. Some Cunard passengers who had purchased less expensive tickets slept on the saloon benches when they were curtained off at night. Whether sleeping in a stateroom or on a saloon berth, one summoned a steward anonymously, to which the steward replied, "What number, sir or madam?" The bulkhead separating each pair of staterooms held a candle to illuminate both cabins at once: stewards doused these candles at midnight. Dickens refers to this source of light as a "large bull's eye" (round pane of glass) "just over the looking-glass" (mirror).[11] The Dickens's stateroom had a porthole which could be opened in pleasant weather. There was very limited plumbing, and no hot water. Passengers in the first Cunard steamers enjoyed facilities which were comparable to those for cabin passengers in contemporary sailing vessels, with a few advantages such as the fresh milk and cream, and the services of a pastry chef; however their conditions were not nearly so comfortable as those offered in the transatlantic service of Cunard and its competitors sixty years later.[12]

There is an important part of the little community aboard *Britannia* that Dickens hardly mentions: the men who worked her engines. The engine room was stiflingly hot, regardless of the temperature on deck. The work of the stokers, who had to shovel coal into the furnaces which heated the boilers, was exhausting and exacting. The traditional sailors' routine of "watch on, watch off," working and resting alternately every four hours, did not give the "black gang" (so-called because the coal turned their skin and clothes black) adequate time to cool down and rest. Therefore the black gang in coal-fired steamers worked a different watch routine; four hours on and eight hours off. The crew who worked on deck continued to work alternate four-hour watches. Crew meals could still be served at the same times as they were in pure sailing vessels: one of the engine-room shifts ate their meal in the middle of their eight hours off.

Even with eight hours off between four-hour shifts in the engine room, stokers had a hard life. In the decades following Dickens's passage in *Britannia*, many of the stokers in British and other European steamers were Liverpool Irish, Chinese, or Lascars (men from India). In American steamers, many of the stokers were of African descent. The international character of the maritime world's engine room crews changed the ethnographic map of the world. Chinese stokers who "swallowed the anchor" (gave up seafaring life) and married local women were a significant minority in the Netherlands. During World War II, African American sailors, mostly engine-room workers, performed jazz and blues in Liverpool nightclubs. Liverpool folklorist Tony Davis believes that Liverpudlian music aficionados of the 1940s knew more about Southern Black music than did most contemporary Americans. A close acquaintance of Liverpudlians with American music contributed to the "Skiffle" music craze of Liverpool in the 1950s, out of which grew the Quarrymen/Beatles and other groups of the British Invasion of 1964.[13]

The Great Britain and the Great Eastern

Larger steamers followed in the footsteps of the *Great Western* and the *Britannia*. Brunel's next big transatlantic steamer was the *Great Britain*, with a hull of wrought iron and screw propulsion. When she entered service in 1845, she was the longest passenger vessel afloat, a record her 322-foot hull

Figure 6.2. The Steamship *Great Eastern*. Artist: Charles Parsons. Published by Currier & Ives c. 1858. Hand-colored lithograph. Reproduction Number: LC-DIG-pga-00795 in Collection: Popular Graphic Prints. Courtesy of Library of Congress Digital Collections. http://www.loc.gov/pictures/item/2002699730/.

held for nine years. Iron had many advantages over wood, including cost. In mid-nineteenth-century Britain, wood was becoming more costly as iron was becoming cheaper. Wrought iron even has some advantages over steel. While steel is stronger pound for pound than wrought iron, it is also more prone to rust. The *Great Britain* still survives, beautifully restored in Bristol. She is one of several nineteenth-century vessels still extant, whose hulls are of wrought iron.

Brunel far surpassed the *Great Britain* in 1858 with *Great Eastern*, one of the engineering marvels of the nineteenth century. Christened the *Leviathan* but soon renamed *Great Eastern*, Brunel's masterpiece had double hulls and watertight bulkheads running thwartship and fore and aft, rendering her one of the safest hulls of her own or of subsequent ages. Her hull was of original construction, being constructed without keel or ribs. The *Great Eastern* was 692 feet long, with a loaded displacement of 27,400 tons, designed to carry two thousand passengers. She combined screw, paddlewheels, and sails on six masts. While the *Great Eastern* has been described as the world's first ocean liner, her paddlewheels, bluff sides, sailing masts and other features make her look more like an enormous mid-nineteenth-century steamer. Her career was dogged by difficulties, many of them resulting from her enormous size. In 1861, the *Great Eastern* was caught in the grip of an epic Atlantic hurricane, a storm that would have destroyed a smaller, less sturdy ship. The *Great Eastern*, though intended to be more stable than other vessels, had a tendency to roll, and this came into play when she was in the clutches of this epic storm. A swan whose coop had been smashed ended up in the grand saloon, and battered itself to death trying to fly out of it. A freak wave threw two cows, their pens smashed to splinters, into the ladies saloon, where they were eventually killed, hoisted out, and heaved overboard.

> The rocking movement comes on again with renewed force. The passengers catch hold of the tables for support. The tables are not fastened. . . . Tables give way . . . Stewards rush to the rescue, but in two minutes every piece of crockery on the table is smashed, knives and forks fly about in reckless confusion, and the scene closes by a general accumulation of tables, chairs, crockery, passengers and stewards in the middle of the saloon.[14]

The situation worsened in the following days, with compartments, cabins and staterooms flooded. Everyone and everything was soaked in seawater. Two casks of fish oil, not properly secured, got loose and broken, permeating the entire cavernous vessel with its scent. The passengers had not eaten in some time. Cooks were thrown against their stoves, but they managed nonetheless to prepare a simple stew for the passengers. There was no more intact crockery. Barrels of smashed crockery were rolled into the saloon: passengers were encouraged to find the biggest fragments in which to eat their stew. Barrels of ship's biscuit were lashed to the bulkheads, from which the passengers could help themselves.[15]

Her paddles and rudder disabled, the *Great Eastern* eventually got back to Cobh, then known as Queenstown, the deepwater port of Cork. Four years later she was put to work laying a transatlantic telegraph cable, arguably her most successful employment. Late in her career she ended up as a beached billboard and showboat in Liverpool, and was finally scrapped in 1886.[16]

P&O Line: Passages to the Mediterranean, India, and Australia

Another early shipping line was the Peninsular and Oriental Steam Navigation Company, which in 1837 secured a mail contract from the British Admiralty to carry mail between Britain and the Iberian Peninsula, that is Spain and Portugal. The company flag, which still flies today, combines the colors of the Spanish and Portuguese flags of 1837.[17] The mail contract was expanded to include Alexandria in Egypt, and the company expanded into cargo and passenger service. Through many mergers and demergers, and episodes of diversification that have embraced banking, grocery store chains, and more, this company has survived to the present day with its name and flag intact.

There were other British shipping lines operating steamers in the Indian Ocean. The largest of these was the British India Steam Navigation Company, which was eventually absorbed into the P&O Line.

The Suez Canal

The opening of the Suez Canal in 1869 made steam travel to India and Australia much easier. Prior to the completion of the canal, passengers were compelled to travel overland between Alexandria and the Red Sea, boarding a new steamer after their trip across the desert. Until 1888, the Post Office (which had taken over responsibility for overseas mail from the Admiralty in 1860) required the mail bags to travel overland and not through the canal, from Port Said (a new port built on the soil dug out for the canal) to Suez. At least the passengers could remain on board as their steamers transited the canal.[18]

The Collins Line

American steamers operated on a number of short runs, for example from the cities of the eastern seaboard to Panama, and from Panama to California, during the California Gold Rush of 1849. Traveling this way was faster than taking a sailing ship around Cape Horn, but it was also more dangerous. Many would-be-forty-niners perished of malaria and tropical fevers in Panama, while waiting to find a place on a steamer bound for their destination.

Pleasure steamers proliferated on the Hudson and in New York Harbor, as well in other protected waters. As the design of steamers improved, steamers competed successfully with sailing vessels in more and more offshore routes. During the Mexican-American War of 1847, steamers were used to transport troops to Mexico; by the time of the American Civil War less than twenty years later, steamers had almost completely replaced sailing vessels as they carried troops, mails, and munitions between the northern states and federal outposts in the southern states.

In the 1860s, vessels were built for operation in shallow water that were sometimes driven by a pair of smaller-diameter screws instead of one large screw. Twin-screw vessels could be built with shallow draft, allowing them to compete with paddle-wheel steamers in shallow waters.

By 1850, American steamers offered competition in the transatlantic passenger business. Edward Knight Collins secured a subsidy from Congress to carry mail, and the Collins's New York & Liverpool United States' Mail Steamship Company (popularly known as the Collins Line) built four side-wheel steamers which were larger and more comfortable than the Cunard steamers. The *Atlantic, Arctic, Baltic,* and *Pacific* had roomier staterooms, improved ventilation, an on-board barber, and steam heat. In port, their saloons were elegantly equipped with fine carpets and brocade curtains, which however were replaced with coconut mats and canvas curtains at sea.

Sadly, the Collins Line steamers came to grief. The *Arctic* sank off the coast of Newfoundland in 1854, following a collision with a French iron-hulled screw steamer. Collin's wife, daughter, and youngest son were among those who lost their lives. In January 1856, the *Pacific* disappeared after departing Liverpool. The only trace of her was a bottle that washed ashore on the Hebridean island of Uist in 1861, containing this touching message:

"On board the Pacific from Liverpool to N.Y.—Ship going down. Confusion on board—icebergs around us on every side. I know I cannot escape. I write the cause of our loss that friends may not live in suspense. The finder will please get it published. W.M. GRAHAM." Congress withdrew its subsidy of the Collins Line, and the transatlantic passenger business was dominated by British and European steamers for some time to come.

Mark Twain Goes to Sea

In 1867, Mark Twain (the nom de plume of Samuel Langhorne Clemens) joined a large party of Americans who made an excursion to and around the Mediterranean, something like the cruises of a later era. The vessel chartered for this adventure was the sidewheel steamer *Quaker City*, a vessel somewhat like the *Britannia* in overall design, built in Philadelphia (hence her name) in 1854; used to blockade Confederate ports and hunt for Confederate commerce raiders during the American Civil War; then returned to passenger service shortly before Mark Twain became her most famous passenger. Mark Twain memorialized his journey in *Innocents Abroad*.

Transatlantic steamer travel had become more common in the twenty-five years since Dickens made his crossing. Mark Twain had been to sea before, and was one of the few passengers who was not seasick on the outward leg of the journey. As he writes:

By some happy fortune I was not seasick.—That was a thing to be proud of. I had not always escaped before. If there is one thing in the world that will make a man peculiarly and insufferably self-conceited, it is to have his stomach behave itself, the first day at sea, when nearly all his comrades are seasick . . . We all like to see people seasick when we are not, ourselves. Playing whist by the cabin lamps when it is storming outside is pleasant; walking the quarterdeck in the moonlight is pleasant; smoking in the breezy foretop is pleasant when one is not afraid to go up there; but these are all feeble and commonplace compared with the joy of seeing people suffering the miseries of seasickness.[19]

Mark Twain described his stateroom:

We selected a stateroom forward of the wheel, on the starboard side, "below decks." It had two berths in it, a dismal dead-light, a sink with a washbowl in it, and a long, sumptuously cushioned locker, which was to do service as a sofa—partly—and partly as a hiding place for our things. Notwithstanding all this furniture, there was still room to turn around in, but not to swing a cat in, at least with entire security to the cat. However, the room was large, for a ship's stateroom, and was in every way satisfactory.[20]

This stateroom aboard *Quaker City* greatly resembled Dickens's stateroom aboard *Britannia*.

Mark Twain painted a vivid picture of the shipboard meal and recreation routine aboard *Quaker City*:

At seven bells the first gong rang; at eight there was breakfast, for such as were not too seasick to eat it. . . . From eleven o'clock until luncheon, and from luncheon until dinner at six in the evening, the employments and amusements were various. Some reading was done, and much smoking and sewing, though not by the same parties . . . in the smoking room there were always parties of gentlemen playing euchre, draughts and dominoes, especially dominoes, that delightfully harmless game; and down on the main deck, "for'rard"—for'rard of the chicken-coops and the cattle—we had what was called "horse billiards." Horse billiards is a fine game . . . By 7 o'clock in the evening, dinner was about over; an hour's promenade on the upper deck followed; then the gong sounded and a large majority of the party repaired to the after cabin (upper), a handsome saloon fifty or sixty feet long, for prayers. The unregenerated called this saloon the "Synagogue."[21]

A number of details about this narrative are interesting. Chickens and cattle were carried aboard, probably furnishing fresh milk, cream, and eggs during the voyage, and possibly fresh meat. Mark Twain mentions the purchase of cattle in Alexandria, possibly because the cattle carried on board from North America had been eaten by then.[22] Meal times were announced with a gong.

What Twain called "Horse Billiards," "a mixture of shuffleboard and hop-scotch" is the game that came to be called Shuffleboard aboard the liners and cruise ships of the twentieth century. To Charles Dickens and Mark Twain, Shuffleboard was the ancient English tavern game of Shove Groat or Shove Ha'penny. By the 1920s, the seagoing version that Mark Twain calls "Horse Billiards" having usurped the name of Shuffleboard, was a staple amusement of transatlantic liners as well as summer camps ashore.

Mark Twain describes seasick passengers consuming tea and toast topside in the lee of the paddle wheel. He mentions tea and coffee on the return voyage, when a passenger complains of the weakness of the ship's coffee, but the captain informs him that "It is inferior—for coffee—but it is pretty fair tea."[23]

There were attempts at dancing on the upper deck, under awnings, on starlit evenings. To the music of a melodeon, clarinet, and accordion, some of the passengers attempted to dance on deck:

> When the ship rolled to starboard the whole platoon of dancers came charging down to starboard with it, and brought up in mass at the rail; and when it rolled to port they went floundering down to port with the same unanimity of sentiment. Waltzers spun around precariously for a matter of fifteen seconds and then went scurrying down to the rail as if they meant to go overboard. The Virginia Reel, as performed on board the *Quaker City*, had more genuine reel about it than any reel I ever saw before, and was as full of interest to the spectator as it was full of desperate chances and hairbreadth escapes to the participant. We gave up dancing, finally.[24]

Mark Twain mentions that they stocked up on fresh oranges, lemons, figs, and apricots when they stopped in the Azores.[25] Mark Twain did not name the actual dishes served aboard *Quaker City* in 1867, but the fare was probably similar to that served aboard *Britannia* twenty-five years earlier.

Steamers at War: Shell-guns, Propellers, and Lifting Screws

Steam had great potential for the navies of the world. An armed vessel that was independent of the wind could attack and retreat in most any direction at will, and could maneuver itself into positions where it could pound a wind-powered enemy while receiving little return fire. Robert Fulton designed a steam-powered harbor defense vessel, the *Demologos*, for service during the War of 1812.[26]

During the first half of the nineteenth century, paddle wheel steamers were added to the naval fleets of the world. Steam did not replace sail in warship design overnight. There were many reasons for this: one of the principal reasons being the inefficiency of early steam engines. Until the development of the triple-expansion engine, in which the same steam pushes on three cylinders in succession and is then returned to be reheated in a closed system, steamers required an enormous supply of coal to fuel their engines. This in turn limited the range of early steam warships. With the general adoption of the triple-expansion engine after 1880, steamers could go much further on their coal supply.

Another factor that hindered the proliferation of the steam warship was the vulnerability of the paddle wheels. A steamer could be crippled by having its paddlewheels damaged, and the paddlewheels were usually mounted right in harm's way, near the center of the vessel. A battle fought in Campeche Bay, Yucatan in 1843 between two British-built paddlewheel steamers of the Mexican Navy on one side, and two sailing warships of the Republic of Texas Navy on the other, went rather badly for the steamers.

The Mexican vessels at Campeche Bay incorporated another innovation in addition to their steam propulsion: shell guns. French general Henri-Joseph Paixhans had developed a new type of gun in the 1820s, firing explosive shells that were detonated by a timed fuse set in motion by the ignition of the gun's charge. Intended to give the French Navy an advantage over the British Navy, Paixhans's shell-gun was quickly adopted by all the navies of the world. Smoothbore shell-guns sacrificed range and accuracy. In the Battle of Campeche Bay, the Texian vessels, armed with traditional guns firing solid shot, inflicted a great deal of damage on their shell-firing opponents. By the mid-nineteenth century, shell guns were produced with rifled bores, which increased their range and accuracy.

A solution to the vulnerability of paddlewheel warships was the screw or propeller. By the second quarter of the nineteenth century, screw steamers appeared alongside their paddlewheel siblings. The screw or propeller was of course much less likely to be damaged by enemy gunfire. Debates ensued between proponents of both methods of propelling a steam vessel. In 1845 the British Admiralty held a tug-of-war between two steam sloops of similar size and power, the screw sloop *Rattler* and the paddlewheel-driven *Alecto*. The *Rattler* dragged the *Alecto* backwards at a speed of almost three knots, and thereafter most new steam warships were equipped with screws rather than paddlewheels.[27]

With the superior efficiency of the screw proven, most oceanic steam passenger vessels in the latter half of the nineteenth century were driven by screws. Paddlewheels still had an advantage in very shallow waters, and they remained popular in steamers designed for rivers, lakes, and bays.

An interesting design feature of long-range cruising vessels of the mid-nineteenth century is the lifting screw. Screw steamers using sail power to stretch their coal supplies were hampered by the screw, fixed to the drive-shaft, a source of drag. To eliminate this drag, many steamers were equipped with a "lifting screw," in which the screw was held in a rectangular frame. When operating under sail, the driveshaft was shifted forward, and the screw was lifted out of the water in its frame. When the engine was to be used again, the screw in its frame was lowered back into the water, the driveshaft shifted aft to engage the screw, and the vessel could continue under steam power. Steamers of this era without lifting screws could not operate efficiently under sail. During the American Civil War, Confederate captain Raphael Semmes initially operated CSS *Sumter*, a steamer without a lifting screw. His second command, CSS *Alabama*, was a purpose-built cruiser with a lifting screw. With the *Alabama* Semmes's speed and range was greatly improved. Semmes himself stated that the *Alabama* could carry only enough coal to steam for eighteen days; thus her performance under sail was of vital importance.[28] Later on, sailing vessels with engines were equipped with feathering screws, which could be disengaged from the engine without the necessity of lifting them out of the water.

CSS *Alabama* also carried a condenser to convert salt water into fresh, an expanded version of the condenser on the *Victory*'s Brodie stove.[29]

Changes in warship design made for changes in the eating and sleeping accommodations of the crew. HMS *Warrior*, commissioned in 1860, was like her sister HMS *Black Prince*, an enormous ironclad screw-driven steamer. Most of *Warrior*'s guns were nonetheless in the traditional broadside arrange-ment on a lower deck, within an armored casemate.[30] *Warrior*'s crew slept in hammocks and dined on hanging tables slung between the guns, just as the men of the British Navy did on capital ships fifty years earlier. As currently restored, the crew's utensils are changed from those of Nelson's day: round tin plates and tin cups replacing the square wooden plates and horn cups that were in use fifty years earlier.

Changes in the design and arrangement of guns produced changes in where the crew ate. HMS *Captain*, roughly contemporary with *Warrior*, had four enormous guns in two armored turrets on deck.[31]

USS *Monitor* had two guns in one revolving turret. With all of her limited hull space abaft the turret taken up by machinery, the officers and crew were accommodated forward in spaces that communicated with a single central wardroom.

American Naval Rations
during the Civil War

It is interesting to study the issue of food and drink in the U.S. Navy during the American Civil War. Here is what was approved by the U.S. Congress on July 18, 1861:

> One pound of salt pork, with half a pint of beans or peas; one pound salt beef, with half a pound of flour, and two ounces of dried apples or other fruit; or three quarters of preserved (canned) meat, with half a pound of rice, two ounces of butter, and one ounce of desiccated (dehydrated) vegetables; or three quarters pound preserved meat, two ounces of butter, and two ounces of desiccated potato; together with fourteen ounces of biscuit (hardtack), one quarter of an ounce of tea, or one ounce of coffee or cocoa, two ounces of sugar, and a gill (four ounces) of sprits (grog); and a weekly allowance of half a pound of pickles, half a pint of molasses, and half a pint of vinegar.[32]

This is only a Congress-approved suggestion, and actual issues may have been different, using locally available resources. This is a slightly greater ration than that recommended for soldiers at the same time. Several things are worthy of note: the "preserved meat" could be salt meat; but is very likely that it is canned/tinned meat that is intended. "Desiccated vegetables" were also issued to soldiers, who generally disliked it and nicknamed this issue "desecrated vegetables."[33] The "dessicated vegetables" came as a small greenish brick wrapped in paper. The desiccated potato is an interesting item, as are the pickles. It is likely that coffee was issued more often than tea or cocoa. Sailors who had spent time in merchant ships would have been accustomed to sweetening their coffee with molasses. The spirits were just as likely to be corn or rye whiskey as the traditional rum.[34]

The Congressional records show what basic materials were recommended for seamen in the United States Navy during the Civil War. For a day-to-day record of actual food issues, we turn to the journal kept by Charles Brother, a private in the United States Marine Corps, who kept a journal during 144 days he spent serving in the steamer *Hartford* in 1864. Private Brother recorded what he was served for dinner aboard the *Hartford* almost every day from March 14 to the Battle of Mobile Bay on August 5. USS *Hartford* was David Farragut's flagship in that battle: Farragut may (or may not) have uttered his famous words, "Damn the torpedoes: Full Speed Ahead!" within earshot of Private Charles Brother. From Private Brother's journal entries, the following pattern of food issues (for dinner, the mid-day principal meal of the day) emerges:

Monday—Pork and Beans
Tuesday—Duff
Wednesday—Pork and Beans
Thursday—Bully Beef, coffee
Friday—Duff
Saturday—Pork and Beans
Sunday—Bully Beef, coffee

There are variations in this routine. After receiving "fresh beef, vegetables, and ice," from supply ships, the *Hartford* issued "Fresh Grub" to the crew for the following one, two, or three days in place of the usual food. These issues of fresh food comprised seventeen of the one hundred and forty-four days covered in Private Brother's journal. On two days, "Potatoe Sause" (probably a hash based on minced potatoes) was substituted; on five days, "Sea Pie" (a form of baked lobscouse, as described in an earlier chapter). On six Sundays, the Hartford's crew received "Dandyfunk" instead of, or in addition to, their usual bully beef. As described in chapter 4, this was probably an elaborate form of "duff." On four Sundays, boiled rice was issued. On just two days, Private Brother recorded an issue of "Salt Horse" served with duff. "Salt horse" was the beef soaked in casks of brine that remained a staple in the diet of contemporary merchant sailors throughout the nineteenth century. Bully beef was boiled beef, usually sirloin, round, or flank steak which had been boiled, sometimes roasted as well, and then preserved in tin containers. It is interesting that the men of the *Hartford* ate so much tinned beef, when merchant sailors continued to make do with "salt horse" soaked in brine casks. It would appear that Uncle Sam in wartime had deeper pockets than most sailing ship owners. Private Brothers does not mention biscuit by name, but it probably accompanied most of the dinners he notes in his journal. On one occasion he notes "soft tack" or bread.[35]

While Private Brother's accounts of reprovisioning are terse, a Union sailor offered a more detailed account of his ship being resupplied by the steamer *Massachusetts*:

We . . . hear that letter, papers, fresh meat and ice awaits us, on the good old Bay State steamer Massachusetts. We prepare to lower boat and get our goodies . . . The boat returns well laden with barrels of potatoes, quarter [sic] of beef, and chunks of ice, but no mail.[36]

Farewell to Grog in the United States Navy

The issue of grog, water mixed with rum, whiskey, or other spirits, had been an institution of the United States Navy from its inception. One American sailor described the issue:

Grog was served out twice a day, in the morning before breakfast and again at night before piping down for supper. When the Boatswain piped for grog time, the crew fell into line and marched in single file, before the ship's steward, who dealt out [to] each [a] share as he came up. Each man received one gill [four ounces] in a small round measure. The boys often tried to trick the steward by falling in line again and thereby getting a double ration, but they were not always successful in this, for the steward, master-at-arms, and a marine stood by to see that each man got his ration and that no man was served twice.[37]

This merry scene was not to last.

Flag Officer Andrew H. Foote led a crusade for temperance in the United States Navy. In 1843, as First Lieutenant aboard the newly built fifty-gun sailing frigate *Cumberland*, Foote was largely responsible for making the *Cumberland* the first "Temperance Ship" (i.e., no alcohol on board) in the United States Navy. This was the same *Cumberland* that was rammed and sunk nineteen years later at Hampton Roads, by the Confederate ironclad *Virginia*. After the abolition of the importation of slaves from Africa in January 1808, American Navy vessels joined those of the British Navy in patrolling the waters off the West Coast of Africa, searching for slave smugglers. Foote was active in this anti-slave-smuggling patrol as commander of the USS *Perry* from 1849 to 1851. Foote published a book, "Africa and the American Flag" in 1854, which argued for enhanced and more vigorous American participation in the prevention of the slave trade from Africa, as well as for increased support of Liberia.[38] Many civilians in the Temperance Movement were also opposed to slavery; during the United States in the 1840s and 1850s, the two causes tended to go together. In this regard Foote, who had attained the rank of admiral by the middle of the Civil War, was characteristic of his era.

Since 1831, sailors in the United States Navy had been given the option to receive a pay supplement instead of grog. In July 1862, Congress passed legislation to stop the issue of grog altogether in United States Navy vessels on September 1, 1862. All sailors were to receive a five cents a day pay raise to compensate them for the stoppage of grog. An unidentified sailor remembered the day:

I well remember the day we received the news that grog was abolished . . . Curses not so loud, but deep, were indulged in by old tars, some of whom had seen years of service, and who, by custom, had become habituated to their allowance of grog, that the very expectation of it was accompanied by a feeling of pleasure. It was a long time before the men forgot the actions of Congress, and in fact, they never ceased to talk about it.[39]

Date	Monday	Tuesday	Wednesday	Thursday	Friday	Saturday	Sunday
March 14-20, 1864	Pork & Beans	No Duff, Bully Beef instead	Pork & Beans	Duff	Duff	Pork & Beans	Bully Beef, Coffee
March 21-27, 1864	Pork & Beans	Duff	Pork & Beans	Bully Beef, Coffee	Duff	Pork & Beans	Bully Beef, Coffee
March 28-April 3, 1864	Pork & Beans	Duff	Pork & Beans	Bully Beef, Coffee	Duff	Pork & Beans	Bully Beef, Coffee
April 4-10, 1864	Pork & Beans	Duff	Pork & Beans	Bully Beef, Coffee (got fresh beef, ice, vegetables)	Fresh Grub	No food entry	Fresh Grub
April 11-17, 1864	Pork & Beans	Duff	Pork & Beans	Ate ashore: Pork & Beans	Duff	Pork & Beans	Bully Beef, Boiled Spuds for dinner, Dandyfunk for supper
April 18-24, 1864	Pork & Beans	Duff	Pork & Beans	Bully Beef, Coffee	Duff	Pork & Beans	Boiled Rice
April 25-May 1, 1864	Pork & Beans	Pork & Beans	Pork & Beans	Bully Beef, Coffee	Duff	Pork & Beans	Bully Beef, Rice (got fresh beef, ice, and vegetables)
May 2-8, 1864	Fresh Grub (Small Stores Drawn)	Duff	Pork & Beans	Pork & Beans	Duff	Pork & Beans	Bully Beef, Rice
May 9-15, 1864	Pork & Beans	Sea Pie	Pork & Beans	Bully Beef, Coffee	Sea Pie	Pork & Beans	Fresh Grub for dinner, Dandyfunk for supper

Figure 6.3. Civil War Ration Chart. Researched and compiled by author Simon Spalding, based on the journal entries on food and reprovisioning by USMC Private Charles Brothers. Source: Navy Department, Naval History Division, *Civil War Naval Chronology: 1861–1865* (Washington, DC: U.S. Government Printing Office, 1971), VI: 47–83.

Date	Monday	Tuesday	Wednesday	Thursday	Friday	Saturday	Sunday
May 16-22, 1864	Fresh Grub	Fresh Grub	Pork & Beans	Bully Beef, Coffee	Duff	Pork & Beans	Bully Beef, Dandyfunk
May 23-29, 1864	Pork & Beans	Duff (got ice, fresh beef, and vegetables)	Fresh Grub	Fresh Grub	Fresh Grub	Pork & Beans	Bully Beef, Dandyfunk
May 30-June 5, 1864	Pork & Beans	Duff, Salt Horse	Pork & Beans	Bully Beef, Coffee	Duff	Pork & Beans (supply ship arrived)	Fresh Grub
June 6-12, 1864	Pork & Beans	Duff, Fresh Grub	Fresh Grub	Fresh Grub	Salt Horse, No Duff	Pork & Beans (cleaned mess kits)	Bully Beef, Dandyfunk
June 13-19, 1864	Pork & Beans	Duff	Pork & Beans	Bully Beef, Coffee	Sea Pie	Pork & Beans	Bully Beef, Coffee
June 20-26, 1864	Pork & Beans	Sea Pie	Pork & Beans	Bully Beef, Coffee	Duff	Pork & Beans	Bully Beef, Rice
June 27-July 3, 1864	Pork & Beans	Duff	Pork & Beans	Bully Beef, Coffee	Action. No food entry. (supply ship arrived)	Fresh Grub	Fresh Grub
July 4-10, 1864	No journal entry.	Duff	Pork & Beans	Bully Beef, Coffee	Duff	Pork & Beans	Bully Beef, Coffee
July 11-17, 1864	Pork & Beans	No food entry	Pork & Beans	Bully Beef (supply ship arrived)	Fresh Grub, 'potato sause' for breakfast.	Pork & Beans	Dandyfunk
July 18-24, 1864	Pork & Beans	No food entry	Pork & Beans	Bully Beef, Coffee, Ham	Sea Pie	Pork & Beans	Bully Beef, Coffee
July 25-31, 1864	Pork & Beans	No food entry	Pork & Beans	Bully Beef, Coffee	Duff	Pork & Beans	Bully Beef, Coffee
August 1-5, 1864	Pork & Beans	Duff	Pork & Beans	Bully Beef, Coffee	Battle of Mobile Bay. Journal ends.		

Clearly a great number of the men serving in the United States Navy in 1862 did not share the sentiments of Andrew Foote.

On August 31, 1862, the grog ration was issued for the last time in the United States Navy. Throughout the ships of the navy, many of them on station around the Southern coasts where they blockaded ports held by the Southern Confederacy, mournful celebrations were held in honor of the soon-to-be-stopped grog ration. Aboard USS *Portsmouth* a song, composed by one of her officers by the name of Caspar Schenk, was sung at the wardroom table. The song has been enshrined in the traditions of the United States Navy, sung to the melody of the old English drinking song, "Landlord, Fill the Flowing Bowl":

> Come, messmates, pass the bottle 'round
> Our time is short, remember,
> For our grog must stop, and our spirits stop,
> On the first day of September.
> Refrain:
> For tonight we'll merry, merry be,
> For tonight we'll merry, merry be,
> For tonight we'll merry, merry be,
> Tomorrow we'll be sober.
>
> Farewell old rye, 'tis a sad, sad word,
> But alas it must be spoken,
> The ruby cup must be given up,
> And the demijohn be broken.
>
> Jack's happy days will soon be gone,
> To return again, oh never!
> For they've raised his pay five cents a day,
> But stopped his grog forever.
>
> Yet memory oft' will backward turn,
> And dwell with fondness partial,
> On the days when gin was not a sin,
> Nor cocktails brought courts-martial.

(Boatswain's Mates pipe "All Hands Splice the Main Brace")

> All hands to splice the main brace, call,
> But splice it now in sorrow,
> For the spirit-room key will be laid away
> Forever, on to-morrow.[40]

The song actually overstates its case. Cocktails in the wardroom, consumed off-duty, were still permitted, and most certainly did not bring courts-martial for those officers imbibing. Thus officers could still consume alcohol in the wardroom while off-duty until 1914, when much stricter measures against alcohol were put in place in the United States Navy.

Improvements in Steam Engines

By the 1870s, steamers were being built with compound engines, in which the steam passed through several (usually three) cylinders in succession, then was returned to the boiler to be heated up again. This greatly increased the efficiency of steam engines, as well as making them smoother in operation, as the cylinders were offset in their crank cycle. The improvement in engine design and efficiency obviated the auxiliary sailing rigs of earlier steamers, and produced other changes. The triple-expansion engine became the normal form of reciprocating steam engine for decades to come, up to and including the "Liberty Ships" built in the United States during World War II.

HMS *Devastation* of 1873 had a triple-expansion engine, just one signal mast with no sails, an armored steel hull, and her 12-inch guns in two turrets before and abaft an armored superstructure. This design became the shape of things to come in large warships for the next sixty-five years.[41]

The triple-expansion engine also affected passenger ship design. The *City of Paris* (1888) and her sister *City of New York* were long (560 feet long) and lean, built of steel, with a long superstructure with an open mezzanine deck, twin screws, lifeboats in davits, and three funnels. The shape of ocean liners to come had been established.[42] With more efficient engines, passenger steamers became more economical to operate, and it is in this era that steamers swept the immigrant trade from sailing vessels. Of course, the more reliable schedules and the centrally prepared food, included in the ticket price, were important inducements.

During the second half of the nineteenth Century, most large warships carried their largest guns in turrets, and the men dined below in a "mess-room" that evolved into a larger, plainer version of the officers' wardroom. A photo of the messroom of the U.S. cruiser *Olympia* from 1899 shows men eating from a hanging table, one man eating while he sits on a sea chest. The mess table is along the fore-and-aft axis of the *Olympia*, not thwartship as was necessary when mess tables hung between guns mounted in broadside. Not long after, mess tables were no longer hung from the ceiling, but bolted to the floor.

Here is a contemporary messroom from another U. S. warship, the battleship *Maine* in 1896. The men of the Maine are sitting on folding camp

Figure 6.4. S.S. *City of Paris*. While shown with sails set, they were rarely used in practice. Painting by Antonio Jacobsen, 1889. Source: http://www.bonhams.com/auctions/20482/lot/114/. Courtesy of Wikimedia Commons. Public domain. http://commons.wikimedia.org/wiki/File:City_of_Paris,_by_Antonio_Nicolo_Gasparo_Jacobsen.jpg.

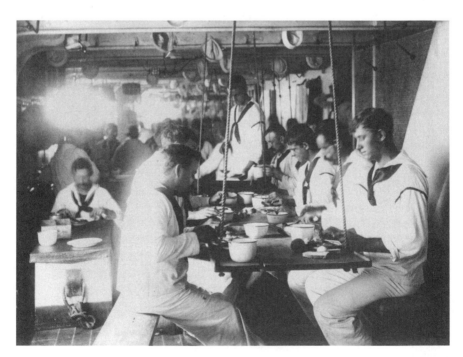

Figure 6.5. Crew's Mess on USS *Olympia*, 1899. Note that sailors are eating at a table suspended by ropes. Photographer: Frances Benjamin Johnston, 1864–1952. Reproduction Number: LC-USZ62-128415 in Collection: Johnston (Frances Benjamin) Collection. Courtesy of Library of Congress Digital Collections. http://www.loc.gov/pictures/item/2001698162/.

stools, and eating off a folding table. This is another solution to the void left by the elimination of densely-placed broadside guns, and the tables that hung between them. Two years later, the *Maine* blew up and sank in Havana harbor, precipitating the Spanish-American War.

Canning: A New Method to Preserve Food Ashore and at Sea

The early years of the nineteenth century also witnessed new developments in the preservation of food. The British blockade of French ports during the Napoleonic Wars resulted in critical shortages of food in the French Navy, and in France generally. Napoleon Bonaparte created a Society for the Encouragement of Industry, which issued one of its first prizes to Nicholas Appert, who developed a technique for storing food sealed in champagne bottles. He then put the bottles in baths of boiling water. Although Louis Pasteur's research was not to show how heat could sterilize food for another fifty years or so, Appert's process accomplished a kind of pasteurization. The French Navy was an early patron of these bottled foods, and in 1807 they took peas, beans, and vegetable soup bottled by Appert on a voyage to the Caribbean, with very satisfactory results.[43]

In 1813 Bryan Donkin and John Hall in England preserved food by similar methods, but using containers of tin-plated iron instead of champagne bottles. The tinned food received the approbation of the Royal Society, the Royal Family, and the Royal Navy. Tins of Donkin & Hall's preserved food accompanied Admiral Ross and Otto von Kotzebue to the Arctic, and in 1818 the British Navy purchased 23,779 cans of meat and vegetables. The canned/tinned food was made available to the public in 1830, with tomatoes, peas, and sardines available in this new long-lasting form. Sales to the public were initially slow. The cans were individually made by hand and consequently quite expensive: they required a hammer and chisel to open. After 1841 chlorine salts in the boiling water speeded up the sterilization process, and the price began to drop.[44] It was in 1847 that the British Navy officially adopted tinned meat as regular issue aboard ordinary ships.[45]

The canned/tinned food industry suffered a setback in 1845, when deaths in the Franklin Expedition were blamed on bad food.[46] Recent studies of corpses and cans from that ill-fated expedition have shown that the cans, which were not from Donkin's company, were made with excessive amounts of lead solder, and the bodies of expedition members were found to exhibit lead poisoning. It appears that lead poisoning from inferior cans not only damaged their health, but may have impaired their judgment as well, resulting in fatally flawed decisions and choices.[47]

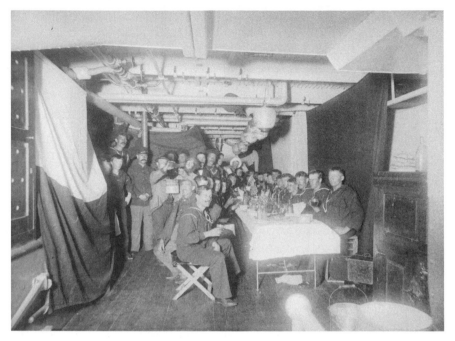

Figure 6.6. USS *Maine* sailors' mess, 1896. The men are using folding benches and table; another approach to messroom seating after the era of the broadside gun. Photographer: Edward H. Hart. Detroit Publishing Company. Reproduction Number: LC-DIG-det-4a14369 in Collection: Detroit Publishing Company. Courtesy of Library of Congress Digital Collections. http://www.loc.gov/pictures/item/det1994001068/PP/.

Another setback to canned food came in 1855, when 5,000 cans of food intended for British troops in Crimea where found to be spoiled, apparently from inadequate heating during the sterilization process.[48]

Bully Beef

By the end of the nineteenth century, tinned meat had generally replaced salt beef in barrels in the world's navies; and it was replacing, or at least supplementing, salt beef in casks in merchant vessels, especially those operating under steam. British merchant sailors named this new product after famous female murder victims. Thus they called tinned beef "Fanny Adams" after a girl murdered in Hampshire in 1867. Seven pound tins of mutton were called "Harriet Lane" after a young woman murdered in Whitechapel, London, in 1874.[49] In the British Navy and Army, the tinned beef, usually boiled and sometimes roasted as well, was usually known as "Bully Beef" a term probably based on French *boeuf boilli*. Under this name, tinned beef has continued as a staple of British military rations up to the present. A similar product, called corned beef in American usage, remains a staple of American military and civilian cuisine. Corned beef hash, comprised of minced potatoes, tinned beef, some minced onions and sometimes other vegetables fried on a grill, remains an American favorite breakfast to this day, a standard menu item in short-order "greasy spoon" restaurants, soda fountain counters, and diners across North America. Corned beef hash is often served with a fried egg.

Canned Salmon and the Alaska Packers

Canning became a major industry on the West Coast of North America in the second half of the nineteenth Century. The salmon canning industry on the West Coast of North America began on the heels of the California Gold Rush. In 1852, William Hume, Perry Woodson, and James Booker, began a small salmon fishing and canning business near Sacramento. They were joined by Andrew S. Hapgood, a lobster canner from Maine, in 1864, and the business got going in earnest with a production of 2,000 cases of forty-eight cans per case the first year. Business was still slow, as San Francisco merchants were reluctant to sell the product, and the salmon supply in the Sacramento River was limited. In 1866 the firm, now incorporated as Hapgood, Hume & Co. began fishing and canning in Astoria, Oregon, at the mouth of the Columbia River. Here the salmon catch was enormous, and production increased dramatically. The salmon fishing and canning industry spread to Washington and British Columbia in the 1870s and 1880s. The cans were made by hand, labor which was mostly done in the winter. The workers in gutting, boning, and preparation of the fish, as well as making and sealing the cans, were a combination of local men and women, mostly Haida and other Native Americans; and a growing population of Chinese workers. Sadly, the Chinese workers endured a great deal of race prejudice as they were willing to work for lower pay than Caucasian workers.[50]

In 1904 a mechanical can-making machine, the invention of E.A. "Iron Chink" Smith, began service in 1904. This machine, known locally (and regrettably) as "The Iron Chink," or almost as regrettably as "The Iron Chinaman," spread throughout the Pacific Northwest canneries. It did not put the Chinese workers out of business however, as Chinese and some Japanese workers continued to process the fish and pack them into the cans.[51]

The Alaska Packers Association was formed in San Francisco, and it included a variety of independent canneries whose salmon was marketed under the individual canneries' names. The Alaska Packers were famous for their fleet of sailing vessels, known collectively as the "Star Fleet." Sailing ships were in-expensive, so these were purchased and operated by the Alaska Packers, sailing out of San Francisco at the beginning of the season, and carrying Chinese work-ers to perform the canning operations. After 1900, most of the wooden-hulled ships were replaced by British-built steel sailing vessels, for example the *Star of Russia, Star of Italy, Star of Bengal,* and *Star of France.* The company liked the "Star of" theme, so subsequent purchases were renamed *Star of Alaska, Star of Finland,* and so on. In the case of the *Star of Alaska* (the *Balclutha,* her origi-nal and present name), a shelter deck was constructed to provide additional habitation for the cannery workers, and this area (and the cannery worker accommodation in other vessels), was known as "Chinatown" to the sailing crew. The Chinese workers slept in bunk beds, and had their own cooks.[52]

The Alaska Packers' Star Fleet extended the working life of many old sail-ing vessels, two of which survive today. The company continued to employ sailing vessels until 1927, at which point they were replaced by powered ves-sels. The *Star of Alaska* was exhibited for some time as *Pacific Queen*: in 1959 she was purchased and restored by the San Francisco Maritime Association, and was opened to the public as a floating museum under her original name *Balclutha.* She is the centerpiece of the San Francisco Maritime Museum's collection of historic vessels, on Hyde Street Pier near Fisherman's Wharf. The *Star of India* (ex-*Euterpe*) is preserved as the centerpiece of the San Diego Maritime Museum. This vessel, built of wrought iron in 1863, still occasion-ally sails. Other Alaska Packers survived the transition to motor propulsion in various ways: the *Star of Scotland* (ex-*Kenilworth*) served as a floating fishing pier and live bait store anchored off Santa Monica until 1938, as a floating casino between 1938 and 1941; then she was re-rigged as a six-masted schoo-ner and put into cargo-carrying service. She was sunk by German submarine *U-159* in the South Atlantic in November 1942.[53] These vessels owed their extended lives to the canning industry, and to the technological advances that made canned salmon a more attractive food ashore than salt cod.

A Momentous Century

The nineteenth century saw momentous changes in seafaring and in seago-ing food. Steam power was experimental early in the century, but by the end of the century the majority of the world's passengers, as well as perishable or precious cargoes, were transported by steam-powered vessels. These vessels were aided by progress in the designs of their engines, and by the construc-tion of canals in critical locations. By the end of the century, sail-driven vessels were operating in trades in which speed and reliability were not vital, and in the carriage of bulky, low-value cargoes. During this century,

Figure 6.7. Dining Saloon on Steam Schooner *Wapama*. Note the swiveling chairs, and the raised edges on the table of this early twentieth-century coastal steamer. Reproduction Number: HAER CAL,21-SAUS,1—17 in Collection: Historic American Buildings Survey/Historic American Engineering Record/Historic American Landscapes Survey. Courtesy of Library of Congress Digital Collections. http://www.loc.gov/pictures/item/ca1521.photos.013125p/.

the preservation of food for long periods of time was revolutionized by the development of canning. Wooden casks of brine, like the sailing vessels that had relied on them, were largely replaced by lighter, disposable metal containers. The relative freshness of canned foods improved the flavor and the nutritional value of food at sea.

This photograph shows the dining saloon of the *Wapama*, a small coastal steamer that carried cargo and passengers on the West Coast of North America in the early twentieth century. Note the table, swiveling chairs, and condiment rack. The table has raised edges or "fiddles" to keep plates from sliding off.

A Final Word

An editorial from an Australian newspaper commented on immigrants who had complained about the food and other conditions aboard the steamers they had taken. The unidentified poet defends "steamship food" and other conditions.

SOME COMPLAINTS INVESTIGATED

Some weeks ago in Europe
The task at which he worked
Nourished the genii of discontent
That in his bosom lurked:
The long, long, day. His small, small wage
Were more than he could stand;
"So down with his pick, and up with swag,
Here's for a better land!"
The steamship fare was small enough,
For that his thanks were due
To those prepared to welcome him
To climes and interests new;
But discontent on idleness
Thrives better than on toil;
That genii in his and other breasts
Was still intent on spoil,
So he, and others like himself.
Grumbled and sneered and swore
At steamship food that perhaps surpassed
All they had known before.
Beds, cabins, everything, in fact.
He slammed with equal vim,
Yet perhaps he did it just because
They were too good for him.[54]

SEVEN

Ocean Liners and Refrigeration

The turn of the twentieth century witnessed the evolution of one of the icons of the age, the ocean liner. The ocean liner, as well as her siblings of more modest size, carried passengers in greater speed and comfort than the steamships of the preceding century. These improved ships made faster, safer, and more comfortable travel accessible to immigrants. While passenger steamers evolved into ocean liners, a more subtle, but very important evolution was taking place in the development of refrigeration. Perishable cargos could be carried around the globe, changing the relationship of different regions and making the world's food supply a less local and more global concern. The preservation of the food consumed at sea was also transformed by refrigeration. Food, whether a commercial cargo or the sustenance of crew or passengers, was altered by the widespread use of mechanical, and later by electric, refrigeration.

The Ocean Liner Evolves

The *City of New York* and *City of Paris* were built for Britain's Inman Line of transatlantic steamers, and represented the transition from nineteenth-century steamship to ocean liner. They were powered by twin triple-expansion engines, driving twin screws. This made them more resilient to engine or driveshaft malfunctions: their sails were less essential as auxiliary propulsion, and were reduced. The two sisters were built of steel, near Glasgow in Scotland: the *City of New York* was christened by Winston Churchill's American-born

Figure 7.1. Sign advertising travel on the Cunard line, c. 1875. Reproduction Number: LC-DIG-pga-01235 in Collection: Popular Graphic Arts. Courtesy of Library of Congress Digital Collections. http://www.loc.gov/pictures/item/2003680949/.

mother. They were built for the Inman Line, a competitor of Cunard Company and the White Star Line for the lucrative and popular transatlantic passenger trade. Through a series of mergers and takeovers these two British steamers spent much of their careers under American ownership. Each 560 feet long, with a central superstructure sporting a long mezzanine deck surmounted by triple funnels, these two outstanding vessels looked much like scaled-down versions of the ocean liners of the next generation.[1]

As the steamship evolved into the ocean liner, the food service evolved along with size and design of the vessels themselves. When Dickens crossed the Atlantic aboard *Britannia* in 1842, the food for the 115 passengers simply was relatively simple and straightforward. There was a difference in sleeping accommodations, with less expensive tickets for those who elected to sleep on the cabin furniture behind a curtain, more expensive for those such as the Dickens family who elected to sleep in a stateroom. The food service, as Dickens describes, was on the order of a boarding-house, with steaming tureens and trays brought to the saloon's two long communal tables. As steamships were built larger, they took over the immigrant trade from sailing vessels, and offered different classes of service. Passengers in staterooms were divided into first and second classes, with separate dining rooms, and assigned to different sections of the mezzanine decks and other ship's facilities. The first-class cabins were located close to the center of the ship, where the effects of rolling and pitching were felt less acutely. The service for passengers with inexpensive tickets, in what was called "steerage" in the nineteenth century and what was usually called "third class" aboard liners of the early twentieth century, was a great improvement over the conditions experienced in sailing immigrant ships of the early to mid-nineteenth century. Third-class accommodations were plain but sturdy and clean: these passengers shared halls or cabins with bunks; without the wood paneling of the first- and second-class cabins but (when they had cabins) usually including a washbasin and other essentials. Third-class passengers generally dined in clean plain white-painted dining rooms reserved for their class, on long tables bolted to the deck. The walls usually held a few framed copies of the shipping lines' publicity. The food was plain but wholesome and abundant, served boarding-house style. Immigrants of this era may have eaten better during their passages than they did ashore. It should be born in mind as well, that aboard liners traveling at twenty knots or more, passage across the Atlantic was much shorter than in sailing vessels or even early steamers. Whatever crowding and lack of privacy the third-class passengers experienced was briefer than it was for their predecessors, a matter of days rather than weeks.

The owners of ocean liners did well to look after their third-class passengers. The Admiralty mail contracts and the third-class passenger fares were the most profitable parts of the vessels' operations. Some liners, such as *La Provence* in 1906, put their steerage passengers in big halls where bunk beds were adjacent to tables and benches bolted to the deck.[2] On the *Olympic* and the *Titanic*, the third-class passengers were accommodated in cabins, plainer versions of the cabins in second class. Aboard *Vaterland*, third-class passengers had their own kitchen, dining room, and stewards. The German liners carried the bulk of continental émigrés from Europe, and Albert Ballin of HAPAG-Lloyd even established a fifteen-acre Emigrant Village on the Elbe River, for passengers waiting to cross.[3]

Steamship food service in the nineteenth century had been like the food service in contemporary hotels. There were simultaneous seatings at large communal tables. Hotel guests or passengers might be offered some choice between selections which were already prepared. Passengers in early steamships were accustomed to these conditions ashore, when they dined at hotels.

Persons of means in the eighteenth century could dine on whatever they liked prepared by their own personal cook. Persons of great wealth could employ a trained cook capable of preparing fashionable and elaborate dishes, with the help of additional kitchen staff. After the Bourbon Restoration in

France, a growing bourgeoisie wanted to enjoy, occasionally at least, the high living that had previously been enjoyed by French aristocracy. Thus was born the French restaurant, in which all the ingredients for dishes on a printed menu were on hand, ready to be cooked to order at any time of day. In 1830, two Swiss immigrants to New York opened a Restaurant Française next to their pastry and coffee shop on William Street. Patrons sat at their own cloth-covered tables, dining on cooked-to-order food at a small table for just their own party. Giovanni and Pietro Del-Monico's Restaurant Française was a success, inspiring imitators and introducing a new style of dining to the affluent American public. The Del-Monico's pastry shop and restaurant expanded to become one of New York's most fashionable restaurant-hotels by the middle of the century.[4]

Deluxe a la carte dining, with food cooked to order and served immediately, came to transatlantic service in 1904. It was introduced not by the British, but by the Germans; specifically, by the Hamburg-Amerika Line (HAPAG, for Hamburg-Amerikanische Packetfahrt Actiens-Gessellschaft), guided by the organizational genius Albert Ballin. If "God is in the details," Ballin was the high priest of passenger service at sea. When he crossed the Atlantic on one of his own ships, as he routinely did, a barrage of memos was sure to follow, on a myriad of ways that service could be improved. For example, he suggested that a sandwich of Westphalian ham should accompany the traditional 11:00 a.m. cup of bouillon served on deck; that breakfast toast should be served in warm napkins; and that butter dishes needed to be larger.[5]

Albert Ballin spoke English, and was keenly observant of his English competitors. Not content to keep pace with British transatlantic service, Ballin was determined to outpace his Anglo-Saxon rivals. He was not alone in this: his German competitors of the North German Lloyd strove to surpass their British competitors as well as their fellow Germans. During the first decade of the twentieth century, the Blue Ribband (the record transatlantic time, which was now institutionalized and cited in advertisements for passenger lines) was passed back and forth between these two German lines.[6]

Beginning with the Paris Ritz Hotel in 1898, Ritz Hotels sprung up in Paris, London, and then in the great cities of Europe and North America. Representing the pinnacle of stylish luxury, the Ritz chain set a new standard for the wealthy of that era. The Ritz Hotels were set apart by, among a myriad of exquisite details, the close collaboration of Cesar Ritz, the hotelier, and his architect, Charles Mewes. Spaces public and private were sculpted by Mewes into new standards of elegance and comfort. Ritz and Mewes made their mark in London in 1900, when they were engaged to rebuild the interior of the Carlton Hotel. A centerpiece of their redesign was the Ritz-Carlton Grill, at which Albert Ballin dined.

For HAPAG's new liner *Amerika*, Albert Ballin turned to Ritz's architect Charles Mewes. *Amerika* was intended, like her competitors of the White Star Line, to set a new standard of elegance and luxury, and the French architect was given a free hand to design the new liner's interior spaces. Like other great German liners of that era, the *Amerika* was built in the British Isles, by the same Harland & Wolff yard in Belfast that later built the ill-fated *Titanic*.

Mewes, though born in Strasbourg, spoke only French. For his British work he worked in partnership with fellow architect Arthur Davis in London; for German work, with a partner in Cologne.[7]

The most striking innovation aboard *Amerika* was the creation of a *crème de la crème* restaurant, where first-class passengers could dine at any time of the day or night, being served food cooked to order from the menu. Passengers could sit at any one of twenty-five separate tables, between expansive windows on three sides. Serving tables or "islands" camouflaged the stanchions between decks, and the room was adorned with Ormolu sconces and deep blue carpet. The walls were sheathed in cream-and-gold wallpaper and polished mahogany, and the tables had individual lamps, with the Carlton crest used throughout as an ornamental motif.

Amerika's restaurant was an enormous success on her maiden voyage; in fact Ballin ordered that the restaurant kitchen be expanded immediately. Thenceforward, HAPAG offered a $25 discount from the first-class fare to passengers who elected to do all their dining in the restaurant.

With the addition of a cooked-to-order Hotel Ritz-Carlton restaurant, the galley organization for big transatlantic liners established:

- a galley in which the food for third-class passengers was prepared.
- a galley in which the food was prepared for first- and second-class passengers. Though these passengers were seated in different dining rooms and the food selections were not the same, their food was usually prepared in the same galley.
- a kitchen in which food was cooked to order for first-class patrons of the restaurant.

This cooking and dining arrangement was followed in British and French as well as German super-liners of the early twentieth century. Boardinghouse-style fare was prepared in the third-class kitchen, served in the third-class dining area(s). The first- and second-class fare was prepared in one galley, which could facilitate substitutions, if needed, in menu items for these two classes. First-class passengers who chose to dine in the a la carte restaurant had their selections cooked to order in a special kitchen dedicated to the restaurant.[8]

Cunard Company faced stiffer competition at the turn of the century than it had when Charles Dickens took passage aboard *Britannia*. After 1903, the fastest transatlantic steamers were four ships of North German Lloyd. American railroad mogul J. P. Morgan had bought up a number of small shipping lines, 25 percent of the Holland-America Line, and the White Star Line, making the White Star Line a formidable competitor. Cunard's management wanted to regain supremacy over the transatlantic passenger business, and they determined to do this with a pair of steamers of original design. The sisters *Mauretania* and *Lusitania*, built near Glasgow, were bigger and faster than any passenger vessels built before.[9]

The key to the speed of the "Mary" and the "Lucy," as their crews called them, was a new type of engine. The steam turbine engine was the brainchild of the tireless, brilliant English engineer Charles Algernon Parsons. In essence, the steam turbine is a series of wheels rimmed with slanted vanes. Jets of steam released in a concentrated stream set successive wheels into rapid rotation, and the steam turbine offers greater speed and more power for its size than reciprocating steam engines. Parsons proved the value of his engine by making a surprise appearance with his speedy (34.5 knots, equivalent to 40 mph—the fastest vessel of the nineteenth century) launch *Turbinia* at the Jubilee Naval Review in Portsmouth in 1897, easily outrunning any vessel sent to catch him.[10] The navy had to concede the value of Parsons's engine, and in 1906, launched a new turbine-powered battleship, HMS *Dreadnought*, whose efficient, compact turbine power plant allowed her more firepower and armor than any previous warship.[11]

The *Mauretania* and *Lusitania* were originally planned for reciprocating engines, but were redesigned to accommodate the new higher-performance turbine engines. In the process, they also gained an additional funnel; they were built with four funnels rather than the originally planned three.[12]

Mauretania and *Lusitania* set a new standard in transatlantic liners. When they entered service in 1907, the *Mauretania* and *Lusitania* were the largest moving structures ever built. The *Mauretania* was 790 feet long, and 31,938 gross register tons. Her four turbines developed 68,000 shaft horsepower (later increased), directly driving four propellers. She carried 2,165 passengers: 563 in first class, 464 in second class, and 1,138 in third class. The new Cunard liners incorporated features that were to set a standard for liners of that era, such as skylights, and an electric elevator for first-class passengers. A third and larger sister, *Aquitania*, entered service in May 1914, just in time for service in World War I as a troopship and hospital ship. She served as a troopship again in World War II. When she was finally scrapped in 1950, the *Aquitania* had enjoyed the longest service life of any twentieth-century liner: her record for service longevity stood until the *QE2* broke her record in 2004.

The White Star Line responded with its own series of super-liners. The first launched was the *Olympic* in 1911, followed in 1912 by her sister *Titanic*. *Titanic*'s tragic sinking on her maiden voyage after a collision with an iceberg was the greatest peacetime maritime disaster in history, and has been written about extensively. The third sister, *Britannic*, incorporated a number of safety features inspired by the loss of her ill-fated sister. These features saved lives when the *Britannic* sank in 1915. The *Britannic*, slightly larger than her sisters, never saw service in her intended role as a transatlantic liner; she was immediately pressed into war service as a hospital ship, and she sank after striking a German naval mine near the Greek Island of Kea. The White Star Liners boasted three first-class elevators to the Cunard's one. In passenger service they boasted sixty chefs and assistants plus thirty-six support staff.[13] Like the *Great Eastern* with its screw, paddle wheels, and sails, the White Star Line trio combined different modes of propulsion. The central screw was driven by

Figure 7.2. Triple-screw (propeller) steamer *Olympic* of the White Star Line. Detroit Publishing Co., c. 1910–1915. Reproduction Number: LC-DIG-ppmsca-19060 in Collection: Miscellaneous Items in High Demand. Courtesy of Library of Congress Digital Collections. http://www.loc.gov/pictures/item/2008680520/.

a turbine, while the two outboard screws were driven by reciprocating steam engines. Though these three liners were slightly slower than the Cunard's *Mauretania* and *Lusitania*, they were larger and even more luxurious.

Dinner Bell, Gong, or Bugle

On Cunard liners of the early twentieth century, dinner was announced by a bell, as it was when Charles Dickens was a passenger aboard *Britannia*. The White Star Line introduced a different method of announcing meals: a smartly uniformed bugler called passengers to their meals, alleged playing the tune "The Roast Beef of Olde England."[14] There is something puzzling about the oft-repeated tale of this tune announcing meals on White Star liners. The tune, as played in the days of Nelson on fiddles and fifes of the Royal Navy, would be quite difficult, perhaps impossible, to play on a keyless bugle. Photographs of White Star buglers clearly show the traditional instrument without keys, so either the tune was somehow simplified to suit the instrument, or some other tune or bugle call was substituted. Later on a gong replaced the bugle on White Star liners.[15]

More Competition from Germany

May 1913 Hamburg-Amerika Line built three new super-liners for transatlantic service. The first of these was *Imperator*, then her two sisters *Vaterland* in 1913, and *Bismarck* in 1914. Like their Cunard brethren, they were powered by turbine engines driving quadruple screws. They had Mewes-designed interior spaces, and a Ritz-Carlton restaurant. The *Vaterland* had an ingenious internal arrangement; the uptakes for her engine exhaust were divided, passing to either side of dining spaces which could be designed without allowing for the passage of exhaust uptakes along the centerline. After World War I these liners became prizes of war. The *Imperator*, after serving the United States as a troopship, became Cunard's *Berengaria*. Thus she complied with Cunard's tradition of –ia endings, though named for a queen, Richard the First's consort, rather than for a country or kingdom as other Cunard liners were. The *Bismarck* was turned over to the White Star Line, who gave her an –ic ending to fit their naming tradition, and *Bismarck* became *Majestic*.[16] In 1917, the *Vaterland* was taken over by the United States, becoming the U.S. troopship and postwar liner *Leviathan* (nicknamed *Levi Nathan* by her crews).[17]

A notable event aboard the *Imperator* was a dinner to celebrate the twentieth wedding anniversary of the legendary stage magician and escape artist Harry Houdini on June 22, 1914. The front cover of the menu features an imposing image of the liner.

Figure 7.3. S.S. *Imperator* of the Hamburg-Amerika Line. Cover of twentieth anniversary dinner invitation of Mr. and Mrs. Harry Houdini. June 22, 1914. On June 18 of that year, the Houdinis sailed from Europe to New York. Houdini performed on board the ship on June 21—a performance attended by fellow passenger, former President Theodore Roosevelt. Reproduction Number: LC-USZC2-4893, LC-USZC2-4892, LC-USZC2-4894 in Collection: Miscellaneous Items in High Demand. Courtesy of Library of Congress Digital Collections. http://www.loc.gov/pictures/item/96519251/.

Cooks aboard the Hamburg-Amerika Line prepared the following meal in honor of Mr. and Mrs. Houdini:

Menu
Beluga Caviar in Ice
Potage Diplomate
Fillet of Sole a la Meuniere
Chicken en Casserole
Lettuce Salad
Asparagus, Sauce Hollandaise
Westphalian Ham
Peaches a la Melba
Dessert[18]

British registry liners were built with deck reinforcements so that they could carry guns in wartime, being classified by the Royal Navy as auxiliary cruisers. Several of them were painted in "dazzle" camouflage, wild patterns breaking up the ship's lines so as to confuse an enemy submarine captain looking through a periscope. The *Lusitania*, carrying ticketed passengers though armed as an auxiliary cruiser, was sunk by a German submarine in 1915, the same year that *Britannic* was lost. *Olympic* and *Mauretania* both served as troopships. After the war, most big liners converted from coal-firing to oil-firing. This eliminated many engine-room jobs, though these were the most back-breaking, dirty jobs at sea.

There was a shift in the demographic of post–World War I passengers, particularly in third class. Company literature fastidiously avoided the term "steerage," favoring instead "tourist third class." Tourists, teachers, students, and young Americans wanting to explore Europe inexpensively shared accommodations with successful immigrants revisiting their home countries. The same sort of passengers who would fly coach in the 1960s were opting for the less expensive tourist third-class berths in the transatlantic liners of the 1920s. By the 1920s transatlantic liners offered simple cabins for this class, more or less a no-frills version of second-class accommodations.[19] Exclusive luxury for the wealthiest passengers was played down; for example, *Imperator/Berengeria*'s Ritz-Carlton restaurant was converted to a ballroom.[20]

In the years between the two world wars, travel by transatlantic liner took on a glamorous quality as film stars and other celebrities traveled in their favorite liners. Marlene Dietrich favored the *Normandie*, while Cary Grant, and the Duke and Duchess of Windsor, the former Edward VIII and Wallis Simpson, favored the *Queen Mary*.[21]

"Why Don't You Make a Ship Look Like a Ship?"

It may surprise modern readers that this question was asked of the builders of the great ocean liners of this era. To modern eyes, the graceful lines of early twentieth-century liners are the very essence of what a "ship" ought to look like. However, at that time steamships with masts and sails were still in service, and so the giant liners looked like "floating hotels" to their human contemporaries. Arthur Davis, the British architect who was Mewes's partner, defined and discussed the phenomenon in 1922.

> When I was first engaged, some fifteen years ago, to start this work. . . . I said to the directors of the company, "Why don't you make a ship look like a ship?"

. . . But the answer I was given was that the people who use these ships are not pirates, they do not dance hornpipes; they are mostly seasick American ladies, and the one thing they want to forget when they are on the vessel is that they are on a ship at all. . . . The people who travel on these large ships are the people who live in hotels; they are not ships for sailors or yachtsmen or people who enjoy the sea. . . . I suggest to you that the transatlantic liner is not merely a ship, she is a floating town with 3,000 passengers of all kinds, with all sorts of tastes, and those who enjoy being there are distinctly in the minority. If we could get ships to look inside like ships, and get people to enjoy the sea, it would be a very good thing; but all we can do, as things are, is to give them gigantic floating hotels.[22]

P&O Line

The P&O Line grew during the late nineteenth century, expanding service in the Mediterranean to Alexandria in Egypt. The *Hindostan*, launched in 1842, offered service between Suez and Calcutta, and was soon joined by the *Bentinck* and the *Precursor*.[23] Novelist William Thackeray, writing about his Mediterranean travels aboard the P&O steamship *Lady Mary Wood* in 1844, paraphrased a popular saying of the day when he wrote, "The sun never sets on a P&O ship."[24] He also summed up his experience as "So easy, so charming and I think profitable—it leaves such a store of pleasant recollections for after days."[25]

Other famous P&O passengers included Florence Nightingale, who shipped in the steamer *Vectis* from Marseilles to Constantinople (modern Istanbul) during the Crimean War.[26] Following the Sepoy Mutiny of 1857, 6,000 troops traveled to India in P&O ships; like all India passengers before the completion of the Suez Canal, they disembarked at Alexandria, traveled over the desert, and boarded a new vessel in Suez.

The P&O Line was awarded a mail contract to Australia in 1852, with the steamship *Chusan* (a name which was repeated in P&O service) the first to bring British mail to Melbourne and Sydney. Some P&O cargoes were less felicitous, for between 1847 and 1858, P&O shipped 642,000 cases of Bengal and Malwa opium to the Far East.[27]

Vessels bound for the Indian Ocean were fitted out differently than those in Atlantic service. P&O ships had double doors on their staterooms, a solid outer door and an inner door with adjustable louvers. By leaving the outer door open and the inner door closed, passengers could increase the ventilation in their cabins without loss of privacy. Awnings of canvas were rigged over the deck, cooling the decks and also the interior spaces. Dining rooms were fitted with *punkahs*, the traditional ceiling fan of India, consisting of a tasseled cloth hanging from a suspended rod. By moving the rod back and forth by pulling on a cord, stewards could fan their passengers while they dined.[28] The principal dust jacket illustration for this book features a dining scene aboard the P&O liner *Himalaya* in 1891, while encountering heavy weather in the Bay of Biscay. Fiddles are fitted to the tables, and the *punkah*, not yet needed at this stage of the voyage, is nonetheless visible over the diners' heads.

The heat was so intense in the Red Sea that passengers often slept on deck, with bedding they brought themselves, during the hottest parts of their journey. It was customary for ladies to sleep on one side of the deck, gentlemen on the other.[29] By 1900, trip by steamer offered times of just over three weeks from England to Bombay, and forty-four days to Sydney.[30]

The P&O Line, as well as the British India Line and other lines serving this route, recruited crew members from India, favoring different ethnic groups for different elements of the crew. Indian workers were known as "Lascars" in the maritime world. Deck crews were generally Hindus. Engine room workers were usually Muslims, from regions which comprise modern Pakistan. The engine crew was supervised by a "Serang," who was usually a long-time fixture in the ship and often made steamers a family business. As an example, Sarfaraz Khan, chief engine room serang in the P&O liner *Arcadia*, served for thirty-six years, and had seventeen relatives working in P&O vessels.[31]

Christians from Goa were the preferred Lascars for work in the galleys and for stewards. Their Christian religion made them comfortable handling all forms of meat and fish, which could have been an obstacle for Muslims and Hindus. Among these Goa Christians was usually the chief steward or purser. He was responsible for the ordering of food and other comestibles, an enormous responsibility.[32]

British India Steam Navigation Company and the Orient Line

In the early twentieth century, the P&O Line took over the British India Steam Navigation Company, which was then the largest British shipping line. British India, like P&O, was reorganized from an earlier company, and incorporated under this name in 1856. Like P&O, British India had been quick to take advantage of the completion of the Suez Canal to carry passengers and cargo to India and Australia without the overland trip from the Mediterranean to the Red Sea. P &O also gained controlling interest in the Orient Line, which gave it the Australia mail contracts, and a number of East African routes as well.[33]

The Origins of "Posh": An Apocryphal Legend

In the late nineteenth and early twentieth century, it has been said that passengers who wanted sun through their portholes on the way to and from Britain and India or Australia, would book staterooms on the port side on the outbound journey, and then on the starboard side on the homeward-bound leg. Some versions of the legend even state that passengers' tickets were stamped "P.O.S.H." to indicate which side of the vessel the passenger was to occupy on the outward and homeward voyages. The popular imagination has bestowed on the adjective posh meaning high-born, wealthy, or aristocratic, a derivation of "Port-Out-Starboard-Home." Linguistic historians do not agree, but the legend holds that this adjective derives from steamer travel through the Mediterranean Sea to the Indian Ocean, so that these "posh" travelers would travel in greater comfort. In fact, travelers to India and Australia did not book their return passages together with their outbound ones, so there was no "return ticket" to be stamped with the legendary (though apocryphal) letters "P.O.S.H." The expression "posha dandy," in circulation in London circa 1895, may be the origin of the term "posh," which became current in British English during World War I.

The Captain's Table, and Other Dining Locations

Once outward bound, passengers (in first class at least) would request a reservation in the dining room. On those liners which had a second floor or balcony in the dining room (e.g., *Berengaria*, *France*, *Paris* and *Mauretania*), seating there was desired by celebrities, as it was a somewhat more private area, and diners could enter and depart the balcony unobtrusively. Another popular choice was a seat in one of the "outside" tables. Chief stewards usually placed their less experienced subordinates toward the middle of the dining rooms where they could keep an eye on them. Experienced transatlantic passengers knew that the more experienced stewards waited on the "outside" tables. Mothers traveling with marriageable daughters were known to seek seating with well-off eligible bachelors. Passengers eager to rub elbows with celebrities would also try to arrange seating near famous passengers.

Only inexperienced passengers would request a seat at the captain's table, the most prestigious table of all. Seats there were by invitation only; a seat at the captain's table could be declined but never requested. Pursers and even company officials got involved in the selection of seats there: it was highly desirable to avoid seating passengers together who had clashed ashore. The most famous gaffe of this nature occurred aboard the *Majestic* when a divorced politician found himself seated at the captain's table next to his ex-wife's co-respondent. Henri Villar, purser of various French liners between the two world wars, was famous for his encyclopedic memory for names and scandals, and his deftness in choosing suitable dining companions.[34]

Typical Food Service on a Transatlantic Liner circa 1912

The exact conditions of food service on the great transatlantic liners varied somewhat from ship to ship, line to line, and year to year. We will take the White Star liners *Olympic* and *Titanic* as our point of departure. The *Titanic* of course needs no introduction. Several motion pictures, countless books, numerous museum and other exhibitions, and public fascination with the maiden voyage of that doomed ship has made her probably the most written about liner of all time. Her nearly identical sister *Olympic* had a long and varied career, and the food service of these two liners was similar in most regards to their competitors.

Figure 7.4. "He Meant Well" by Samuel D. Ehrhart, 1862–1937. Published by J. Ottmann Lith. Co., 1904. Here the captain of an ocean liner offers a dinner toast to the health of "captain's table" passengers who are more than a little queasy from the motion of the ship. Reproduction Number: LC-DIG-ppmsca-25848 in Collection: Miscellaneous Items in High Demand. Courtesy of Library of Congress Digital Collections. http://www.loc.gov/pictures/item/2011645532/.

Third-Class Fare

Our tour of food service aboard a transatlantic liner will begin with the 1,000 or so passengers whose business was the most profitable for the owners: third class. This class of ticket was no longer called "steerage" in 1912, and was not to be named "tourist class" until after World War I. There were still ships in service in 1912 in which third-class passengers were lodged in big dormitory-like halls with racks of bunk beds, with eating tables and benches bolted to the deck in the same compartment. On the big White Star liners, third-class passengers enjoyed better accommodations. They slept in plain cabins built to accommodate as few as two or as many as ten passengers. Single men were lodged forward, families, couples, and single women aft. They had access to fresh air on the foredeck and poop deck, and dined in multiple seatings in the third-class dining saloon, a plain clean white-painted hall served by stewards. Passengers received simple "table tickets" that assigned them to a specific seating though not to a specific seat; these tickets were printed in English, German, Swedish, and Finnish.[35]

In third class, breakfast might consist of an offering of oatmeal porridge and milk, "Swedish Bread" (probably knaekebrod, that is crisp rye or wheat flatbread) with butter and marmalade, and a choice of tea or coffee.[36] Breakfast often included, in addition, a hearty ingredient such as smoked herring and potatoes, Irish stew, or fried tripe and onions; a different offering on different days.[37]

Dinner, the main meal of the day, typically began with a soup: from day to day, it might be pea, vegetable, rice, or bouillon. The main course could be (again depending on the day) corned beef and cabbage; roast pork with sage and onions; steak and kidney pie, or fricassee rabbit and bacon. On Fridays there was usually a choice of a fish dish with egg salad, or cold cuts of meat with pickles. These would be accompanied by a vegetable (lima beans, green peas, carrots, green beans, or cabbage) and boiled potatoes, as well as a dessert of plum pudding, rice pudding, semolina pudding, or stewed fruit. No beverage is specified, so water may be assumed. Except for the choice of either meat or fish on Friday, only one choice of entrée was available on any given day.[38]

The next meal was tea, which included a daily main course of curried mutton and rice, sausage and mashed potatoes (bangers and mash, to British and Irish passengers), cod fish cakes (on Friday), rabbit pie, or a "Ragout of Beef, Potatoes, and Pickles."[39] This was accompanied by either fresh bread and butter or "Swedish Bread" (or both on some days).[40] This was sometimes accompanied by a jam of rhubarb, rhubarb and ginger, or plum and apple.

Dessert could be either apples, oranges, rice with apricots, prunes, or apples; or a plum, semolina, or "Cerealine" pudding.[41] Currant buns were sometimes offered. With this meal, tea was of course the beverage. A late supper was offered every evening of Cabin biscuits and cheese, with gruel and/or coffee. Fresh fish was offered in place of cod cakes when available.[42]

An interesting note on White Star third-class fare, is the following note: "Kosher Meat Supplied and Cooked for Jewish Passengers as required."[43] It appears that on the White Star Line circa 1912 at least, there was a Kosher option. While this was on an advertisement to induce prospective passengers to travel with the White Star Line, there is corroborating evidence that actual food service closely matched this plan. Third-Class Menus for the Titanic on April 12 and April 14, 1912 closely match the White Star Line's "Specimen Bill of Fare."[44]

Second-Class Fare

The *Olympic* and *Titanic* were designed to carry up to 614 second-class passengers. This class of service was equated with the middle class—professional people, schoolmasters, tradesmen. The second-class dining room on the White Star super-liners was elegant, spanning the full beam of the ship, so that sunlight could enter through portholes. Rectangular tables accommodated eight diners apiece.[45] The dining room featured oak paneling, an elegant patterned ceiling overhead, cloth tablecloths and table linen, and swiveling wooden chairs securely bolted to the deck. The china was emblazoned with the White Star Line name and company flag, flower vases adorned the tables. It has been observed that second-class dining on the *Olympic* and her sisters may have been comparable to first-class dining on smaller vessels. On the big White Star liners as on others, a shared galley for first- and second-class food preparation must have been handy if substitutions of vegetables or other items needed to be made.[46]

In second class, the dinner menu offered more than one choice of entrée, starch, vegetable, and dessert. The menus usually show them all together without indicating which items are to be chosen from a selection. Perhaps passengers could be allowed to combine half-portions of, for example, two different offerings of vegetable or starch. This can be confusing, with several possible interpretations of what an actual passenger's meal could have been. Based on this author's interpretation, *Titanic*'s second-class dinner on April 14, 1912 included a soup course with consommé tapioca (pieces of tapioca floating in beef broth), an entrée with a choice of either baked haddock with sharp sauce, curried chicken with rice, spring lamb with mint sauce, or roast turkey with cranberry sauce.[47] This could be accompanied by a selection of green peas or pureed turnips; and boiled potatoes, roast potatoes, or boiled rice. For dessert there was a choice of plum pudding, "Cocoanut Sandwich," wine jelly, or "American" ice cream.[48] Finally, there were assorted nuts, fresh fruit, cheese and biscuits, and coffee.[49]

It is interesting to note that while the third-class fare included Scandinavian and German choices, the second-class fare reflects dishes familiar to the tastes of either British (haddock, plum pudding) or American (turkey with cranberry sauce, American-style ice cream) passengers. Second-class passengers were likely to be American or British professional people with middle class tastes in food.[50]

First-Class Fare

The *Olympic* and *Titanic* had accommodation for 833 first-class passengers, who could enter the dining room by the elegant forward grand staircase, or by one of three first-class elevators. In first class, the meals were far more lavish than in second class, including more luxurious ingredients, more courses, and more choices. A first-class breakfast menu from the *Titanic* survives from April 11, 1912. This meal started with baked apples, fresh fruit, stewed prunes, Quaker Oats, boiled hominy, and puffed rice.[51] These dishes were followed by a choice of fresh herring, Findon haddock, or smoked salmon. Next came a hearty selection of grilled mutton, kidneys and bacon, or grilled ham, grilled salmon, lamb collops, or vegetable stew. This is followed by a choice of fried, shirred, poached, and boiled eggs. Passengers were then given an option of plain or tomato omelets to order or sirloin steak and mutton chops to order. These were accompanied by a choice of mashed, sauté, and jacket potatoes. There was also cold meat, Vienna and graham rolls, soda and sultana (golden raisin) scones, corn bread, buckwheat cakes (probably pancakes in American style). These items were served with black currant conserve, Narbonne honey, and Oxford marmalade. A final offering was a thankfully light one: watercress. It is interesting to see how both in first- and second-class menus that popular American choices appear next to British ones.[52]

The first-class luncheon on the *Titanic* was equally substantial. A surviving menu from April 14, 1912, tells us that luncheon began with a choice of two soups (consommé fermier or cockie leekie), followed by a choice of entrees: fillets of brill, egg a l'argenteuil, chicken à la Maryland, or corned beef. It appears that this was served with vegetables and dumplings. If those choices did not appeal, passengers could also choose grilled mutton chops with mashed, fried, or baked jacket potatoes. Sweets at luncheon included custard pudding, apple meringue, or a pastry. Passengers who did not want made to order food could also choose from dishes on a buffet, ranging from salmon, ham, and veal pie, and brawn to bologna sausage, Virginia and Cumberland ham, and corned ox tongue. Buffet diners had choices of lettuce, beetroot, or tomatoes on the side. Cheeses were also served with the first-class luncheon: Cheshire, Stilton, Gorgonzola, Edam, Camembert, Roquefort, St. Ivel, and Cheddar. Passengers could pay extra for beer with their lunch: cold Munich lager cost 3d (thrupence for a half pint) or 6d (sixpence for a pint) a tankard.[53]

A first-class menu from the last dinner served aboard the *Titanic* has survived, and it suggests an eleven-course meal, with alternate choices for some courses. Each course was probably accompanied by a different wine. Here the dominant ethnic accent is French *haute cuisine*, suited to the tastes of the high-born and the high-living. It is interesting to have menus for the same meal on the same day for first- and second-class passengers. Knowing that the dishes for both classes were prepared in the same galley, it is likely that the boiled rice came from the same pot for both classes, and that the beef consommé was likewise the same for both classes, with more costly flotsam in the first-class version. According to a first-class menu from the *Titanic*, dinner included a first course of varied hors d'œuvres and oysters, a soup or second course of "Consommé Olga" or cream of barley, and a third course (the fish course) of salmon served with mousseline sauce and cucumbers.[54] Following the fish, the fourth course featured entrée choices: filet mignon, "Chicken Lyonnaise," or "Vegetable Marrow Farci."[55] The fifth course was a choice of lamb with mint sauce, roast duckling in apple sauce, or beef sirloin with "Chateau Potatoes," served with green peas or creamed carrots, boiled rice, "Parmentier," or boiled new potatoes.[56] The sixth course was a punch or sorbet, followed by a seventh course of roast squab and watercress. Asparagus salad with a Champagne-saffron vinaigrette comprised the eighth course and cold paté de foie gras and celery made up the ninth course. The meal finished with choices of sweets—"Waldorf Pudding," peaches in "Chartreuse" jelly, éclairs, and "French" ice cream.[57] We may assume that coffee was served after dessert, as had been customary in France since the mid-nineteenth century.[58]

The Ritz-Carlton Restaurant

For those seeking the last word in luxury, first-class passengers could choose to dine in the Ritz-Carlton à la carte restaurant. This room featured décor of beautifully carved hardwoods with gilded accents, elegantly upholstered chairs in Louis XVI style, with small round tables for two to four diners to sit together. First-class passengers who elected to eat all their meals in the restaurant could apply for a rebate at the end of their voyage. The food here was cooked to order and served right from the restaurant kitchen. The *Olympic*'s restaurant was so popular that it was expanded early in that liner's career. A surviving menu for the *Olympic*'s restaurant is entirely in French. Diners could construct their own meal from a combination of the dishes offered, with as few or as many courses as they liked.[59]

Some great liners included additional meal spaces such as a Café Parisien, Verandah Café and so on, where one could order up a light snack as one would at a Continental sidewalk café. In later years the Cunard Line offered passengers a choice between American, Canadian, or British Bacon, and perhaps other varieties as well.

On P&O ships, headed to India and Australia, the meals would have been essentially similar to those described above, but with the more-frequent appearance of Indian or Indian-inspired dishes such as curries and mulligatawny soup.[60] Many passengers probably had their first introductions to Indian cuisine aboard a P&O liner, and this helped to make curries and other Indian foods an integral part of the British diet.

In the years between the world wars, fashions changed as more young passengers chose to travel "Tourist Third Class," and the deluxe a la carte restaurants waned in popularity. Immigrants, previously the most profitable sector of the transatlantic liners' passengers, dropped off as American immigration laws became less inclusive.

New ships were built, such as *Normandie* and the *Queen Mary*, which reduced the number of funnels (the fourth funnels of *Olympic*, *Titanic*, and *Britannic* were nonfunctional anyhow), but increased overall size. Some ships were taken off transatlantic service to work more leisurely routes, such as *Aquitania* making trips to the Mediterranean. New liners were oil-fired, and coal-fired steamers that remained in service were converted from coal to oil. More changes were in store for big passenger vessels.

Refrigeration

The demand for refrigeration in the United States began with the harvesting and distribution of ice by Frederic Tudor from the 1820s on. Tudor harvested ice from New England lakes, and shipped it in insulating materials to icehouses in Charleston, New Orleans, Savannah, and Havana. Ice could be carried to individual homes in horse-drawn wagons. People bought iceboxes to keep their dairy products, fish, meat, and fruits fresh longer. This created a demand for ice or cooling which fueled the development of refrigeration.[61]

Another factor in the development of refrigeration was Great Britain's growing population. Britain began to experience food shortages in the 1870s, as her population's needs began to outstrip her agricultural production. A slump in the world's wool market was affecting New Zealand and Australia, and enterprising individuals sought ways to refrigerate meat from Down Under while it was transported to Great Britain.[62]

A number of inventors had developed devices that used the condensation of liquefied gases such as ammonia, alcohol, and ether in a closed system to lower the temperature of water and make it freeze into ice. The American physician John Gorrie, the French Ferdinand Carre, and the British-born Australian journalist James Harrison each developed ice-making machines on this principle.[63]

In 1882 William Soltau Davidson, a British-born New Zealander, equipped the sailing ship *Dunedin* with compression refrigeration, and successfully transported a shipment of New Zealand lamb and mutton to Great Britain. The *Dunedin* was joined by a sister ship *Marlborough*, and in short order by rivals and competitors from the New Zealander *Mataurua* to the German steamer *Marsala*. The steamer *Strathleven*, equipped with refrigeration, carried Australian meat to Britain at more or less the same time. New Zealand and Australia became major producers of Great Britain's meat supply.[64]

Refrigeration was applied to the maritime transport of fruit, and ships equipped with refrigeration carried bananas, citrus, and other fruit from the tropics to colder climes. By the early twentieth century, the world's food supply had become global, with even perishable foodstuffs from one part of the globe being available far from their place of origin.[65]

The principles of refrigeration were applied to small units in ships. Steam could be used to power the compression of gases, and so, for example, the U.S. cruiser *Olympia*, built in 1892, is equipped with a steam-powered ice maker. The ice could then be used to keep perishable foodstuffs fresh.

The *Olympic* and her sisters boasted separate refrigerators for the different perishable foods: meat, fish, fruit, vegetables, dairy products, eggs (the latter were to be turned once a day until they were used) each had their own refrigerators, and there was separate cold storage for wines.[66]

Staggering Quantities of Food

The sheer quantities of food required to stock big ocean liners are staggering as are the staffing requirements to prepare and serve it. Liners such as the *Olympic* and the *Titanic* made their Atlantic passages, with the following typical quantities of essential ingredients:

Figure 7.5. Steam-powered refrigeration compressor or ice machine on USS *Olympia*. Reproduction Number: HAER PA,51-PHILA,714—40 in Collection: Historic American Buildings Survey/Historic American Engineering Record/Historic American Landscapes Survey. Courtesy of Library of Congress Digital Collections. http://www.loc.gov/pictures/item/pa3529.photos.360742p/.

15,000 bottles of ale and beer
36,000 apples
100 loaves of bread
2,200 lbs. of coffee
600 gallons of condensed milk
40,000 fresh eggs
250 barrels of flour
7,500 pounds of ham and bacon
75,000 lbs. of fresh meat
11,000 lbs. of fresh fish
4,000 lbs. of salted and dried fish
25,000 lbs. of poultry
40 tons of potatoes
10,000 lbs. of sugar[67]

A generation later, the list of food supplies for the *Queen Mary* making a westbound Atlantic crossing included the following:

20 tons of beef
25 tons of potatoes
70,000 eggs
1,000 jars of jam
5 tons of bacon and ham
160 gallons of salad oil
9 tons of fish
500 lbs. of smoked salmon
$4^1/_2$ tons of lamb[68]
The list goes on and on, in staggering profusion.

Conclusion

In the half-century leading up to World War II, mankind produced the largest moving objects heretofore constructed, and carried thousands of people across the Atlantic, as well as through the Mediterranean Sea and Indian Ocean. Some traveled in sumptuous luxury, and others in simple austerity. The steam turbine replaced the multiple-expansion reciprocating engine in big passenger vessels as in warships, and after World War I oil replaced coal as the fuel employed to heat the steam. Refrigeration changed the way the world ate, making fruit and ice available around the world, almost anywhere and anytime. In so doing, refrigeration created new types of ships, new routes, and also changed the food available for sailors and passengers alike to eat while they were on the sea.

This chapter ends with a song about a working lifestyle long past, that of the engine room crew in the days of coal-fired ocean liners. The song is slightly mysterious, as it is set in 1924, by which time the *Mauritania* had been converted from coal to oil. Nonetheless, it paints a picture of life in the engine room of one of the great early twentieth-century liners, when they were still coal-fired. Traditionally, many of the chief engineers of the transatlantic liners were Scottish, and many of the stokers were Liverpool Irish, working bare-chested while wearing thick gloves and wooden clogs.[69]

"Firing the Mauritania"

'Twas in nineteen hundred and twenty four
I found myself in Liverpool on the floor
So I went to the Cunard office door
And got a job on the *Mauritania*

Chorus: She surely was a slaver:
Ah, to Hell with the *Mauritania*!

The *Mauritania*'s a beautiful sight
She's got sixty-four fires a-burning bright
And you'll shovel the coal from morning to night
Trying to fire the *Mauritania*

Her coal was hard and full of slate
And that's what's beaten the four-to-eight
It very soon wearied the four-to-eight
Trying to fire the *Mauritania*

The eight-to-twelve were much better men
But they were knackered by half past ten
So tired and weary by half past ten
Trying to fire the *Mauritania*

The fan's on the bum and fire won't draw
And that's what's beaten the twelve-to-four
It very soon buggered the twelve-to-four
Trying to fire the *Mauritania*

So come all you firemen, listen to me
A Cunard liner spells purgatory
So stick close to the coast, don't go deep sea
Trying to fire the *Mauritania*.[70]

EIGHT

New Technologies

Submarines, Cruise Ships, and Containerization

During the twentieth century, new technologies were applied to the movement of people and cargoes over the water, and to the world's navies. Ships were built that could launch airplanes, and that could submerge and attack other ships from below the surface of the sea. Airplanes provided competition for the passenger trade, and passenger ships evolved in new directions, for travelers who sailed in them for changing reasons. The cruise ship industry evolved out of the waning passenger ship industry, like a phoenix from the ashes of its funeral pyre. The use of steel containers for freight changed the shipping of cargo, and contributed to a more global economy.

At the same time, small boats became more popular as an outdoor recreation. Some chose to experience traditional sailing vessels, whether as passengers, training for naval service, or as an opportunity to recreate a maritime past.

Royal Navy Cocoa

By the two world wars, the British Navy had a well-established tradition of serving cocoa to crewmen on watch (awake and working) at four bells in the night watch and mid watch (i.e., 10:00 p.m. or 2200 hours, and 2:00 a.m. or 0200 hours), and often at four bells in the morning watch (i.e., 6:00 a.m. or 0600 hours) as well. The 0600 hours cup, usually of coffee, was a well-established American merchant ship tradition by 1877 when Frederick Pease

Figure 8.1. Sailors eating aboard the yacht *Emerald*, no date. Courtesy of San Francisco Maritime NHP, Image B10.30817n (SAFR 21374).

Harlow described it. Cocoa is documented as a navy food clear back to the time of Admiral Nelson; however the tradition of serving it at these specific times has proven elusive to date precisely.

Royal Navy cocoa in the Manual of Naval Cookery published in 1930: "Cocoa as a beverage is more nourishing than tea or coffee, but not so stimulating. It is more nourishing because it contains fat and starch. The Service cocoa contains all the cocoa fat, and arrowroot and refined sugar are added. The slight stimulation derived from cocoa is due to the active principle of Theo-bromine. It also has an astringent similar to Tannin in action."[1] The drink was prepared at sea by breaking Navy chocolate, issued in block form, into small pieces and combining it with the cocoa/arrowroot paste, which is then heated with a little water to make a thick paste. A teaspoonful of this paste is combined with half a pint of boiling water, simmered for half an hour, and then served with milk and sugar, very hot.[2] This concoction is sometimes known as "kye" or "kai" in naval service, with occasional additions of custard powder (possibly the arrowroot) and occasional other additives. Steam from a steam drain could give it an espresso-like quality. The origins of the nickname are mysterious, but may relate to the legendary Persian king Kai Khusrow, who possessed a magical cup.

The German navies of both world wars imitated the British Navy in many regards. The issue of a hot beverage halfway through the night and middle watches was traditional in German ships too; however it was coffee and not cocoa which was served to German sailors.

A "Cup o' Joe" Replaces the Wardroom Tipple in the United States Navy

One of the most controversial figures of the early twentieth-century United States Navy was the secretary of the navy from 1913 to 1921, a Woodrow Wilson appointee from North Carolina named Josephus Daniels. Daniels was a newspaperman with no experience of the sea, but an ardent believer in a number of causes. He was vilified then, and praised today, for his support of Women's Suffrage: he was one of the more visible male champions of votes for women. He was praised by some then, and is vilified today, for his white supremacist views. These views tainted the editorial policy and reporting of his newspaper, the Raleigh *News & Observer*, which encouraged the passage of Jim Crow and other racially discriminatory laws in North Carolina. His parsimony, and his lack of knowledge of the sea and ships, won him no friends in the fleet; but his assistant secretary, future president Franklin Delano Roosevelt, did a great deal to buffer him from the resentment of his subordinates.[3] Daniels investigated identical bids by three contractors for providing armor plate for the battleship *Arizona*, and enforced competitive bidding by these and other contractors. By so doing, Daniels claimed to have reduced the cost of *Arizona*'s armor plate by $1.1 million.[4] A reformer at heart, Daniels ordered every ship and shore station to establish compulsory classes in basic subjects, and voluntary classes in advanced subjects. Daniels also required that several places in the Naval Academy (for prospective officers) be set aside for talented enlisted men.[5] This is the text of the menu whose cover is shown in figure 8.2.

MENU
Dinner, July 4th, 1935

Sweet Pickles	Ripe Olives	Stuffed Celery
Fruit Cocktail		
Roast Turkey	Giblet Gravy	
Cranberry Sauce		
Cornbread Dressing		
Creamed Mashed Potatoes	Mashed Turnips	
Combination Fresh Vegetable Salad	Russian Dressing	
Ice Cream and Cake		
Hot Rolls	Butter	
Coffee[6]		

Figure 8.2. USS *Arizona* Fourth of July dinner menu cover. July 4, 1935. This is the vessel on which Josephus Daniels claimed to have saved the American taxpayer over a million dollars. Sunk by the Japanese at Pearl Harbor, the *Arizona* is now a memorial to those who lost their lives there. Author's collection.

Josephus Daniels made culinary history with another reform. Enlisted men had been denied the grog ration since 1862, but officers were still allowed to consume privately purchased alcohol in the wardroom, off duty. Feeling this to be discriminatory against the enlisted men, Daniels issued General Order No. 99, to take effect on July 1, 1914:

> The use or introduction for drinking purposes of alcoholic liquors on board any naval vessel, or within any navy yard or station, is strictly prohibited, and commanding officers will be held directly responsible for the enforcement of this order.[7]

The order was issued a month in advance of its execution, which challenged some naval personnel to consume the existing stocks in time. Raucous and elaborate celebrations were held on the eve of July 1, such as mock burials at sea of empty bottles, and even of whole coffins filled with "dead soldiers." Aboard the battleship *North Dakota*, one of eleven American battleships at Veracruz, Mexico, there was a lively party in the wardroom. At one point, the Executive Officer walked in, wearing a baseball catcher's mask and chest protector, and proposed a toast to Josephus Daniels. He was pelted with "rolls, sandwiches and anything else handy."[8]

Secretary Daniels was also memorialized in song. Popular verses were added to the song, "The Armored Cruiser Squadron," and widely sung through the fleet:

> Away, away with sword and drum,
> Here we come, full of rum
> Looking for something to put on the bum
> In the Armored Cruiser Squadron.
>
> Josephus Daniels is a goose,
> If he thinks he can induce,
> Us to drink his damn grape juice
> In the Armored Cruiser Squadron.[9]

The most enduring tribute to Secretary Daniels may stem from a misattributed quotation. Daniels is alleged to have said that "nothing stronger than coffee" would be served in United States Navy ships after General Order No. 99. He may have said this, or he may not have. As he was widely *believed* to have said it, the men of the United States began calling coffee "Joe" in his honor: or so the legend goes. This soon became an enduring Navy tradition, like calling a toilet a "head" (possibly derived from the era of sailing navies, when the crew privies were located in the beakhead, just forward of the cutwater), and the expression crept into civilian American usage as well. As if Josephus Daniels's legacy was not sufficiently confused already, some have questioned the etymology of the naval use of "cup o' Joe," claiming that the idiom predates General Order 99. This may be true. Other culinary traditions of the sea stem from apocryphal origins, for example, saluting Admiral Horatio Nelson by giving the name "Nelson's Blood" to rum (though his body was actually kept in a cask of brandy). Then too, there is the apocryphal origin of the adjective "posh." Saluting Secretary Josephus Daniels by giving his name to coffee may reflect what people believe; rather than what history recorded, or failed to record.

Passenger Service Changes, and the Cruise Ship Evolves

It is challenging to say where passenger service ends, and "cruises" begin. The "expedition"; which Mark Twain and a boatload of other Americans took to

Figure 8.3. A cartoon lampooning alcohol and the Navy under Secretary of the Navy Josephus Daniels. "No Drink in the Navy" by Hy Mayer, 1868–1954. Puck Publishing Corporation. May 9, 1914. Reproduction Number: LC-DIG-ppmsca-28049 in Collection: Miscellaneous Items in High Demand. Courtesy of Library of Congress Digital Collections. http://www.loc.gov/pictures/item/2011649785/.

the Mediterranean aboard the steamship *Quaker City* could be described as a cruise, though the author and his fellow passengers sometimes slept ashore, and used land transportation. Numerous trips offered by the P&O Line in the nineteenth century could also be considered "cruises," in which passengers were offered leisurely voyages to more than one destination.

The National Prohibition Act

It may be said that what sets a cruise apart from a passage is that in the cruise, the journey itself is the destination. An event that did a great deal to blur the distinction between journey and destination, and to blur many other things besides, was the passage of the Eighteenth Amendment in the United States in 1919, to take effect along with its partner the National Prohibition Act (better known as the Volstead Act), in January 1920. Few pieces of American legislation define an era as much as Prohibition, and its repeal by the Twenty-First Amendment in 1933. As seen in the previous chapter, the prohibition of alcohol in the United States and aboard U.S.-registered ships was a great selling factor for the passenger ships of other nations. Americans joined other travelers in a virtual boycott of American ships in the Atlantic. As a newspaperman said of the crew of the *President Harding*, "It hurt them to think Americans deserted them to go on foreign lines merely because they could not, as one officer remarked, 'wait seven days for a drink.'"[10] Where those American passengers went, and what use they made of those seven days, is evident in a British newspaperman's report of the arrival of the famous Cunard liner *Mauretania* in 1920: "[She] has docked at Southampton with empty bins. A record stock of wines and spirits has been utterly consumed by American passengers."[11]

Other forces were at work to change the nature of passenger service at sea. American immigration laws became stricter, and the pre-war flood of European immigrants was replaced by a post-war trickle. For all the press attention to the goings-on of the privileged first-class passengers, it was the third-class business that provided the bulk of the owners' profits. To complicate matters, the big ocean lines busily set about replacing ships lost during the war, and converting old liners from coal to oil. The investment in carrying capacity outpaced the need; now the major lines had more carrying capacity than their transatlantic business could fill.[12]

Before World War I, cruise and excursion voyages were only offered on big new ships off-season: other times of year, this duty was relegated to old vessels on their way to the scrapyard. This changed after the war. Cunard put *Aquitania*, the third sister of *Lusitania* and *Mauretania*, into service in the Mediterranean. The Germans had already anticipated the trend with the Hamburg America Line's conversion of the transatlantic *Deutschland* into the Caribbean-service *Victoria Louise*, in 1912. The German liner had half her engines removed, her public rooms expanded, and (anticipating a trend) was repainted white. Just prior to the war, the Hamburg America Line also introduced 125-day world cruises in the ships *Cleveland* and *Cincinnati*, converted from three-class service to one-class service. Cunard, Canadian Pacific, and Red Star Line also offered world cruises off-season.[13]

In the Pacific, there were Asian immigrants sufficient to keep American and Japanese passenger ships operating in the black. Canadian Pacific and the P&O Line also provided service in the Pacific. The Matson Line offered passenger service to Hawai'i and the South Pacific. The Aloha Tower, a Honolulu landmark which has been likened to a Pacific Statue of Liberty, welcomed immigrants and tourists from 1926 on.[14]

While Europeans continued to dominate transatlantic service, some American lines found niches in certain runs: the Grace Line sailed to the Caribbean and South America; Moore McCormick to South America; and the American Export Line to the Mediterranean.[15] United Fruit Company took passengers to their tropical destinations as well.[16]

During Prohibition, a number of passenger lines offered short, cheap "booze cruises" from American ports to destinations such as Nova Scotia, Nassau, and Bermuda. For the most part, these were offered in superannuated vessels that were not entirely suited to warm-weather cruising, lacking air conditioning and warm-weather cruising amenities such as swimming pools. However, the passengers were free to drink themselves into oblivion: in this period, that suited many American passengers just fine.[17] As a steward on the Hamburg-America liner *Reliance* observed, Americans "learned about Daiquiri cocktails at Havana, rum swizzles at Trinidad, and punch at Kingston."[18] In the unlikely event that American passengers forgot to show up for their tutelage in mixed drinks, Facundo Bacardi sent wireless invitations to his distillery to arriving U.S.-registered ships as they arrived in Havana.[19]

The stock market crash of 1929 caused a worldwide depression which further reduced the demand for three-class transatlantic service. For those who could afford it, the shorter trips to destinations in the Caribbean and Hawai'i offered an affordable travel opportunity. The same was true of Mediterranean trips for Europeans. During the 1930s the offerings of these trips expanded. The advertising still stressed the destinations the passengers would visit, more than the shipboard experience itself.[20] Nonetheless, the foundations of the cruise ship industry were being laid during the 1920s and 1930s.

Two new Italian Liners Point
the Way to the Future

In the 1930s, the transatlantic liners experienced competition from Italy. The *Rex* and the *Conte de Savoia* were graceful, comfortable, and fast: they held the coveted Blue Ribband for the fastest westbound transatlantic times from 1933 to 1935. The run between New York and Italy entailed a few days cruising in the Mediterranean, and the Italian liners, while fast, also featured more open, airy spaces. At a time when other passenger lines' advertising pictured formal-looking business travelers promenading the decks with their elegant wives, the astute Italians' advertising showed colorfully dressed vacationers vigorously enjoying leisure activities.[21]

Merchant Marine Act of 1920,
Known as the Jones Act

This piece of legislation authored by Senator Wesley Jones (Republican, from Washington State) was designed primarily to protect American merchant sailors and American maritime carrier from foreign competition. The provisions of the act regarding "cabotage" produced some interesting reactions by those organizing booze cruises, trips offshore specifically for the purpose of allowing American refugees from the Volstead Act to drink to their heart's content. "Cabotage" is a loan word from French, meaning coastal shipping. Laws of cabotage are usually designed to protect the domestic shipping of one coastal country from competition from another. Laws of Cabotage can be complicated, especially when applied to air travel: for example, while there were two Germanies, Pan American Airlines used East Berlin's Tegel Airport when flying to Berlin from West German airports, because of West Germany's rights of cabotage. Under the Merchant Marine Act of 1920 (better known as the Jones Act), foreign-registered ships (the only kind who could legally serve alcohol to their passengers) had to touch foreign soil if they were going to sail between two (or the same) United States port(s). This resulted in booze cruises from American ports making stops in some non–U.S.-owned islands of questionable charm and interest: these stops were legal necessities for cruising from and to American ports with thirsty American passengers. Another effect of the Jones Act was to give U.S. flagships a virtual monopoly on service between the U.S. West Coast and Hawai'i, as there were no convenient non–U.S.-territory islands on the way.

Competition from the Air

Irving Berlin in his song "I'll See You in C-U-B-A" urged Americans to visit Havana, providing a musical siren call to that destination for Americans eager to enjoy high life outside the cellar of the neighborhood speakeasy. In November 1920, Inglis Moore Uppercu, a Cadillac dealer from New York, offered a faster alternative to sea travel. Uppercu formed Aeromarine Airways, one of the first regularly scheduled, U.S.-based international airlines. A trio of wooden-hulled biplane flying boats, picturesquely named *Niña*, *Pinta*, and *Santa Maria*, whisked Americans in wicker armchairs from Miami to Havana, Bimini, and other bibulous destinations.[22] After Pan American Airways began service from Key West to Havana in 1927, this fledgling airline launched an advertising campaign jointly with Bacardi, under the slogan "Fly with us to Havana and you can bathe in Bacardi rum two hours from now."[23] Thus Prohibition not only contributed to the transition from sea travel to cruising, but it also helped jump-start the principal competitor to sea travel, the commercial airline. Reflecting popular awareness of expanded choices in travel, the line "hop on a ship" in Irving Berlin's song was widely performed and recorded as "take a plane or a ship." Prohibition was repealed in 1933, ironically spearheaded by Josephus Daniels's former assistant Franklin Delano Roosevelt. Prohibition ended, but many changes in passenger travel, at sea and in the air, had already been set in motion.

Messmen in the United States Navy

Jim Crow laws, which segregated much of American society from the 1890s on, made changes in the United States Navy, and specifically in its food service. The American Navy of the War of 1812 and the 1861–1865 Civil War included a large proportion of African American sailors. By the time of World War I, the United States Navy had become a "white" service. In 1932, Captain Abram Claude opened the Navy to African American messman who served the officers in the wardroom, as stewards served passengers in civilian vessels. This duty had been served mostly by noncitizen Filipino messmen since 1919.[24] While Claude's open door was a long way from combat duty, it did readmit African Americans into the segregated United States Navy, and many of the Negro messmen served in combat capacities anyhow. Messmen had positions at guns at General Quarters, and Asian and African American messmen manned guns, and in many cases died, in the Japanese attack on Pearl Harbor in 1941.[25] Doris "Dorie" Miller, promoted from mess attendant to main cook in the battleship *West Virginia*, served a .50 caliber machine gun heroically at Pearl Harbor, earning the Navy Cross and passing into legend.[26]

The American armed forces were eventually desegregated following President Harry Truman's Executive Order 9981. The Vietnam conflict was the first American war since 1900 fought with a fully racially integrated navy.

The Evolution of the Practical Submarine

The submarine has existed in the human imagination for quite some time. William Bourne may have created a submersible rowing craft in sixteenth-century London, and David Bushnell created a one-man submersible called the *Turtle*, which attempted to drill a hole in a British Navy vessel during the War of American Independence. During the nineteenth century, a new generation of imaginative genius was applied to the problem of creating and propelling a craft which could submerge and (even more important) resurface at will. Robert Fulton designed submarines that would use a sail on the surface, with its operator hand-cranking the propeller when submerged. Wilhelm Bauer's *Brandtaucher* was a brilliant design, with two men operating treadmills, like outsize hamster wheels, to turn the propeller. Bauer's parsimonious superiors stripped his design of water-ballast tanks, so that the ballast water sloshed around freely under duckboards. This proved to be a fatal flaw. To the short-lived Confederate States Navy goes the laurel for the first vessel sunk by a submarine: the USS *Housatonic* was sunk by the *Hunley*, a tiny metal tube in which the crew of eight hand-cranked the propeller. The French Navy developed *Plongeur*, a vessel which ran on compressed air, which also served to blow the ballast water tanks; and then later a tiny all-electric submarine *Gymnote*. Jules Verne studied a model of *Plongeur* and consulted with the future developers of *Gymnote* for his novel *20,000 Leagues Under the Sea*. A gyroscopic compass was developed for the submerged navigation of *Gymnote*. John Holland, born in Ireland but an immigrant to the United States, developed submarines that used an internal combustion engine on the surface, combined with batteries to run an electric motor while submerged, and an air compressor to blow ballast tanks. Submarines of the Holland pattern were acquired by both the American and British navies. Holland's competitor Simon Lake designed American submarines which incorporated other important design features, such as the escape trunk, the conning tower, and the retracting periscope. The German Navy built submarines with kerosene engines, which left a tall, unstealthy plume of white exhaust smoke. When the Germans developed the diesel engine, the practical modern submarine had arrived. By the outbreak of World War I every major navy had submarines with diesel engines for surface running, batteries and an electric motor for running submerged, and air compressors to blow the water out of tanks between an inner "pressure hull" and an outer hull.

Submarines began carrying cooking facilities early on. In 1912, U-9, one of the German Navy's kerosene-powered boats, had a small electric hot plate on board: but it rarely, if ever, worked.[27] By World War II, American submarines had working all-electric galleys, with freezer and refrigerator compartments under the galley deck. Submarines developed routines for serving everyone in the very limited space available. American submarines divided the crew into three divisions, who worked four hours on, eight hours off in rotation. The meals were prepared, then served in three seatings to each division in turn: first the division that was about to go on watch; then the division that was between watches; and finally the division coming off watch. Each division had about ten to twelve minutes to eat. This system worked to feed all eighty or so enlisted men in a timely manner. Some submarines, operating in enemy territory and mostly attacking at night, ran their watch routine "in reverse": dimming their lights during the day, and serving meals at night. Most American submarine cooking was done on the surface, as this made for more efficient venting of the galley smells.

During World War II, American submarines—whose patrols lasted sixty to ninety days, made an effort to serve good food. Many U.S. submarines carried an ice cream maker, as did U.S. Navy surface ships. One ice cream-capable American submarine, the *Pampanito*, is now a museum vessel in San Francisco. For crew members who might be hungry between meals, it was customary to keep a coffee pot on at all hours, and to have the makings of sandwiches, and sometimes pastry, available around the clock. This recalls the bread barge filled with ship's biscuit of 150 years before.

One class of American submarine was not popular; the S-boats that fled the Philippines shortly after the attack on Pearl Harbor and operated out of Australia, known to their crews as "pig boats." These were old World War I vintage boats, with limited ventilation and cramped interior spaces. Many of their food issues were Australian or Dutch: some of these, such as rabbit and mutton, and Bitter Orange and Bitter Lemon soft drinks, were not popular with American sailors.

On any submarine, squeezing the food into the pressure hull packed with torpedoes, ammunition, air compressors, batteries, electric motor, diesel engine, fuel, crewmen, and much more, was a challenge. American boats left port with food crammed into shower stalls, around the engine, and in the crew members' cubic foot of personal locker space. Extra items such as canned fruit sometimes ended up in bunks or ditty bags until needed. German submarines sometimes had loaves of bread in nets, and sausages hanging from pipes, creating an impression like the Hanging Gardens of Babylon.[28]

The Ge-dunk Bar and NAAFI

On larger American Navy vessels, there was a Ge-dunk bar (pronounced with a hard "g," rhymes with "be-sunk") where sailors could purchase ice cream, candy, and sweets. A friend of the author's who served in the battleship *Alabama* remembered his crew calling ice cream "ge-dunk." Other veterans remember "ge-dunk" as a generic name for any of the snacks and extras available for purchase, with the sailor working the register known as "the gedunk guy" or "gedunka-roo." The origins of the term are obscure, possibly from a comic strip character Harold Teen who ate "gedunk sundaes" at his local soda fountain; or perhaps from the sound that vending machines made. The term was current by 1931, when it appeared in *Leatherneck Magazine*: it is still used in the U.S. Navy.[29]

The British had their own equivalent of the Ge-dunk bar. The NAAFI (Navy, Army and Air Force Institutes), formed in 1921, evolved from the World War I Army Canteen Committee. NAAFI functions somewhat like the USO in American service, providing pubs, lounges, and other welcome extras, including drinks and snacks. In the British Armed Services, the snacks purchased at NAAFI facilities are sometimes called "nutty."[30]

Changes in Naval Food Service

When World War II began the British Navy still did much of its mealtime organization as it had for over a century. Mess cooks still collected their messes' food from the galley, performing extra preparation at the mess tables; men still lived, slept, and ate in one increasingly cramped messroom. Lend-lease, in which destroyers were transferred from the American to British service, compelled the British crews of those vessels to adapt to some of the American-style structures of those vessels: fold-down bunks or racks instead of hammocks, and meals served from a galley adjoining a dedicated dining area. The American vessels had other amenities that were new to British destroyer crews, such as machine laundries, mechanical potato peelers, and soda fountains. Since World War II, the U.S. and the U.K. navies (and probably most every other navy) have implemented cafeteria-style service, in which the men walk past steam trays between the galley and the messroom. This arrangement is efficient of time, space, and manpower.[31]

While officers ate the same food as the crew, they still ate separately, even though the wardroom in an American warship was essentially a smaller version of the crew's messroom. A song popular with American navy sailors during World War II, based on an older folksong about convicts transported to Australia, poked fun at some of these lingering naval traditions. After lampooning the practice of calling a motor launch a "barge" if it carried an admiral, and a "gig" if it carried a captain, one verse pokes fun at the separate but equal messroom and wardroom:

> The crew they all eat in the messroom,
> But the captain won't eat with the mob:
> It's not that he eats any better:
> He doesn't want us to know he's a slob!

Jungle Juice

Jungle Juice began as a military expression for homemade alcohol, probably because it was concocted by sailors, marines, and soldiers in the jungles of the South Pacific in World War II. Raisins are a preferred ingredient, though any sort of canned fruit will do. It is very important that the container in which fermentation takes place be vented. Otherwise, it is likely to explode: explosions in military installations tend to attract unwanted attention.[32] In more recent civilian usage, Jungle Juice is used as an expression for a communal punchbowl mix of fruit juices, "Everclear," sweet liqueurs, and any number of other ingredients. In its original military meaning, it is the name for the alcohol itself, which is concocted and not purchased.

Ancient Improvisations Get New Names

Shortages of favorite foods, intermittent supply, and difficult conditions have reduced sea cooks to simple expedients for centuries. Just as thirteenth-century Catalan-Aragonese galley cooks tossed all the ingredients requiring cooking into a single cauldron and served it up with biscuits, twentieth-century sea cooks combined ground beef, bully beef, or other meat with whatever else was edible in a single pot, and served it over toasted bread or a hamburger bun. These improvisations became known as "Chipped Beef on Toast," "S___ on a Shingle" (or S.O.S. for short), "Chicken on a Raft," and other colorful nicknames. Under the new name "Sloppy Joe," this naval staple became a familiar item in postwar school cafeterias, where faculty members with military experience could be heard to chuckle, "We called it something different in the Navy."

Postwar Liners and Cruise Ships

World War II left the Germans, Japanese, and Italians without the means of operating passenger service (most of their ships had been sunk), and other states somewhat limited. The P&O Line recovered, running passengers and cargo to Hong Kong and Australia. The Australian government operated a famous scheme to bring in much-needed workers, by offering a subsidized passage from Britain for Britons who were willing to spend at least two years in Australia. The cost of the passage to the immigrants was only ten pounds: therefore they were known in Australia as "Ten Pound Poms." This scheme not only generated more labor force for Australia, but it took strain off the British economy, still reeling from the war, and effectively subsidized the P&O Line. With adjustments in the price of the fare, the scheme lasted for decades.[33]

American passenger carriers came into their own after World War II. British and European passenger fleets were decimated by the war. American ports were undamaged, American industry robust, and economy vigorous. In the postwar years, the American Export Line offered trips to the Mediterranean; their liner *Constitution* carried Grace Kelly on her way to Monaco to marry Prince Rainier. Moore-McCormack lines offered trips to South America, while the "white ships" of the Matson Line offered trips to Hawai'i and the South Seas. The Grace Line offered departures every Friday from Manhattan, bound for the Southern Hemisphere. The American President Line offered hundred-day world cruises. The world cruise became something of an American icon: many older couples of that era looked forward to celebrating their retirement with a world cruise.[34]

There were also less glamorous ways to travel by sea in comfort. The Grace Line operated passenger-cargo liners that carried fifty-two passengers in air-conditioned staterooms with private baths, and even a swimming pool.[35] The "banana boats" of United Fruit and the gray-hulled "coffee boats" of the Delta Line offered trips in freighters with capacity for twelve or more passengers.[36] The "Golden Bear" freighters of the Pacific Far East Line (which was later to take over two Matson passenger liners during the 1970s) also carried twelve passengers apiece to destinations in the Far East.

The United States Line held a particularly prominent position among American passenger lines of the 1950s and 1960s, with the prestige of even their magnificent twenty-two knot SS *America* surpassed by the flagship of American passenger liners, the SS *United States*. The *United States* was the masterpiece of American naval architect William Francis Gibbs: she finally won the transatlantic Blue Riband for her country on her maiden voyage in 1952. At 990 feet long, this liner was designed to function if needed as a high-speed (up to 38.32 knots) troop transport. The "Big U" had a superstructure of lightweight aluminum, and her lean, lanky form emanated assurance and speed from every angle.[37]

Figure 8.4. SS *United States* menu cover. Wednesday, November 24, 1954. The meal is described as a "Gala Dinner," and mentions that the ship's clocks will be reset that evening. This probably represented the final and most grand dinner before the end of a crossing, in an era when this liner was the "flagship" of a vast fleet of American passenger vessels. Author's collection.

This is a Gala Dinner Menu from the SS *United States* for Wednesday, November 24, 1954:

Whistable Oysters on the Half Shell
Supreme of Fresh Fruit in Kirschwasser   Fresh Crabmeat Cocktail
Beluga Malossol Caviar on Ice   Foie Gras in Aspic
Iced Table Celery   Queen and Ripe Olives
* * *

Kangaroo Tail Soup   Veloute "Bismarck"
* * *

Lobster a l'United States en Cassolette, Fleurons
Paupiette of Dover Sole, Bonne Femme
* * *

Partridge a l'Anglaise
Bread Sauce, Wild Rice, Glaced Marrons, Currant Jelly
* * *

Benedictine Sherbet, Wafers
* * *

French Poularde, Giblet Sauce, Cranberry Jelly
Roast English Southdown Lamb au Jus, Mint Jelly
* * *

Filet Mignon, Sauce Bearnaise, Mushrooms Sauté
* * *

California Asparagus, Hollandaise
Petits Bois [sic—meant to be pois)   Fresh Stewed Tomatoes
Mousseline, French Fried, Baked Idaho, Parsley or Candied Sweet Potatoes
* * *

Avocado Pear, Florida Dressing
* * *

Preserved Bartlett Pears
* * *

Bombe Glace, Harlequin   Mignardises
* * *

Roquefort or Neufchatel Cheese and Toasted Crackers
* * *

Assorted Nuts   After Dinner Mints   Table Raisins
Stuffed Figs   Crystallized Ginger   Stuffed Dates
Hot House Grapes on Ice
* * *

Café Turc

It should be born in mind that this was a particularly festive meal aboard the flagship of American passenger service. Food service in most passenger ships of this era reflected contemporary American tastes. Starting with cocktails in which whiskey-based drinks and martinis predominated (rum- and tequila-based "umbrella drinks" were rare), dinner usually consisted of the favored deluxe entrees of the time, such as lobster tail and popular cuts of steak. Side dishes tended to be the standard ones of the era, and there was usually a choice of dessert. A special final flourish could be Baked Alaska, vanilla ice cream with sponge cake topped with meringue, then briefly baked to brown the meringue, which insulates the ice cream and prevents it from melting. The name was coined by Charles Ranhofer, *chef de cuisine* for Delmonico's Restaurant in 1876, in honor of the territory recently purchased from Russia by the United States. A festive variation, Bombe Alaska, is splashed with dark rum: with lights dimmed, the rum is set alight and the dessert is flambéed.

By the 1960s there was formidable foreign competition for these vessels: *France* and Cunard's *QE2* were two new superliners of the decade. By this time the bulk of passenger trade was already fleeing to the air. In October 1958, Pan Am began regular service with the new Boeing 707 jetliner. The 707 and the DC-8 offered non-stop transatlantic service, and the young and hip travelers of the 1960s were known as "jetsetters." Companies offering travel by sea tried to lure passengers with slogans such as "Why just go there—when you can *cruise* there?" but the young ignored the appeal, and chose to "just go there" quickly and cheaply by jetliner.

Freighters and Container Ships

World War I did a great deal to eclipse sailing vessels as carriers of cargo. The German Navy used their submarine fleet to blockade Britain, and a disproportionate number of their victims were sailing vessels, which were easy targets. Toward the end of the war, transatlantic merchant shipping steamed in convoys for protection, and sailing ships were too slow and too subject to the wind to participate. By the end of the war, sail had disappeared almost entirely from most of the world's principal sea lanes.

The steam or motor freighter still carried masts. No longer carrying sails, masts with cargo booms were vital in unloading cargo from the hold through hatches, usually in cargo nets or on pallets.

During World War II, the United States built freighters and tankers to standard patterns, in staggering numbers that out-produced the German submarine fleet's capacity to sink them. Sections of hull were prefabricated in a variety of locations, and assembled at the shipyards in record time. Much of this work was done by women, nicknamed Rosie the Riveter, though more and more of the shipyard work was accomplished by welding. "Wendy the Welder" might have been a more accurate nickname for the women (and men) who kept ships coming faster than the Axis could sink them. Liberty ships had triple-expansion engines, and were based on small British tramp steamers. Victory ships were slightly faster, usually powered by turbine engines. A still larger standard design was the C-2 freighter, with turbine or diesel engines. Tankers were also made to a standard pattern, for example the T-2.

Many of these wartime vessels saw post-war civilian use. One war-surplus T-2 tanker, renamed *Ideal-X*, was put to historic use in April 1956, when Malcolm P. McLean, a trucking entrepreneur from North Carolina, arranged for her to carry a deck cargo of fifty-eight metal containers, actually truck trailers detached from their chassis, from Port Newark to Houston. This was a civilian application of a concept that had been used by the U.S. Armed

Forces during the war. The deck cargo of the *Ideal-X* arrived in fine style: the trailers were attached to new chassis and were driven off. McLean followed up in 1957 with an improved vessel, a C-2 freighter converted to hold 226 containers of standard forty-foot-long pattern, named *Gateway City*. In 1958 the Matson Line followed suit with the *Hawaiian Merchant*, followed by the Grace Line's *Santa Eliana* and *Santa Leonor*, also converted from war-surplus C-2 freighters. McLean renamed his shipping company Sea-Land in 1960, and that name has endured to the present.[38]

During the 1960s, more and more cargo traveled by container. Containerization changed the handling of cargo in myriad ways. It made warehouse-style docks redundant, and large gantry cranes of new design essential. Seaports built container facilities, big open flat yards to which the ships moored alongside, instead of the traditional finger-piers surmounted by sheds. Ports such as Seattle, which were quick to develop container facilities, gained an advantage over traditional finger-pier ports. Damage and pilferage were greatly reduced, and time-in-port for freighters shortened from days or weeks to a matter of hours. This reduced the number of jobs for longshoremen, and drastically changed the lifestyle of the working sailor. With a turn-around time in port of only a day or two, containership sailors only had time for a meal or two ashore, perhaps an hour or two for sightseeing.

Nuclear Submarines

Until 1954, submarines could have been more precisely described as submersibles: they were essentially surface vessels that could be submerged for periods whose duration varied from one vessel to another. With the first nuclear-powered submarine SSN *Nautilus*, submarines were able to cruise submerged for long periods, without the diesel-electric boats' need to run on the surface to recharge batteries. The nuclear reactor heats water into steam, which drives a turbine, and is then reheated and reused. This is only one of several "closed systems" in a nuclear submarine.

American nuclear submarines use a modification of the watch and mess routine used aboard submarines in World War II and the Korean War. The crew is still divided into three divisions, who now work a six-hour watch and then rest for twelve hours. Running submerged for days, weeks, and even months at a time, the crew adapts to this eighteen-hour-day routine, in which day and night are no longer relevant. The system of serving each division in rapid succession is still in place. In addition to breakfast, lunch, and dinner, "Midrats"—an offering of food usually using leftovers from the other meals—is served a few hours after dinner.

American submarines are just proud of serving "the best food in the Navy." Submarine cooks, now called culinary specialists, make a special effort to maintain the high reputation of their service. Of course, the menu choices can become somewhat monotonous toward the end of a patrol, when fresh ingredients are running low and some ingredients have been used up. Nonetheless, the culinary specialists of the submarine service are justly proud of their reputation for serving the best food in the service.

The Cruise Ship Rallies

Throughout the 1960s, cruises and passenger travel by sea came to have a stodgy reputation, associated with retired couples and a "square" mind-set. This began to change toward the end of the decade, as new companies such as Ted Arison's Norwegian Caribbean Line marketed their cruises from Miami on a national basis.[39] In 1967 Royal Caribbean Cruises entered the market with brand-new, motor yacht-looking cruise ships, offering fourteen-day Caribbean cruises departing Miami on alternate Saturdays. Royal Caribbean promoted their ships a full year before they entered service, which helped to fill available berths when the ships became operational. Royal Viking offered a Skald Club with special programs for repeat passengers, a full ten years before the first airline frequent-flyer program.[40]

In 1968, the Costa family, operating a pair of ships out of San Juan, Puerto Rico, teamed up with Simmons Group Journeys of New York to offer a new option in the cruise business: the air/sea package. It was an innovative marketing strategy to get Americans from the Northeast to go on cruises: passengers could purchase one ticket which included airfare to and from the port of embarkation, a hotel room there, and the cruise itself. This revolutionized the marketing of cruises, making them accessible from practically anywhere. Air/sea fares also increased consumer confidence with the "one-ticket-covers-it-all" approach.[41] As more customers flew to Miami to embark on cruises, Miami edged ahead of New York in the number of passenger departures in 1974.[42] Miami is still the principal U.S. passenger seaport at the time of this writing.

The cruise business opened new areas to tourism. In the late 1960s Chuck West's Alaska Cruise Line offered seasonal cruises of Alaska's Inside Passage, departing from Vancouver, British Columbia. In 1970 this operation was taken over by the venerable Holland America Line.[43]

In 1972 Ted Arison began a new venture with his vessel *Mardi Gras*, which was in fact the old *Empress of Canada*, remodeled from two-class transatlantic service to one-class cruising. His new company used the name

Carnival, and christened its fleet "The Fun Ships" to attract a younger crowd to the cruising experience. The targeted market might have been young, but the vessels themselves were old. Carnival's first ships were conversions of elderly vessels, as the first container ships were. The ships were less expensive, and the savings were passed on to consumers. This in turn made cruises more popular with young single people, and families with children.[44]

As new, purpose-built cruise ships replaced the converted old ships, a definite look emerged for modern cruise ships. Forward, cruise ship bows looked like large modern motor yachts, with a slanted stem, underwater bulb-bow, and a superstructure that slanted back from a short foredeck. Abaft the bow, the new generation cruise ships were flat-sheered and slab-sided, like a cross between a high-rise hotel and a container ship. This remains the look of the modern cruise ship.

The Love Boat

In 1977, cruise lines got a major makeover in the minds of the American public with the television series *The Love Boat*, partially filmed aboard two cruise ships of the Princess Line, *Pacific Princess* and *Island Princess*. Starring Gavin McLeod as Captain Merril Stubing, the series probably did more than any advertising campaign to give the cruise a new image in the minds of the public. The series ran a whopping ten and a half years, and is still in worldwide syndication.[45]

Food Service in the Cruise Ship Industry

With the renaissance of the cruise industry from the 1970s on, a whole industry of food service has grown up within and around it, based mostly in Miami.

The turnaround time for a typical cruise ship would be the envy of even a container ship port. Cruise ships arrive at 8:00 a.m., and offload their passengers. Immediately the complete food inventory for the next cruise, right down to new mustard and ketchup packets, is stowed and ready for departure by 4:00 p.m. the same day. Cruise ships no longer dump garbage at sea, so food waste material is offloaded during the phenomenally fast turnaround in port. The meals for the whole cruise have been planned, and are standardized from one vessel to another within each cruise line. Which food is served on which day of the cruise is also standardized within the ships of each cruise line. This degree of uniformity, combined with "just in time" food ordering, makes for a bare minimum of wastage. Unlike a hotel restaurant, a cruise line knows exactly where its clientele will be eating while under way. The entire food inventory for the cruise is loaded in Miami: for a variety of reasons, cruise ships do not reprovision in their "away ports."[46]

Many of the meals in the cruise business are handled buffet-style, reminiscent of food service in modern navies; though much more relaxed, and with more time to enjoy the meal. The institution of the midnight buffet on many cruise ships is also reminiscent of recent naval practice, that is the "Midrats" served in the modern United States Navy. For many years, cruise operators such as P&O have catered to special dietary needs, whether Kosher, Muslim, or Hindu fare is required, or a specific allergen avoided.[47] In recent years, vegetarian and vegan menu options have been offered on cruises, and there are even all-vegetarian cruises.[48]

The customer satisfaction for food service in the cruise industry is impressive, surpassing that for food service in hotels.[49] Food is one of the factors that is most important to the satisfaction of cruise passengers, and this is one area in which the industry shines in customer surveys. In the 1970s, cruise ship menu offerings were much like those of ocean liners a generation earlier: a choice of two or three entrees, with standard sides, and perhaps a choice of dessert. By the 1990s, luxury cruise lines such as Seabourn and others were offering gourmet dining up to the old ocean liner standards, while even the bargain-priced cruises offered a wide selection of dishes.[50] In more recent years, Seabourn has developed what it calls "Nouvelle Classic" cuisine, an adaptation of current trends in expensive restaurants ashore.[51] Smaller portions do not necessarily produce lower costs for the operators: "Nouvelle Classic" cuisine can produce an expenditure for the raw food (exclusive of labor and overhead) of twenty to thirty dollars, as opposed to eight to eleven dollars per passenger per day in the mass-market cruise sector.[52]

If cruise ship passengers still want to stuff themselves, they have multiple opportunities to do so. Passengers can, and sometimes do, eat one breakfast in their cabins, and an additional one in the dining room. They can eat lunch twice, on deck and in the dining room; and enjoy an eight-course dinner. Between-meal snacks, midnight buffets, and twenty-four-hour room service are also available.[53]

Recent trends in cruise ship food service have stressed variety. Some passengers want to eat sumptuously, as did their predecessors. Others are more health conscious, and may want healthy choices.

There is a degree of organizational sleight-of-hand in cruise ship food service, in those cases where food is brought to the table rather than self-served at a buffet. The illusion created will be that of personal service in an elegant restaurant, because the ordering is "multiple choice": passengers may be choosing from three soups, two salads, a pasta, seven entrees, and six desserts.

The cruise line has provided for just the number of the different choices that is statistically likely, based on the millions served from the same menu on the same cruise. As two well-informed authors put it, "If it's Italian Night on the *Ecstasy*, Carnival's management know precisely how many of the 2,400 passengers on board will order the Steak Genoa, the Veal Parmigiana, the Pollo Novello Alla Diavola, the Poached Filet of Sole, and the other three entrées, and they have baked exactly the right number of Cappuccino Pies and Amaretto Cakes."[54] This magic act is supervised by an on-board food and beverage manager, and directed by an executive chef who ensures that the recipes (often accompanied by photographs showing the prescribed presentation of each item) are followed to the letter.[55]

Cruise Ships into the Twenty-First Century

Since 2000, the economies of cruise ship operation have allowed cruises to compete for the North American family's vacation budget with family-oriented theme parks. In 1998 the Walt Disney Company, having ended its relationship with Premier Cruise Line, launched its own cruise line, Disney Cruises aka Magical Cruise Company Limited. Disney Cruises now owns its own island in the Bahamas, Castaway Cay, an exclusive port of call for the Disney ships.

Food is a major selling point for cruise lines. At the time of writing, on-line advertisements for the leading cruise ship line lead off with "Tasty food . . ." while promising "amazing destinations," "shipboard activities," and other enticements, it is the "tasty food" that leads off the advertising copy, even when the other attractions and the accompanying photo vary.

Special cruises are now offered based on dietary preference, sexual preference, religion, and every conceivable reason for a thousand or more passengers to choose to be on the same floating hotel for fourteen days. Vegetarian cruises have already been mentioned. An example is the "Holistic Holiday at Sea," presented by the Taste of Health Foundation in conjunction with Costa Cruises. On these specialty cruises, macrobiotic head chef Mark Hanna has developed a vegan menu which, in conjunction with exercise programs and on-board holistic health speakers, are designed to leave their passengers feeling healthier at the end of their cruise than at its beginning. Holistic Holiday at Sea has even produced its own cookbook, *Greens & Grains on the Deep Blue Sea*. The entrees include such choices as "Grilled Tempeh with Mustard Greens," "Millet Croquettes with Tofu Tartar Sauce," and "Sautéed Seitan with Shiitake Mushrooms."[56]

Some firms offer cruises based on sexual preference: in 2014, there were multiple cruise agencies offering cruises specifically for the gay and lesbian community. Cruises are also offered based on religious preference. Several firms offer Christian cruises (Couples Retreat, Ladies Retreat, and Christian singles cruises). A wide variety of Jewish cruises include Passover cruises, Jewish Heritage cruises, and Jewish singles cruises. Muslim Salaam cruises run to a private island in the Bahamas.

The cruise concept has been applied to new waterways. In the early twenty-first century, cruise vessels of shallow draft operate in the Inland Waterway of the eastern United States, some of their trips having a history and heritage theme, with an on-board historian/tour guide. River cruises in China, Russia, and elsewhere in Europe are increasingly popular.

Cruise ship food has a duality in the public mind. On the one hand, "tasty food" remains the key selling point in carefully researched advertisements. On the other hand, public apprehension about cruises, motivated by recent mishaps, often centers on the food as well. Recent incidents of norovirus, and more rarely ETEC (enterotoxigenic E. coli) on cruises have caused some consumer apprehension. Nonetheless, cruises remain one of the most popular vacation options for Americans generally, with the food as the premiere attraction.

Present Day Cruises:
Ten Brands, One Company

At the same time that cruises are offered in increasing profusion, the actual ownership of passenger lines is becoming more centralized. Since the 1990s, Carnival has taken over several of its former competitors. In 2014, no less than ten cruise ship brands, some with venerable names and histories, are subsidiaries of Carnival Corporation & plc. These include Cunard, Costa Cruises, Holland America Line, Princess Cruises, Aida, and P&O Cruises. P&O continues to operate its own ferries and cargo ships.

The Sailing Alternative

From 1947 to 2007, Windjammer Barefoot Cruises offered one- and two-week trips in the Caribbean and Bahamas on a six-ship fleet of sailing vessels. The company lost their flagship to Hurricane Mitch in 1998, and went bankrupt in 2007. The Maine Windjammer Association serves the owners of several traditional schooners that offer a taste of traditional sailing to their passengers, who can join the crew in hauling on halyards and other traditional tasks. The four ships of Windstar Cruises offer an imaginative compromise; graceful vessels that are both cruise ship (though with a leaner profile than the usual floating high-rise hotel) and sailing vessel. The Windstar vessels use their sails whenever possible, using a powerful modern staysail rig trimmed by electric servos from the bridge. These vessels feature pools and offer on-deck dining. Food service for around 300 passengers compares favorably with conventional cruise ships.

Sail Training

Most of the world's navies have used training on sailing vessels as part of the basic training for service at sea: it builds teamwork and cooperation while imbuing cadets with an intimate sense of the traditions of the sea. This experience has been shared with other young people through a variety of programs, offering sail training for a week or two through such programs as the Sea Scouts, Sea Education Association, and VisionQuest. Food preparation and food service in naval sail training vessels resembles what the cadets may expect in their nation's navy.

Historic vessels sometimes sail regularly with paid passengers aboard, for example the schooner *Pioneer*, which offers two- and three-hour sails in New York's Inner Harbor to the public through its operator, South Street Sea Port Museum. Barque *Elissa* in Galveston, Texas and brig *Niagara* in Erie, Pennsylvania both make seasonal sails with a mix of professional and volunteer crew. Each of these three vessels uses a traditional wood-burning iron stove, not only for reasons of tradition, but for safety as well. When the author served in *Pioneer*'s crew, stoves using liquid fuels were disallowed for the danger of combustible fumes below deck. Cooking aboard for the crew was accomplished under way or at anchor using only the wood-burning stove. An electric hot plate was available when at the dock and connected with shore power.

The author has sailed twice in the Polish Sea Scouts' sailing vessel *Zawisza Czarny*, a vessel with refrigerator and freezer spaces, and a small but well-equipped electric galley. On a transatlantic trip in 1992, the fresh-water condenser malfunctioned, water from the bilges flooded the crew compartment, and the choice of foodstuffs narrowed as the voyage went on: fortunately the cook was Andrzej "Arni" Przybek, one of the most talented, imaginative, and good-natured cooks on the Seven Seas.

Small Boats

Small boat galleys are a feature of most sailing yachts and practically all motor yachts. These are often electric, though there are also small boat galleys that use propane tanks. A popular accessory for warm-water sailboats is a charcoal grill on the taffrail; this serves for grilling steaks, fish, or other food

Figure 8.5. Eating Utensils. While some of these are reproductions, they represent the kind of equipment used by common sailors during the Age of Sail. The sailor's sheath knife has a rounded back and blunt point, so it can be used much like a fork. The coffee/tea mug is twentieth-century, and of standard Polish pattern for use at sea, without a handle for reduced breakage and easier stacking. Author's collection. Photograph by Simon Spalding.

out in the open, where the cooking smells are wafted away in the breeze. It is reminiscent of the sheet-metal *fogón* of Columbus's and Magellan's day, a metal firebox for cooking above decks.[57]

One of the most popular open-water small boats to emerge in the fourth quarter of the twentieth century is the sea kayak, usually made of fiberglass or plywood in shapes based on the traditional hide-covered small boats of Greenland, Siberia, and the Aleutian Islands. Kayakers usually eat energy bars or other snacks out of a pocket, and drink bottled water or other beverages. Larger sizes of sea kayaks have cargo compartments fore and aft of the paddler, in which equipment fits for cooking on the beach, in the tradition of Odysseus and his crew.

Conclusion

Technologies change, yet human needs and human nature remain much the same. A Mesolithic mariner in a dugout canoe would surely not know what to make of a container ship or a ballistic-missile submarine: yet he (or she) would no doubt recognize a sea kayaker as a fellow traveler: they might recognize one another's snack food. The seasick fifteenth-century pilgrim to Santiago de Compostela could surely commiserate with a queasy cruise ship passenger departing Miami. The cheering effect of coming in from a heaving deck and sea spray to a warm, cozy cabin to share hot food and drink with shipmates has come down through the ages, and will remain so long as the seas shall roll, and human beings do business on the great waters.

"SEA FEVER"

I must go down to the seas again, to the lonely sea and the sky,
And all I ask is a tall ship and a star to steer her by;
And the wheel's kick and the wind's song and the white sail's shaking,
And a grey mist on the sea's face and a grey dawn breaking.

I must go down to the seas again, for the call of the running tide
Is a wild call and a clear call that may not be denied;
And all I ask is a windy day with the white clouds flying,
And the flung spray and the blown spume, and the sea-gulls crying.

I must go down to the seas again to the vagrant gypsy life,
To the gull's way and the whale's way where the wind's like a whetted knife;
And all I ask is a merry yarn from a laughing fellow-rover,
And a quiet sleep and a sweet dream when the long trick's over.[58]

Selected Recipes

This recipe section is different from that of other books. I freely admit that I have not tried the recipes for bilge rat, seabird, and jungle juice. For these, and for making your own salt beef at home, please be safe, be legal, and exercise caution and good judgment. What follows are merely a selection of many possible foods and drinks to enjoy at sea, or at home ashore. If you are interested in reconstructing gourmet cuisine from the first-class dining rooms and Ritz-Carlton à la carte restaurants of the great liners, refer to the bibliography, where several excellent books offer just what you need to recreate the last meal aboard the doomed *Titanic*, or aboard other liners of that, and other, eras.

Foods on Ancient Aegean and Mediterranean Ships

While not a great deal is known about the recipes for food eaten at sea, the following have been found in shipwrecks:

Parched grain (probably wheat and barley)
Olive oil (sometimes flavored with oregano)
Olives (the pits spat into the bilges)
Fresh Figs
Feta cheese (a dietary staple)
Fresh fish (possibly for the crew to eat)

The Odyssey describes deer and other game hunted on islands, and roasted (probably along with other foods) on the beach. To relive the meals of these ancient mariners, one can experiment with different combinations of these ingredients, combined and served in different ways.

〰〰 Viking Havnest (*Porridge; circa 800–1200*)

2 cups barley meal
4 cups water
Pinch of salt (optional, and probably not historical)
4 tablespoons (half a stick) of unsalted butter

Stir the barley meal into the water, and continue to stir so that the water becomes cloudy. Bring to a boil over medium heat. Once boiling, simmer at low heat for about 15 minutes, stirring frequently, until the consistency the crew likes. When nearly done, add the butter, stirring in until melted. Serve in wooden bowls, and eat with wooden spoons.

If preparing while *i-viking* in a longship or other open lapstrake boat, I suggest keeping the barley meal in a linen or hempcloth bag, tied tightly, inside a wooden cask. Keep the cask away from the sides of the boat, under the fore or after deck if your boat has these, being careful to keep it dry if possible. Your butter can be kept in a ceramic or wooden jar, with a piece of leather tied over the jar's mouth as a cover. Try to keep your butter cool, under cover if possible. Cook your porridge over a fire on the beach, starting the cooking when the fire is turning to embers. Your pot can hang from an iron tripod, as found on the Oseberg ship burial. When it is time to simmer your porridge, use an s-hook to shorten the pot chain, so as to reduce heat.

Spoons have been found in Viking sites, made of wood with a short handle and a long bowl; these may well be porridge spoons. In Scotland a *spirtle* (also spelled spurtle) is often used to stir porridge; this is a round-section stick of hardwood (usually maple) about 11 inches long and ⅝ of an inch in diameter, rounded at the business end and decoratively turned or carved (usually into a thistle) at the end of the handle. Scots believe that the spirtle dates to medieval times in some form.

If there is no source of fresh water near the beach, be very careful not to waste your fresh water, using just enough for the porridge. The pot can be cleaned later with seawater. If firewood is scarce, make your fire small and put stones around it to focus the heat on your pot. When you raise the pot to simmer it, any fresh fish or small game you have caught can be roasted on sticks, over the embers of the fire.

The pinch of salt was probably not used in the historic period. Salt was difficult to come by in Scandinavia before the Hanseatic League traded it. If barley meal is not available locally, a meal blend including barley is marketed under the name "Roman meal"—Roman Meal is a brand name product, with both words capitalized); and other ground grains may be substituted.

Viking Fish Options

The best fish option is to catch fish under way, gut them, and then spit them on a stick and roast them over the porridge-pot fire on the beach. A good "iron ration" is *skreidh* (stockfish), which you may be able to find with a bit of searching. If you have the good fortune to have a neighborhood Icelandic delicatessen, see if they can supply you with *hardhfiskur*, a popular variation. If neither of these is available, you could use some form of fish (e.g., salmon) jerky as a substitute for stockfish.

Friends of Scandinavian ancestry have asked whether Vikings ate lutefisk or other lye-soaked fish on their travels, and I feel this is extremely unlikely. The preparation of lutefisk involves the use of multiple baths of fresh water (which must be carefully conserved at sea), and it can easily go wrong (producing what the Finns call *saippuakala*, spoiled lutefisk), resulting in something that could cause severe gastric distress. The effects of gastric distress in a crowded open boat in the midst of the ocean are better imagined than described; and the *matsveina* who induced this unhappy condition in his shipmates is sure to be an unpopular fellow for the rest of the voyage.

Stockfish, which is what lutefisk begins with before it is soaked in water and lye, is a good long-keeping food. Bits of it can be gnawed cold like jerky; and being air-dried it requires no desalination. Little chunks of stockfish can be soaked in water for a few minutes; then added to the barley porridge recipe, early on when the porridge is brought to a boil.

Fish à la Boucaine, Taino Barbacoa

This is the cooking technique of the Taino Indians encountered by Columbus and other explorers in the Caribbean, called "barbacoa," which became "barbeque." The same technique is shown in the watercolors of John White painted at the Roanoke settlement in the 1580s. The wooden structure was called "boucaine" in some parts of the Caribbean, and "boucainiers/buccaneers" were Europeans who cooked on a boucaine; that is, had "gone native" to some degree.

Around a small fire, take four straight sticks, two to three feet long, with points at one end and forks at the other; plant them in a square, two feet to a side. Lay two stout straight sticks in the forks, and then lay five or six straight sticks over these. Lay your freshly caught fish over these sticks, turning from time to time. Additional fish can be propped up on sticks on the sides of the fire. Serve when thoroughly cooked.

〰〰 Ship's Biscuit/Biscotto/Bizcocho (all periods)

4 cups whole wheat flour
Approximately 1 cup of water
1 teaspoon salt (optional)

Add very small amounts of water at a time, kneading vigorously so as to activate the glutens in the flour. The salt is optional: your biscuits will keep longer if you leave it out. The biscuit dough will form a very resilient mass, and you may find it expedient to thwack it with a British- or French-style (solid) rolling pin as you knead in the water. Fold and beat the dough repeatedly. Roll the dough into a layer about half an inch thick, then cut out squares, octagons, or circles of about two inches diameter, and prick them with a fork. Bake on an ungreased pan at low heat for at least an hour.

My best batch of ship's biscuits were baked in a gas oven for about 3 hours, with the flame turned down just as low as possible without actually going out. (Check on the flame from time to time, to make sure it has not gone out.) I have made these with both white and whole-wheat flour, and found the whole-wheat ones much more palatable. Prior to about 1800, the flour probably resembled whole-wheat flour rather than white flour in any case.

Keep in a dry place, either in tied linen bags (Medieval Aragonese), wooden casks (Age of Sail 1400–1900), or sealed boxes (Dutch and American Navy after about 1810)—they will keep longer that way). After many months or even years, the biscuits may show signs of infestation: tapping them on the table should evict some of the "bargemen." Small pieces may be broken off the edges and sucked to relieve hunger. The hard centers, known colloquially as "Purser's Nuts" may be found useful as paperweights or projectiles, or sucked to give nourishment during a working watch. Bits that have broken off, left in the bottom of the bag or cask, may be boiled with water into *mazamorra*, a thin gruel that was familiar to Spanish sailors circa 1600. Anything else that is edible may be added, and is sure to improve the flavor and nutritious properties of *mazzamora*.

≈≈ Salsa Dromon (circa 1290)

2 cups dry fava beans (also known as broad beans or horse beans)
2 cups dry chickpeas
3 pints fresh water
One yellow or white onion, cut into roughly ¾-inch squares
Two-to-four cloves garlic, minced
2 tablespoon olive oil
½ teaspoon salt, or more to taste
"Spice": a pinch of cumin, powdered ginger, or any other spice available in thirteenth-century Europe

Soak the fava beans and chickpeas overnight: pour off water and rinse before cooking. In a pot, heat the olive oil, and add the garlic and the "spice," then the onion. After these have been browned, add the fava beans, chickpeas, the water, and the salt. Bring to a boil; then simmer at low heat for 20 minutes or so, stirring frequently. Add additional water if required. Serve with ship's biscuit, and watered wine.

Meat was sometimes added to the salsa, in the proportion of ten grams (about one-third of an ounce) per man. So for each person served, add a third of an ounce of salt meat (e.g., corned beef or salt pork) per person served, cut into small chunks, and add with the beans and chickpeas. This is a very small amount of meat, but it will contribute to the flavor of the dish. "Dromon" was a medieval Mediterranean term for a rowed galley.

≈≈ Menestra à la Galeon Real (circa 1580–1630)

2 cups dry fava beans and/or dry chickpeas
2 cups rice
3 pints fresh water
2-to-4 cloves garlic, minced
2 tablespoon olive oil
1 tablespoon wine vinegar
½ teaspoon salt, or more to taste</ingred>

Soak the legumes overnight: pour off water and rinse before cooking. In a pot, heat olive oil; add the garlic and lightly brown it. Add the legumes, the rice, the water, and the salt. Bring to a boil; then add vinegar and simmer at low heat for 20 minutes or until the rice is done. Serve in wooden bowls.

〜〜 *Burgoo (Royal Navy Porridge)*

2 cups steel-cut oats
4 cups water
1 teaspoon salt
4 tablespoons (half a stick) of unsalted butter
1 tablespoon salt
1 tablespoon sugar or honey (optional)

Add the oats to the water, stirring frequently with a wooden spoon or spirtle. Bring to a boil over medium heat. Once boiling, simmer at low heat for about 15 minutes, stirring frequently, until the consistency the crew likes. When nearly done, add the salt, butter, and sweetening (optional) stirring in until melted. This can be served with a little milk or cream, if desired.

Salt Beef (all periods)

Salt beef may be made at home, but the process is fairly lengthy and is best attempted by cooks familiar with salting and preserving meats. For complete information on how to make salt beef, refer to *Feeding Nelson's Navy* by Janet Macdonald (2006). For easier, tastier, and safer experiments, obtain unsliced pastrami from your local butcher or deli; or use the tinned corned beef that is popular on St. Patrick's Day in North America. The latter will actually resemble the tinned "bully beef" of the nineteenth century to the present, and is a reasonable substitute for salt beef cured in the cask.

Salt Pork

Pork may be preserved like salt beef; but this author advises caution. Dry salt pork, similar to that issued to soldiers in the nineteenth century, is popular in the southeastern United States. If unavailable at a local grocery, ask at Soul Food or Southern-style restaurants if they know of a local supplier. Dry salt pork, though to the uninitiated somewhat resembling salty cardboard, is a good and reasonably safe ingredient for recipes calling for salt pork.

Salt Cod/Bacalhao

Salt Cod is difficult but not impossible to find. If your local fish market does not supply it, check with a local Jamaican or West Indian restaurant that offers "Cullaloo." Salt cod should be soaked in fresh water for about 12 hours before cooking; otherwise it will be unpleasantly salty. Stockfish can be soaked for a shorter time to soften it.

The salt cod can be gently heated in a pan, with a little butter or oil. There is no need to salt it: even after soaking, it is more than salty enough. It can be cut into bite-size pieces, and served with any of these three versions of the traditional sauce:

≈≈ *Fish Sauce à la Taillevent* (*fourteenth-century French*)

Melt unsalted butter, add a dash of powdered ginger and a dash of powdered cloves; then add tiny amounts of mustard powder to taste. Dip chunks of the cod in this sauce.

≈≈ *Fish Sauce à la John Smith* (*sixteenth- to early seventeenth-century English*)

Into half a cup of wine vinegar, add half a teaspoon each of sugar and mustard powder. Add more mustard powder if you like.

≈≈ *Fish Sauce à la Koninklijke Marine* (*eighteenth- to early nineteenth-century Dutch*)

Melt unsalted butter, add mustard powder to taste. Grate nutmeg into the sauce to taste. Feel free to experiment with the sauce, for example, adding a bit of vinegar and sugar to a butter-based sauce, or adding your favorite spices.

Lobscouse

The origins of this dish are still contested: it is popular ashore, and known by this name, throughout Scandinavia; it is also very popular in Liverpool. While ashore, it is made with potatoes. At sea, it is made with bits of ship's biscuit. If, as some believe, it dates back to medieval times, one can approximate a medieval version by substituting diced rutabaga (American and Canadian) or swede (British) for the potatoes.

> 2 pounds salt beef (or corned beef)
> 3 pounds potatoes, cut into 1-inch squares
> 1 onion, chopped into 1-inch squares
> 2 tablespoons butter, olive oil, or slush
> Water

If using traditional salt beef, soak overnight to desalinate. Cut the meat into slices about half an inch thick. Brown the meat in the butter or other cooking fat, grinding black pepper over it. Add the onions and brown them with the meat. Add the potatoes and enough water to just cover the other ingredients. Bring to a boil, stirring occasionally. Cover and cook at low heat for about an hour, stirring occasionally. For more interesting lobscouse and better nutrition, add a chopped carrot and/or parsnip. For a deepwater version, substitute chunks of ship's biscuit, soaked for a couple hours, for the potatoes.

≈≈ *Sea Pie*

This is something like a baked lobscouse. Some Swedish and Finnish versions of "lobscouse" are baked in layers like this recipe for Sea Pie, while some Danish versions of lobscouse are more like the "stew" lobscouse above.

> 2 pounds salt beef (or corned beef), cut into thin slices
> 3 pounds potatoes, cut into thin slices
> 1 onion, chopped into 1-inch squares
> 2 tablespoons butter, olive oil, or slush

In a Dutch oven, flat-bottomed pot, or casserole dish, lay a layer of meat slices on the well-greased bottom. Lay a layer of potatoes and onions over this. Then continue to lay alternating layers of meat and potato/onion. The top layer should be potatoes. Grind a little black pepper over each layer. Add just enough water to come almost up to the top layer, and bake at about 350 degrees for about an hour, or until it seems done.

At sea, it would be normal to substitute bits of ship's biscuit for potatoes. Put them into a bag and hit them with a hammer until they are broken up into quite small fragments, before assembling your Sea Pie.

〰 Crackerhash

2 pounds ship's biscuit, smashed into small bits and soaked for an hour or two in fresh water
1 pound salt beef, salt pork, or any other meat, minced into small bits
1 onion, minced small
pepper and/or other seasoning to taste

Begin by smashing up ship's biscuit with a hammer in a cloth bag. On a hot well-greased griddle or in a well-greased frying pan, brown the onions; then add the beef and/or pork, with a little pepper and/or seasonings. Cook these for a while; then add the ship's biscuit fragments with a cup of water. Continue to cook at high heat until the water is mostly gone; then cook for a little while at low heat, stirring and scraping the bottom regularly. Serve hot from the pan or griddle.

〰 Plain Duff

This is what the crew of the *Akbar* was probably getting in lieu of bread, in 1877. It is basically dough; flour, suet, and water made into a dough, and then boiled in a cloth bag.

2 pounds white or whole wheat flour
1 pound suet or grated pork fat
1 pint water

Combine ingredients in a mixing bowl, mixing thoroughly. Add water if required. Then wrap up the resulting dough into a double cheesecloth bag, tie off the end, and boil in a pot of boiling water for about 3 hours, or until it seems done. This can be served with molasses dribbled over the top.

≈≈ *Plumb Duff*

This is a little more special, for the cabin or for making amends to the forecastle crowd.

    2 pounds white or whole-wheat flour
    1 pound suet or grated pork fat
    ½ quart water
    1 cup raisins, sultanas (golden raisins), and or dried currants
    1 tablespoon molasses
    ½ cup sugar

Boil in a cloth bag like the previous version. Serve topped with applesauce or a hard sauce.

Variations

≈≈ *Dandyfunk*

Add half a teaspoon of powdered ginger, double the molasses, and bake in a pan instead of boiling in a bag.

≈≈ *Spotted Dog (Spotted Dick in English pubs in the 1960s)*

Substitute prunes for the raisins. Boil or bake.

≈≈ *Boiled Baby, Drowned Baby*

Chill the water, double the molasses, and leave out the raisins. Serve with a custard sauce.

≈≈ *Bilge Rat à la Bougainville*

Of course, this is a "desperation recipe," something you are only going to cook if you and your shipmates are in danger of starving to death. Rats are actually rather nutritious; they sold for rather high prices in Paris during the Franco-Prussian War. If cooked and eaten soon after the rat is killed, it is actually slightly antiscorbutic. The Vitamin C breaks down rather quickly after the animal dies, however. Members of Louis-Antoine de Bougainville's

1767–1768 expedition to the South Pacific ate rat when they were short of provisions. For more information about how to prepare rat for the discerning palate, please consult Mrs. *Cook's Book of Recipes for Mariners in Distant Seas: Boiled Jellyfish, Stewed Albatross, and Other Treats for Sailors* by John Dunmore (2006).

〰 Stewed Seabird

Albatross, curlews, petrels, and other seabirds may be eaten in extremis, or even as a staple. Scott's expedition to Antarctica in 1901 was trapped in the ice, and spent a great deal of time on the edge of the Ross Ice Shelf. While there, his men supplemented their stores with penguin; which while an unpleasant repast, saved them from a number of dietary deficiencies that afflicted other polar explorers. For guidance on preparing seabirds, please refer to Mrs. *Cook's Book of Recipes for Mariners in Distant Seas: Boiled Jellyfish, Stewed Albatross, and Other Treats for Sailors* by John Dunmore (2006).

〰 Collops à la Britannia 1842

Dickens writes sparingly of the food aboard the first Cunard transatlantic liner, but he does mention a plate of hot collops. This is a Scottish version of the French *escalopes*, like Italian *scaloppini*.

> 4 slices of veal, or of chicken breast cut thin across the grain
> 6 tablespoons (¾ stick) butter
> lemon peel, zested, grated, or dried
> ¼ cup white wine
> ¼ cup chicken stock
> ⅛ cup cream
> 1 egg yolk
> Ground mace
> Salt and pepper to taste
> A little seasoned flour

Beat the meat slices with a wooden mallet, then roll them in the flour. In a frying pan, melt the butter, and brown the collops in the butter on both sides. Pour the wine and chicken stock over the collops, and add the lemon rind and a pinch of mace. Simmer at low heat for 15–20 minutes. Set the collops aside on a warm platter. Beat the egg yolk with the cream, then add the pan juices from the collops. Pour the warm sauce over the collops, and serve to a famous English novelist of your choice.

〜〜 Pork & Beans à la USS Hartford (1864)

This is what the crew of David Farragut's flagship the *Hartford* ate on Monday, Wednesday, and Saturday in the months leading up to the Battle of Mobile Bay. There is no telling how close this recipe is to what was served on the *Hartford*, but it is bound to be similar. "Damn the torpedoes: Full speed ahead!"

    2 cups dried navy beans or any other sort of dried bean
    2 pounds salt pork, cut into 1-inch squares
    1 peeled onion, cut into ½-inch squares
    2 quarts water
    Salt and pepper (optional)
    2 tablespoons molasses

Soak the beans overnight: pour off water and rinse before cooking. In a pot, heat the water, and add the pork. Bring to a boil, then add the beans and the onions. Bring to a boil again, and then reduce heat and simmer, covered, for about 4 hours, or until done. The pepper adds to the flavor of the dish, but the salt will probably not be needed if Southern-style salt pork is used. Add the molasses after the beans have cooked for about 3 hours.

〜〜 Ragout of Beef, Potatoes, and Pickles à la White Star Line Third Class (1912)

This is the entrée for Sunday Tea (supper) in the White Star Line's third-class specimen bill of fare, and represents the kind of hearty fare offered in that class. White Star really did improve the service in third class, anticipating the "tourist class" of the interwar years. They offered Kosher food in third class on request before World War I, and featured plenty of items that were familiar to Irish, German, and Scandinavian passengers.

    2 tablespoons butter
    2 cloves garlic, minced
    2 onions, minced
    2 carrots, sliced
    1 teaspoon rosemary
    1 teaspoon thyme
    ¼ teaspoon ground nutmeg
    2 pounds stewing or "chuck" beef
    1 cup beef stock

2 cups beef stock
2 cups fresh or frozen peas
1 tablespoon wine vinegar
Salt and black pepper to taste
Pickled red cabbage

In a deep pot, heat the butter, and brown the onions, carrots, garlic, and spices for about 5 minutes. Add the beef, and brown it with the vegetables. Cut the potatoes quite small, and add these, along with the beef stock. Add salt and pepper to taste. Bring to a boil, then cover and simmer on low heat for 90 minutes to 2 hours. Stir in peas and vinegar, cook for 10 minutes or so, until peas are cooked. Serve with red cabbage on the side.

〜〜 *Mulligatawny (nineteenth-century British steamers)*

This was a favorite aboard the ships of the P&O and British India Steamship Companies, carrying Britons to India and Australia, and back home (even though their tickets were *not* stamped "P.O.S.H."). It is an exotic yet mild soup, a gentle introduction to the cuisine of the Indian subcontinent. This is a dish that was already popular in Britain itself by the second half of the nineteenth century.

3 tablespoons olive oil
1 onion, minced
3 cloves of garlic, minced
8 ounces diced tomatoes
¼ teaspoon red pepper
1 tablespoon tomato paste
½ cup lentils
5 cups chicken stock
½ teaspoon ground cloves
1 teaspoon curry powder
⅓ cup raisins
1 cup coconut milk
Grated zest and juice of one lime
Salt and pepper

Fry the garlic and onion in the olive oil in the bottom of the pot. When browned, add the lentils, chicken stock, pepper, tomato paste, raisins, diced tomatoes, the red pepper, and curry powder. Stir all these together, bring to a boil, then cover and simmer for an hour.

Remove half the soup, and puree it in a blender or food processor; then return it to the pot. Add the coconut milk, lime juice, and zest; reheat briefly, then serve in bowls with a lime segment to squeeze into the soup.

≋ Curry and Rice: Madras (nineteenth- and twentieth-century British steamers and liners)

"Curry and rice" appears on the menus of British steamers very early. William Thackeray had curry and rice aboard *Iberia* while steaming between Jaffa and Alexandria on October 12, 1844. It appeared again on the steamship S.S. *German* (Union Steam Ship company) in 1881, and on the luncheon menu of the *Laconia* while cruising the Caribbean in 1929. Curries were usually served at luncheon. After British travelers became familiar with curries on steamships, Indian curries became a staple of British cuisine.

    4 tablespoons olive oil
    3 cloves garlic
    3 onions, peeled and minced
    ¼ teaspoon ground ginger, or four thin slices fresh ginger root
    2 teaspoon cumin
    ¼ teaspoon ground cloves
    1-1/2 teaspoons crushed red pepper (less if a mild curry is desired)
    1 teaspoon paprika
    1 teaspoon turmeric
    1 teaspoon ground coriander
    ¼ teaspoon cinnamon
    2 pounds lamb or mutton cut into ½-inch cubes
    1 cup diced tomatoes
    2 cups coconut milk
    2 cups water
    Salt

Heat the olive oil in a large deep pan, and brown the garlic and onion in the oil. Add the ginger and the spices and cook these together for a minute or two, constantly stirring. Add the lamb, browning it in the spices. Add the coconut milk, the tomatoes, and the water. Bring to a boil, then reduce heat and simmer for 45 minutes to an hour. Add salt (or not) to taste. Serve over plain white rice, with mango chutney.

Drinks

〰 *John Smith's Drink for Sick Men (1627)*

In a pint of boiling water, add a stick of cinnamon, five thin slices of fresh ginger. Continue to boil for about 5 minutes, then remove from heat and add a teaspoon of sugar. Serve to sick crewman. The ginger is antiscorbutic, and will also ease a sore throat.

〰 *Grog*

À la Vernon 1740 ("three water"): Mix 1 part dark rum with 3 parts water.

À la Nelson 1805: Mix 1 part dark rum with 4 parts water, with $1/_2$ teaspoon of sugar and 1 teaspoon of lime or lemon juice per serving.

"P.O.S.H.": An elegant way to drink your citrus and quinine, with dark rum. Mix a glass of Tonic Water with dark rum to taste, and a squeezed lime quarter. Serve over ice.

〰 *"Kai" or Royal Navy Cocoa*

This is a staple of the British Navy, traditionally served at Four Bells in the night and middle watches (10:00 p.m. and 2:00 a.m.). In the German Navy, coffee is served at these times. In the United States Navy, it is customary to keep a coffee pot going in the galley, the bridge, and other locations where the crew stands watch at night.

Baker's Chocolate
Water
Milk
Sugar

Make this into a paste, mixing the cocoa with boiling water to make a thick paste. Add half a pint of boiling water and simmer for 30 minutes. Add milk and sugar, and serve hot.

Some say that arrowroot or custard powder improves this drink, as well as possibly a spritz from a steam drain, and, if available, a splash of dark rum. A Dutch sailor suggested that condensed milk, especially the "Friesian Flag" brand, goes very well with cocoa or coffee at sea.

≋ Jungle Juice

This homemade high-strength alcohol was made by sailors, marines, and soldiers in the World War II island campaigns of the Pacific, which probably accounts for its name. This is not to be confused with the potluck punchbowl concoctions of "Everclear," fruit juice, and other ingredients popular with college students in peacetime. For more information on this drink, refer to *Military High Life: Elegant Food Histories and Recipes* by Agostino von Hassell, Herm Dillon, and Leslie Jean-Bart (2006).

Notes

Chapter 1

1. E. G. Bowen, *Britain and the Western Seaways* (London: Thames and Hudson, 1972), 23.

2. Ibid., 24–25.

3. Ibid., 33, 35.

4. Ibid., 33.

5. Paul Johnstone, *The Sea-craft of Prehistory*, 2nd ed. (London: Routledge & Kegan Paul, 1988), 45–51.

6. Bjorn Landstrom, *The Ship: An Illustrated History* (New York: Doubleday, 1961), 52–55; Johnstone, *The Sea-craft of Prehistory*, 115.

7. Landstrom, *The Ship*, 53.

8. G. J. Marcus, *The Conquest of the North Atlantic* (New York: Oxford University Press, 1981), 24–32; Bowen *Britain and the Western Seaways*, 43–60.

9. Johnstone, *The Sea-craft of Prehistory*, 128.

10. Landstrom, *The Ship*, 14–16.

11. Ibid., 14–15.

12. Johnstone, *The Sea-craft of Prehistory*, 71–72.

13. Landstrom, *The Ship*, 26.

14. Ibid., 26–27.

15. Homer, *The Odyssey*, Book X, http://classics.mit.edu/Homer/odyssey.html.

16. Landstrom, *The Ship*, 30–33.

17. George F. Bass, ed., *Beneath the Seven Seas: Adventures with the Institute of Nautical Archaeology* (London: Thames & Hudson, 2005), 48–55.

18. Cemal Pulak, "Discovering a Royal Ship from the Age of King Tut: Uluburun, Turkey," in Bass, *Beneath the Seven Seas*, 34–47.

19. Pulak, "Discovering a Royal Ship," in Bass, 34–47.

20. Elizabeth Greene, "An Archaic Ship Finally Reaches Port: Pabuç Burnu, Turkey," in Bass, 59–63.

21. Wikipedia article, "Ma'agan Michael Ship," http://en.wikipedia.org/wiki/Ma%27 agan_Michael_Ship.

22. Charles Q. Choi, "Ingredients for Salad Dressing Found in 2,400-Year-Old Shipwreck," November 8, 2007, http://www.livescience.com/2024-ingredients-salad -dressing-2-400-year-shipwreck.

23. Susan Womer Katsev, "Resurrecting an Ancient Greek Ship: Kyrenia, Cyprus," in Bass, 72–79.

24. J. P. Joncheray, *L'Epave "C" de la Chretienne* (Frejus, 1975), 93–94 and figures 7, 9, 10 in George F. Bass and Frederick H. van Doorninck Jr., *Yassi Ada*, Volume I (College Station: Texas A & M University Press, 1982), 95.

25. David Abulafia, *The Great Sea: A Human History of the Mediterranean* (New York: Oxford University Press, 2011), 203.

26. Landstrom, *The Ship*, 48–51.

27. Mark Lallanilla, "Ancient Roman May Hold 2,000-Year-Old Food," August 12, 2013, http://livescience.com/38814-ancient-roman-shipwreck.html.

28. Bass and van Doorninck, Jr., *Yassi Ada*, 313–14.

29. Lionel Casson, *Ships and Seamanship in the Ancient World*, 2nd ed. (Baltimore: Johns Hopkins University Press, 1995), 302–4.

30. Bass and van Doorninck, Jr., *Yassi Ada*, 87–110.

31. Ibid., 315.

32. Marcus, *The Conquest of the North Atlantic* (New York: Oxford University Press, 1981), 44.

33. Landstrom, *The Ship*, 56.

34. Ibid., 58–59; Bertil Almgren et al., *The Viking* (Gothenberg, Sweden: Tre Tryckare, Cagner & Co., 1966), 181.

35. Landstrom, *The Ship*, 60–62.

36. Ibid., 57.

37. Louise Kaempe Henriksen, "Journeyman Cook," March 12, 2007, updated February 12, 2011, http://www.vikingesskibsmuseet.dk/en/the-sea-stallion-past-and -present/the-ships-crew/crewmembers-in-the-viking-age/matsveina/#.UypKWyjDPdk.

38. Henricksen, "Journeyman Cook."

39. Einar Haugen, trans., *Voyages to Vinland: The First American Saga* (New York: Alfred A. Knoff, 1942), 8–9, http://www.archive.org/stream/voyagestovinland 013593mbp/voyagestovinland013593mbp_djvu.txt.

40. Henricksen, "Journeyman Cook."

41. Anton Engbert, Curator Viking Ship Museum Roskilde, e-mail correspondence, March 10, 2014.

42. Casson, *Ships and Seamanship in the Ancient World*, 175–82.

43. Landstrom, *The Ship*, 80–81.

44. Johnstone, *The Sea-craft of Prehistory*, 200–201.

45. Thomas Gladwin, *East Is a Big Bird: Navigation & Logic on Puluwat Atoll* (Cambridge: Harvard University Press), 49–51.

46. Gladwin, *East Is a Big Bird*, 41.

47. Johnstone, *The Sea-craft of Prehistory*, 205.

48. Ibid., 216.

49. Lawrence V. Mott, *Sea Power in the Medieval Mediterranean: The Catalan-Aragonese Fleet in The War of the Sicilian Vespers* (Gainesville: University Press of Florida, 2003), 186–96.

50. Lawrence V. Mott, "Feeding Neptune: Food Supply and Nutrition in the Catalan-Aragonese Fleet" (paper presented at the Forty-Third International Congress on Medieval Studies), 2008.

51. Mott, *Sea Power in the Medieval Mediterranean*, 217.

52. Ibid., 222.

53. Ibid., 220; Mott, "Feeding Neptune," 7.

54. Mott, "Feeding Neptune," 6.

55. Ibid., 5.

56. Ibid., 2; Mott, *Sea Power in the Medieval Mediterranean*, 216–17.

57. Ken Albala, personal communication, May 5, 2014.

58. Mott, "Feeding Neptune," 7.

59. Mott, *Sea Power in the Medieval Mediterranean*, 218–19.

60. Susan Rose, *Medieval Naval Warfare* (New York: Routledge, 2002), 106.

61. Landstrom, *The Ship*, 69–93.

62. Detlev Ellmers, "The Hanseatic Cog of Bremen AD 1380," eutsches Schiffahrtsmuseum, Bremen, http://www.raco.cat/index.php/Drassana/article/viewFile/106096/132585; Landstrom, *The Ship*, 70–73.

63. Marcus, *The Conquest of the North Atlantic*, 132–43.

64. Ibid., 132.

65. Rose, *Medieval Naval Warfare*, 14–15.

66. Ibid., 16.

67. Ibid., 20.

68. Ibid., 18.

69. Ibid., 20.

70. Gavin Menzies, *1421: The Year China Discovered America*, 3rd ed. (New York: Perennial: 2004), 96–97; Louise Levanthes, *When China Ruled the Seas: The Treasure Fleet of the Dragon Throne, 1405–1433*, 2nd ed. (New York: Oxford University Press, 1996), 96–97.

71. Abulafia, *The Great Sea*, 423–26.

72. Ibid.

73. Mark Kurlansky, *Salt: A World History*, 2nd ed. (London: Penguin Books, 2003), 131.

74. Ibid., 140–42.

75. Tobias Gentleman, "England's Way to Win Wealth and to Employ Ships" (London 1614), in E. Arber, R.C. Beasley, and T. Sccombe, *Voyages and Travels Mainly During the 16th and 17th Centuries* (1903), 267, in Wikipedia, "Herring Buss," http://en.wikipedia.org/wiki/Herring_buss.

76. Ibid.

77. Kurlansky, *Salt*, 143.

78. Ibid., 112–115.

79. Daniel J. Boorstin, *The Discovers: A History of Man's Search to Know His World and Himself* (New York: Vintage Books, 1983), 119.

80. William Michael Rossetti, *The Stacions of Rome . . . :And the Pilgrims Sea-voyage . . . with Clene Maydenhood . . . A Supplement to "Political, Religious, and Love Poems,"* and *"Hali Meidenhad,"* editor Frederick James Furnivall (Early English Text Society, 1867).

Chapter 2

1. J. H. Parry, *The Age of Reconnaissance: Discovery, Exploration and Settlement 1450 to 1650*, 2nd ed. (London: University of California Press, 1981), 72; Carla Rahn Phillips, *Six Galleons for the King of Spain: Imperial Defense in the Early Seventeenth Century* (Baltimore: Johns Hopkins University Press, 1986), 165.

2. Parry, *The Age of Reconnaissance*, 70–71.

3. Ibid., 72.

4. Samuel Eliot Morison, *The European Discovery of America: The Northern Voyages A.D. 500–1600* (New York: Oxford University Press, 1971), 131.

5. Ibid., 72.

6. Ibid.

7. Christopher Columbus, *The Log of Christopher Columbus: His Own Account of the Voyage That Changed the World*, trans. by Robert H. Fuson (Camden, ME: International Marine Publishing Company, 1987), 61.

8. Columbus, *The Log of Christopher Columbus*, 61.

9. Parry, *The Age of Reconnaissance*, 72.

10. Columbus, *The Log of Christopher Columbus*, 63.

11. Ibid., 181.

12. Ibid., 175.

13. Reay Tannahill, *Food in History*, 2nd ed. (New York: Stein and Day, 1974), 265–66.

14. Parry, *The Age of Reconnaissance*, 72.

15. Jacob Nagle, *The Nagle Journal: A Diary of the Life of Jacob Nagle, Sailor, from the Year 1775 to 1841*, ed. by John C. Dann (New York: Weidenfeld and Nicolson, 1988), 317.

16. Parry, *The Age of Reconnaissance*, 284.

17. Ibid., 285.

18. Phillips, *Six Galleons for the King of Spain*, 165.

19. Columbus, *The Log of Christopher Columbus*, 185.

20. Parry, *The Age of Reconnaissance*, 73.

21. Peter Kirsch, *The Galleon: The Great Ships of the Armada Era* (London: Conway Maritime Press, 1990), 80.

22. Kirsch, *The Galleon*, 81.

23. Ibid., 79–84.

24. Ibid., 81.

25. Ernle Bradford, *The Story of the Mary Rose* (London: W.W. Norton and Company, 1982), 9–24.

26. Ann Stirland, "The Men of the *Mary Rose*," in Cheryl Fury, *The Social History of English Seamen, 1485–1649* (Woodbridge, Suffolk, UK: Boydell Press, 2013), 56–57, http://books.google.com/books?id=Zt5_no6uC8IC&pg=PA57&lpg=PA57&dq=Mary+Rose+malnutrition+scurvy&source=bl&ots=hxygTh2jtz&sig=_jKQYwOgxv8_ciZJkHvZl2T28QI&hl=en&sa=X&ei=DZsrU5PXCei90AHLhIHwDw&ved=0CDIQ6AEwAg#v=onepage&q=Mary%20Rose%20malnutrition%20scurvy&f=false.

27. *Mary Rose* Trust, "Life on Board—Food and Drink," http://www.maryrose.org/discover-our-collection/her-crew/life-on-board/#Food and Drink-link.

28. *Mary Rose* Trust, "Discover the Mary Rose—Her Crew—The Men of the Mary Rose," http://www.maryrose.org/discover-our-collection/her-crew/.

29. Ibid.

30. Kit Mayers, *North-East Passage to Muscovy: Stephen Borough and the First Tudor Explorations* (Gloucestershire, UK: Sutton, 2005), 36–37.

31. Morison, *The European Discovery of America*, 130.

32. Mayers, *North-East Passage to Muscovy*, 37.

33. Morison, *The European Discovery of America*, 137.

34. Kirsch, *The Galleon*, 74.

35. Corbett, "Papers Relating to the Navy During the Spanish War," 259–260, in Kirsch, *The Galleon*, 77.

36. Ibid., 79.

37. Garrett Mattingly, *The Armada* (Boston: Houghton Mifflin, 1959), 95–109.

38. Winston Graham, *The Spanish Armadas* (London: Collins, 1972), 73.

39. Neville Williams, *The Sea Dogs: Privateers, Plunder & Piracy in the Elizabethan Age* (London: Weidenfeld and Nicolson, 1975), 173.

40. Oppenheim, *A History of the Administration of the Royal Navy*, 384, in Kirsch, *The Galleon*, 75.

41. Ibid., 74.

42. David Howarth, *The Voyage of the Armada: The Spanish Story*, 2nd ed. (New York: Penguin Books, 1981), 132–33.

43. Kirsch, *The Galleon*, 75.

44. Ibid., 74.

45. Email correspondence, Fred Hocker, Chief Curator, Vasa Museum, Stockholm, Sweden, March 14, 2014.

46. Admiralty Library MS 9 in Kirsch, *The Galleon*, 173.

47. Phillips, *Six Galleons for the King of Spain*, 95.

48. Ibid., 97.

49. Ibid., 99.

50. Ibid., 100–1.

51. Ibid., 164.

52. Ibid., 100–1.

53. Ibid., 163.

54. Ibid., 164.

55. Ibid., 167, 169.

56. Ibid., 167.

57. Ibid.

58. Ibid.

59. Ibid.

60. Ibid., 165.

61. Philip Amadas and Arthur Barlowe, *The First Voyage Made to the Coasts of America, with two barks, where in were Captaines M. Philip Amadas and M. Arthur Barlowe, who discovered part of the Countrey now called Virginia, Anno 1584*, 298, in Virtual Jamestown Project, http://etext.lib.virginia.edu/etcbin/jamestown-browse?id=J1014.

62. Richard Grenville, *The Voiage Made by Sir Richard Greenville, for Sir Walter Ralegh, to Virginia, in the yeere 1585, Part 1*, 311, in Virtual Jamestown Project, http://etext.lib.virginia.edu/etcbin/jamestown-browse?id=J1015.

63. John White, *The Fourth Voyage Made to Virginia with Three Ships, in the Yere 1587*, 387, in Virtual Jamestown Project, http://etext.lib.virginia.edu/etcbin/jamestown-browse?id=J1018.

64. White, *The Fourth Voyage Made to Virginia*, 388.

65. Ibid.

66. Ibid.

67. John White, *The Fift Voyage of M. John White into the West Indies and Parts of America Called Virginia, in the yeere 1590*, 415, in Virtual Jamestown Project, http://etext.lib.virginia.edu/etcbin/jamestown-browse?id=J1019.

68. White, *The Fift Voyage of M. John White*, 418.

69. Grenville, *The Voiage Made to Virginia with Three Ships*, 312.

70. Ibid., 313.

71. Grenville, *The Voiage Made to Virginia with Three Ships*, 313.

72. Ibid.

73. Ibid., 314.

74. White, *The Fourth Voyage Made to Virginia*, 390.

75. Grenville, *The Voiage Made to Virginia with Three Ships*, 314.

76. White, *The Fourth Voyage Made to Virginia*, 387.

77. White, *The Fift Voyage of M. John White*, 412.

78. Paul Hulton, *America 1585: The Complete Drawings of John White* (Chapel Hill: University of North Carolina Press, British Museum Publications, 1984), 47–50.

79. Amadas and Barlowe, *The First Voyage Made to the Coasts of America*, 298.

80. White, *The Fourth Voyage Made to Virginia*, 387.

81. Ibid., 387.

82. Ibid., 389.

83. Ibid., 397.

84. White, *The Fift Voyage of M. John White*, 422.

85. White, *The Fourth Voyage Made to Virginia*, 400.

86. Ibid., 401.

87. John Smith, *A Sea Grammar: With the Plaine Exposition of Smiths Accidence for Young Sea-Men* (Sabin Americana Print Editions, Gale Digital Collections) 35.

88. Smith, *A Sea Grammar*, 36.

89. Ibid.

90. Ibid., 38.

91. Ibid., 36.

92. Ibid.

93. Ibid., 38.

94. Ibid.

95. Ibid.

96. Ibid., 38–39.

97. Ibid., 61.

98. Ibid., 84–85.

99. Ibid., 85.

Chapter 3

1. Bjorn Landstrom, *The Ship: An Illustrated History* (New York: Doubleday, 1961), 79, 100–101; J. H. Parry, *The Age of Reconnaissance: Discovery, Exploration, and Settlement 1450 to 1650*, 2nd ed. (London: University of California Press, 1981), 115–17.

2. Parry, *The Age of Reconnaissance*, 121.

3. Landstrom, *The Ship*, 78–79.

4. Carlo M. Cipolla, *Guns, Sails, and Empires: Technological Innovation and Early Phases of European Expansion, 1400–1700* (New York: Minerva Press, 1965), 81–82.

5. Cipolla, *Guns, Sails, and Empires*, 99, 113, 115; Parry, *The Age of Reconnaissance*, 119–20.

6. Ibid., 119–20.

7. Ibid., 114–23.

8. Nathan Miller, *The U.S. Navy: An Illustrated History* (New York: American Heritage; Annapolis: United States Naval Institute Press, 1977), 27–29.

9. Brian Lavery, *Nelson's Navy: The Ships, Men, and Organisation, 1793–1815*, 2nd ed. (London: Conway Maritime Press, 2012), 201.

10. Lavery, *Nelson's Navy*, 203.

11. Janet Macdonald, *Feeding Nelson's Navy*, 2nd ed. (London: Chatham, 2006), 45.

12. Macdonald, *Feeding Nelson's Navy*, 9.

13. Ibid., 31. See also John Masefield, *Sea Life in Nelson's Time* (London: Conway Maritime Press, 1984), 105; and Wordpress, "Navy Cheese," May 15, 2009, http://ageofsail.wordpress.com/category/naval-food/.

14. Macdonald, *Feeding Nelson's Navy*, 10.

15. Ibid.

16. Ibid., 176.

17. Jacob Nagle, *The Nagle Journal: A Diary of the Life of Jacob Nagle, Sailor, from 1775 to 1841*, ed. John C. Dann (New York: Weidenfeld and Nicolson, 1988), 286.

18. Nagle, *The Nagle Journal*, 286.

19. Ibid., 144.

20. Macdonald, *Feeding Nelson's Navy*, 16–18.

21. Masefield, *Sea Life in Nelson's Time*, 103.

22. Macdonald, *Feeding Nelson's Navy*, 17–18.

23. Ibid., 21–22.

24. Ibid., 86–91.

25. Richard Foss, *Rum: A Global History* (London: Reaktion Books, 2012), 60–62; Macdonald, *Feeding Nelson's Navy*, 42; Charles J. Gibowicz, *Mess Night Traditions* (Bloomington, IN: AuthorHouse, 2007), 69–70.

26. Macdonald, *Feeding Nelson's Navy*, 43.

27. Masefield, *Sea Life in Nelson's Time*, 85.

28. Ibid.

29. Webster's Ninth New Collegiate Dictionary, s.v. "slush," 1111.

30. Ibid., s.v. "slush fund," 1112.

31. Macdonald, *Feeding Nelson's Navy*, 105.

32. Albert Greene, "Recollections of the Jersey Prison Ship" (Providence: H.H. Brown, 1829), in Meryl Rutz, "Salt Horse and Ship's Biscuit," January 20, 2014, http://www/navyandmarine.org/ondeck/1776salthorse.htm.

33. Rutz, "Salt Horse and Ship's Biscuit," http://www/navyandmarine.org/ondeck/1776salthorse.htm.

34. Macdonald, *Feeding Nelson's Navy*, 106.

35. Ibid., 190–91. See also Anne Chotzinoff Grossman and Lisa Grossman Thomas, *Lobscouse and Spotted Dog: Which It's A Gastronomic Companion to the Aubrey/Maturin Novels* (New York: W.W. Norton, 1997), 18–20.

36. Grossman and Thomas, *Lobscouse and Spotted Dog*, 92.

37. Ibid., 28–29.

38. Ibid., 92.

39. N. A. M. Rodger, *The Wooden World: An Anatomy of the Georgian Navy*, 2nd ed. (New York: W. W. Norton, 1996), 86.

40. Rodger, *The Wooden World*, 90.

41. Rutz, "Salt Horse and Ship's Biscuit."

42. Lavery, *Nelson's Navy*, 205.

43. Macdonald, *Feeding Nelson's Navy*, 111–12.

44. Lavery, *Nelson's Navy*, 205.

45. Macdonald, *Feeding Nelson's Navy*, 98.

46. Masefield, *Sea Life in Nelson's Time*, 104.

47. Lavery, *Nelson's Navy*, 202.

48. Macdonald, *Feeding Nelson's Navy*, 122.

49. Ibid., 123.

50. Rodger, *The Wooden World*, 73.

51. Ibid.

52. Mary Ellen Snodgrass, *Encyclopedia of Kitchen History* (New York: Fitzroy Dearborn, 2004), 256.

53. Henry Teonge, *Diary of Henry Teonge, Chaplain on Board His Majesty's Ships Assistance, Bristol, and Royal Oak: 1675–1679* (London, 1825), https://archive.org/details/diaryofhenryteon00teon, 130.

54. Nagle, *The Nagle Journal*, 21.

55. Macdonald, *Feeding Nelson's Navy*, 25.

56. Ibid., 155–57.

57. Mary Ellen Snodgrass, *Encyclopedia of Kitchen History* (New York: Fitzroy Dearborn, 2004), 256; J.C. Beaglehole, *The Life of Captain James Cook*, 2nd ed. (Stanford: Stanford University Press, 1974), 135–36.

58. Beaglehole, *The Life of Captain James Cook*, 170–71.

59. Nagle, *The Nagle Journal*. 106.

60. Lavery, *Nelson's Navy*, 206.

61. Macdonald, *Feeding Nelson's Navy*, 145–47.

62. Ibid., 144–45; John Smith, *A Sea Grammar: With the Plaine Exposition of Smiths Accidence for Young Sea-Men* (Sabin Americana Print Editions, Gale Digital Collections), 85.

63. John Smith, *A Sea Grammar*, 85.

64. Macdonald, *Feeding Nelson's Navy*, 141.

65. Ibid., 142.

66. Navy Department Library, "Living Conditions in the 19th Century U.S. Navy, http://www.history.navy.mil/library/online/living_cond.htm.

67. Miller, *The U.S. Navy*, 121.

68. American Seamen's Friend Society, *The Sailor's Magazine and Seamen's Friend*, Volume 38, Number 7, March 1866, http://books.google.com/books?id=59kaAAAAYAAJ&pg=PA200&lpg=PA200&dq=trotter+grog+1781&source=bl&ots=PQw3pjW4Rk&sig=xHku5dcCIL_p1DNMYAMz_iFHJJc&hl=en&sa=X&ei=dmMvU8RSy6HSAdfGgcAB&ved=0CC4Q6AEwAg#v=onepage&q=trotter%20grog%201781&f=false, 200; Oriental University Institute, *The Imperial and Asiatic Quarterly Review and Oriental and Colonial Record*, Volume 11, Number s21 and 22, 1901, http://books.google.com/books?id=1RYoAAAAYAAJ&pg=PA409&lpg=PA409&

dq=trotter+grog+1781&source=bl&ots=d9eK2gtZ1c&sig=kUq77VpOnqzNIoia4nc
YNRW07fo&hl=en&sa=X&ei=dmMvU8RSy6HSAdfGgcAB&ved=0CDYQ6AE
wBQ#v=onepage&q=trotter%20grog%201781&f=false, 409.

Chapter 4

1. Elliot Snow, *Adventures at Sea in the Great Age of Sail: Five Firsthand Narratives* (New York: Dover Publications, 1986), 108.

2. Sandra L. Oliver, *Saltwater Foodways: New Englanders and Their Food at Sea and Ashore in the Nineteenth Century* (Mystic, CT: Mystic Seaport Museum, 1995), 85.

3. Oliver, *Saltwater Foodways*, 85–86.

4. Ibid., 85.

5. Frederick Pease Harlow, *The Making of a Sailor, or Sea Life Aboard a Yankee Square Rigger* (New York: Dover Publications, 1988), 116.

6. Harlow, *The Making of a Sailor*, 120.

7. Ibid.

8. Hugh McCulloch Gregory, *The Sea Serpent Journal: Hugh McCulloch Gregory Voyage Around the World in a Clipper Ship, 1854–1855*, ed. Robert H. Burgess (Charlottesville: University of Virginia Press, 1975), 10–11.

9. Harlow, *The Making of a Sailor*, 116.

10. Ibid., 264.

11. Oliver, *Saltwater Foodways*, 87.

12. Harlow, *The Making of a Sailor*, 116.

13. Oliver, *Saltwater Foodways*, 87.

14. Stan Hugill, *Shanties from the Seven Seas*, 2nd ed. (London: Routledge & Kegan Paul, 1984), 324.

15. Hugill, *Shanties from the Seven Seas*, 236–37.

16. Harlow, *The Making of a Sailor*, 207–8.

17. Ibid., 120.

18. Charles A. Abbey, *Before the Mast in the Clippers: The Diaries of Charles A. Abbey, 1856 to 1860*, ed. Harpur Allen Gosnell (New York: Dover Publications, 1989), 201.

19. Harlow, *The Making of a Sailor*, 147.

20. Stan Hugill, *Songs of the Sea* (Maidenhead, England: McGraw-Hill, 1977), 45.

21. Harlow, *The Making of a Sailor*, 147.

22. Hervey Garrett Smith, *The Arts of the Sailor*, ed. Eugene V. Connett (New York: Barnes & Noble Books, 1979), 18.

23. Harlow, *The Making of a Sailor*, 176.

24. Gregory, *The Sea Serpent Journal*, 21.

25. Ibid.

26. Harlow, *The Making of a Sailor*, 124–25.

27. Ibid., 147.

28. Ibid.

29. Ibid.

30. Hugill, *Songs of the Sea*, 556–57.

31. Hugill, *Shanties from the Seven Seas*, 70–71.

32. Harlow, *The Making of a Sailor*, 145–50.

33. Ibid., 44.

34. Ibid., 166.

35. Gregory, *The Sea Serpent Journal*, 50.

36. Abbey, *Before the Mast in the Clipper*, 216.

37. Harlow, *The Making of a Sailor*, 203.

38. Ibid., 203–4.

39. Ibid., 204–5.

40. Ibid., 203–5.

41. Ibid., 348.

42. Gregory, *The Sea Serpent Journal*, 103.

43. Harlow, *The Making of a Sailor*, 30.

44. Gregory, *The Sea Serpent Journal*, 8.

45. Hugill, *Shanties from the Seven Seas*, 182–83.

46. Abbey, *Before the Mast in the Clippers*, 207.

47. Gregory, *The Sea Serpent Journal*, 16.

48. Ibid., 10–11.

49. Harlow, *The Making of a Sailor*, 195–96.

50. Ibid.

51. Ibid., 147.

52. Oliver, *Saltwater Foodways*, 108.

53. Ibid.

54. Ibid.

55. Hugill, *Songs of the Sea*, 166.

56. Anne Chotzinoff Grossman and Lisa Grossman Thomas, *Lobscouse and Spotted Dog: Which It's A Gastronomic Companion to the Aubrey/Maturin Novels* (New York: W. W. Norton, 1997), 5.

57. Oliver, *Saltwater Foodways*, 109, 116.

58. Harlow, *The Making of a Sailor*, 50.

59. Ibid.

60. Ibid., 145–50.

61. Ibid., 195–96.

62. Abbey, *Before the Mast in the Clipper*, 231.

63. Gregory, *The Sea Serpent Journal*, 50–51.

64. Ibid.

65. Abbey, *Before the Mast in the Clippers*, 206.

66. Harlow, *The Making of a Sailor*, 174.

67. Ibid., 173–75.

68. Ibid., 173.

69. Ibid., 173–74.

70. Ibid., 176.

71. John Smith, *A Sea Grammar: With the Plaine Exposition of Smiths Accidence for Young Sea-Men* (Sabin Americana Print Editions, Gale Digital Collections), 36.

72. Harlow, *The Making of a Sailor*, 187.

73. Ibid.

74. Ibid., 176.

75. Oliver, *Saltwater Foodways*, 107.

76. Harlow, *The Making of a Sailor*, 30.

77. Isaac Norris Hibberd, *Sixteen Times Round Cape Horn: The Reminiscences of Captain Isaac Norris Hibberd*, ed. Frederick H. Hibberd (Mystic, CT: Mystic Seaport Museum, 1980), 8–9.

78. Harlow, *The Making of a Sailor*, 147.

79. Ibid., 128.

80. Hibberd, *Sixteen Times Round Cape Horn*, 33–34.

81. Oliver, *Saltwater Foodways*, 107.

82. Ibid., 108.

83. Harlow, *The Making of a Sailor*, 267.

84. Ibid., 248

85. Bill Beavis and Richard G. McCloskey, *Salty Dog Talk: The Nautical Origins of Everyday Expressions* (London: Adlard Coles, 1983), 81.

86. Michael P. Dyer, Senior Maritime Historian, New Bedford Whaling Museum, e-mail message to author, January 21, 2014.

87. Oliver, *Saltwater Foodways*, 85.

88. Ibid., 124–25.

89. Hugill, *Shanties from the Seven Seas*, 176.

90. Abbey, *Before the Mast in the Clippers*, 77.

91. Hugill, *Songs of the Sea*, 189.

92. Alan Villiers, *The War with Cape Horn*, 2nd ed. (London: Pan Books, 1973), 139–40.

93. Villiers, *The War with Cape Horn*, 140–42.

94. Ibid., 233–38.

95. Hugill, *Shanties from the Seven Seas*, 588–89.

Chapter 5

1. Tripod, "The Slave Trade: Conditions on Slave Ships," March 27, 2014, http://4thebest4e.tripod.com/id15.html.

2. Wikipedia, "Atlantic Slave Trade," http://en.wikipedia.org/wiki/Atlantic_slave_trade.

3. Marcus Rediker, *The Slave Ship: A Human History* (New York: Penguin Books, 2007), 58.

4. Rediker, *The Slave Ship*, 170.

5. Ibid., 237.

6. Ibid., 269.

7. Howard Irving Chapelle, *The Baltimore Clipper: Its Origin and Development*, 2nd ed. (New York: Dover Publications, 1988), 134–35.

8. EyeWitness to History, "Aboard a Slave Ship, 1829," 2000, http://www.eye witnesstohistory.com/slaveship.htm.

9. Ibid.

10. Chapelle, *The Baltimore Clipper*, 136.

11. Andrew W. German, *Voyages: Stories of America and the Sea: A Companion to the Exhibition at Mystic Seaport* (Mystic, CT: Mystic Seaport Museum Inc., 2000), 8–9.

12. Ian Adams and Meredyth Somerville, *Cargoes of Despair and Hope: Scottish Emigration to North America: 1603–1803* (Edinburgh: John Donald, 1993), 100–6.

13. Adams and Somerville, *Cargoes of Despair and Hope*, 106–7.

14. Melvin Maddocks, *The Atlantic Crossing: The Seafarers* (Amsterdam: Time Life Books, 1981), 80.

15. George A. Mackenzie, ed., *From Aberdeen to Ottawa in Eighteen Forty-Five: The Diary of Alexander Muir* (Aberdeen: Aberdeen University Press, 1990), 114.

16. Mackenzie, *From Aberdeen to Ottawa in Eighteen Forty-Five*, 114–15.

17. Maddocks, *The Atlantic Crossing*, 112–17.

18. Ibid., 126–28.

19. Ibid., 120–25.

20. Charles Dickens, *American Notes for General Circulation*, 1842 (London: Penguin Classics, 1985), 262.

21. Ibid.

22. Ibid., 262–63.

23. Ibid., 262.

24. Ibid., 265.

25. Ibid., 265–66.

26. Jeremy Rifkin, *Beyond Beef: The Rise and Fall of the Cattle Culture*, 2nd ed. (New York: Plume, 1993), 56–57.

27. Wikipedia, "Great Famine (Ireland)," March 21, 2014, http://en.wikipedia.org/wiki/Great_Famine_(Ireland).

28. Stan Hugill, *Shanties from the Seven Seas*, 2nd ed. (London: Routledge & Kegan Paul, 1984), 303.

29. Hugill, *Shanties from the Seven Seas*, 300–1.

30. Herman Melville, *Redburn: His First Voyage* (New York: Doubleday Anchor Book, 1957), 231.

31. Ibid.

32. Ibid.

33. Ibid., 254.

34. Ibid., 255.

35. Ibid.

36. Ibid., 282.

37. Him Mark Lai, Genny Lim, and Judy Yung, *Island: Poetry and History of Chinese Immigrants on Angel Island: 1910–1940*, 2nd ed. (San Francisco: HOC DOI Project, Chinese Culture Foundation of San Francisco, 1986), 86.

38. Ibid., 45.

39. Hugh McCulloch Gregory, *The Sea Serpent Journal: Hugh McCulloch Gregory's Voyage Around the World in a Clipper Ship, 1854–1855*, ed. Robert H. Burgess (Charlottesville: University Press of Virginia, 1975), 63–74.

40. Corinne K. Hoexter, *From Canton to California: The Epic of Chinese Immigration* (New York: Four Winds Press, 1976), 35.

41. Charles A. Abbey, *Before the Mast in the Clippers: The Diaries of Charles A. Abbey, 1856 to 1860*, ed. Harpur Allen Gosnell, 2nd ed. (New York: Dover Publications, 1989), 207.

42. Hoexter, *From Canton to California*, 73.

43. Ibid., 76–77.

44. Ibid., 98–100.

45. Ibid., 98.

46. Lai et al., *Island*, 13–14.

47. Ibid., 47.

48. Ibid., 38.

49. Ibid., 130.

50. Kazuo Ito, *Issei: A History of Japanese Immigrants in North America* (Seattle: Japanese Community Service, 1973), 32, in German, *Voyages*, 15–16.

51. Helen Hunt Jackson, *The Helen Jackson Yearbook* (Boston: Robert Brothers, 1895), http://books.google.com/books?id=ELk3AAAAYAAJ&pg=PP1&lpg=PP1&dq=helen+hunt+jackson+the+helen+hunt+jackson+yearbook&source=bl&ots=RN-kGOyyB4&sig=QMjLF0bE7ss4owc_qL-pxonoflM&hl=en&sa=X&ei=D1UvU7usKqXB0gHd7YGgCw&ved=0CDUQ6AEwAg#v=onepage&q=sails%20anchors&f=false, 130.

Chapter 6

1. Bjorn Landstrom, *The Ship: An Illustrated History* (New York: Doubleday, 1961), 230–31.

2. John Maxtone-Graham, *The Only Way to Cross* (New York: Macmillan, 1972), 5.

3. Ibid., 5.

4. Ibid.

5. Charles Dickens, *American Notes for General Circulation*, 1842, 2nd edition (London: Penguin Classics, 1985), 54.

6. Ibid., 54.

7. Ibid., 69.

8. Ibid., 64.

9. Ibid., 69.

10. Ibid., 70.

11. Ibid., 55.

12. Maxtone-Graham, *The Only Way to Cross*, 7.

13. Tony Davis (Liverpool UK folklorist and performer), discussion with the author, August 1992.

14. William B. Forward, Liverpool ship operator, in James Dugan, *The Great Iron Ship* (New York: Harper & Brothers, 1953), 113.

15. Dugan, *The Great Iron Ship*, 116.

16. Ibid., 165–67.

17. Sharon Poole and Andrew Sassoli-Walker, *P&O Cruises: Celebrating 175 Years of Heritage* (Gloucestershire, UK: Amberly, 2011), 11.

18. Ibid., 21.

19. Mark Twain, *The Innocents Abroad* (Hartford, CT: American Publishing Company, 1869), in Project Gutenberg, http://www.gutenberg.org/files/3176/3176-h/3176-h.htm, 19.

20. Ibid., 17.

21. Ibid., 21–22.

22. Ibid., 318.

23. Ibid., 320.

24. Ibid., 24.

25. Ibid., 32.

26. Spencer C. Tucker, ed. Almanac of American Military History (Santa Barbara, CA: ABC-CLIO, 2013), http://books.google.com/books?id=TO2mx314ST0C&pg=PA553&lpg=PA553&dq=Robert+Fulton+steam+powered+defense+vessel+1812&source=bl&ots=LdoUjKJ79l&sig=s1f_yGIydKvGsGNTHTqP0m8GiVs&hl=en&sa=X&ei=0DwZU96CB4ySkQeG4oGYCA&ved=0CDgQ6AEwAw#v=onepage&q=Robert%20Fulton%20steam%20powered%20defense%20vessel%201812&f=false, 553.

27. Landstrom, *The Ship*, 232.

28. Raphael Semmes, Admiral CSN, *Memoirs of Service Afloat* (Seacaucus, NJ: Blue & Grey Press, 1987), 419–20.

29. Ibid., 402–3.

30. Landstrom, *The Ship: An Illustrated History*, 239.

31. Ibid.

32. Dennis J. Ringle, *Life in Mr. Lincoln's Navy* (Annapolis: Naval Institute Press, 1998), 65; Spencer C. Tucker, ed. *The Civil War Naval Encyclopedia* (Santa Barbara, CA: ABC-CLIO, 2011), http://books.google.com/books?id=Ho_8ONL5UgsC&q=food#v=onepage&q=food&f=false, 193.

33. Henry Steele Commager, *The Blue and The Gray*, 2nd ed. (New York: Fairfax Press, 1982), 275.

34. Ibid., 291.

35. Navy Department, Naval History Division, *Civil War Naval Chronology: 1861–1865* (Washington, DC: U.S. Government Printing Office, 1971), VI: 47–83.

36. Anonymous, "Life of a Blockader," *Continental Monthly* 6 (August 1864), 46–55, in Ringle, *Life in Mr. Lincoln's Navy*, 65.

37. Stephen F. Blanding, *Recollections of a Sailor Boy on a Cruise of the Gunboat "Louisiana"* (Providence, RI: E. A. Johnson, 1886), 60, in Ringle, *Life in Mr. Lincoln's Navy*, 70.

38. Tucker, *The Civil War Naval Encyclopedia*, 195.

39. Ibid., 194.

40. The Trident Society, *The Book of Navy Songs*, 3rd ed. (Annapolis: Naval Institute Press, 1955), 86–87.

41. Landstrom, *The Ship: An Illustrated History*, 239.

42. Ibid., 280–81.

43. James Burke, *Connections* (Boston: Little, Brown, 1978), 233–35.

44. Burke, *Connections*, 237.

45. Janet Macdonald, *Feeding Nelson's Navy*, 2nd ed. (London: Chatham, 2006), 172.

46. Burke, *Connections*, 238.

47. Owen Beattie and John Geiger, *Buried in Ice: The Mystery of a Lost Arctic Expedition* (Toronto, CN: Madison Press Books, 1992), 55–60.

48. Burke, *Connections*, 238.

49. Stan Hugill, *Songs of the Sea* (Maidenhead, England: McGraw-Hill, 1977), 166.

50. Ralph W. Andrews and A. K. Larssen, *Fish and Ships: This Was Fishing From the Columbia to Bristol Bay* (Seattle: Superior, 1959), 49–57.

51. Ibid., 58–62.

52. Ibid., 49–62.

53. Lars Bruzelius, The Maritime History Virtual Archives, "Kenilworth," December 30, 1998, http://www.bruzelius.info/Nautica/Ships/Fourmast_ships/Kenilworth(1887).html.

54. Editorial poem, "Some Complaints Investigated," *Brisbane Courier*, September 23, 1911, http://trove.nla.gov.au/ndp/del/page/1571470.

Chapter 7

1. Bjorn Landstrom, *The Ship: An Illustrated History* (New York: Doubleday, 1961), 280–81.

2. Maxtone-Graham, *The Only Way to Cross*, 154.

3. Ibid., 154–55.

4. Edwin G. Burrows and Mike Wallace, *Gotham: A History of New York City to 1898* (New York: Oxford University Press, 1999), 436–37.

5. Maxtone-Graham, *The Only Way to Cross*, 84.

6. Ibid., 11, 43.

7. Ibid., 88.

8. Maxtone-Graham, *The Only Way to Cross*, 11.

9. Ibid.

10. Ken Smith, *Turbinia: The Story of Charles Parsons and His Ocean Greyhound* (Newcastle Upon Tyne, UK: Tyne and Wear Museums, 1996), 17–21.

11. Landstrom, *The Ship*, 244–45.

12. Maxtone-Graham, *The Only Way to Cross*, 15.

13. Rick Archbold and Dana McCauley, *Last Dinner on the Titanic: Menus and Recipes from the Great Liner* (New York: Madison Press, 1997), 21.

14. Archbold and McCauley, *Last Dinner on the Titanic*, 29, 108; Maxtone-Graham, *The Only Way to Cross*, 214.

15. Archbold and McCauley, *Last Dinner on the Titanic*, 76.

16. Maxtone-Graham, *The Only Way to Cross*, 140–41.

17. Ibid., 137.

18. Menu for the twentieth anniversary dinner of Mr. and Mrs. Harry Houdini, June 22, 1914, Reproduction Number: LC-USZC2-4893, LC-USZC2-4892, LC-USZC2-4894 in Collection: Miscellaneous Items in High Demand, Library of Congress Digital Collections, http://www.loc.gov/pictures/item/96519251/.

19. Maxtone-Graham, *The Only Way to Cross*, 168–69.

20. Ibid., 165.

21. Sarah Edington, *The Captain's Table: Life and Dining on the Great Ocean Liners* (London: National Maritime Museum Publishing, 2005), 19.

22. Edington, *The Captain's Table*, 112–17.

23. Sharon Poole and Andrew Sassoli-Walker, *P&O Cruises: Celebrating 175 Years of Heritage* (Gloucestershire, UK: Amberly, 2011), 17.

24. Poole and Sassoli-Walker, *P&O Cruises*, 17.

25. Ibid.

26. Ibid., 19.

27. Wikipedia, "Peninsular and Oriental Steam Navigation Company," last updated March 22, 2014, http://en.wikipedia.org/wiki/Peninsular_and_Oriental _Steam_Navigation_Company.

28. Poole and Sassoli-Walker, *P&O Cruises*, 21.

29. Ibid.

30. Ibid., 24.

31. Edington, *The Captain's Table*, 22.

32. Ibid.

33. Wikipedia, "Peninsular and Oriental Steam Navigation Company," last updated March 22, 2014, http://en.wikipedia.org/wiki/Peninsular_and_Oriental_Steam _Navigation_Company.

34. Maxtone-Graham, *The Only Way to Cross*, 188.

35. Archbold and McCauley, *Last Dinner on the Titanic*, 114.

36. John P. Eaton and Charles A. Haas, *Titanic: Triumph and Tragedy*, 2nd ed. (New York: W.W. Norton, 1994), http://books.google.com/books?id=uia8z RfX1koC&pg=PA116&lpg=PA116&dq=specimen+third+class+bill+of+fare&

source=bl&ots=26t96mUtWa&sig=0fQ169M1pW7csGHkLPXxQDYbV
ro&hl=en&sa=X&ei=CvYgU8-SMsnq0gHk_oDIBg&ved=0CCcQ6AEwAQ#v=
onepage&q=specimen%20third%20class%20bill%20of%20fare&f=false, 116.

37. Ibid.

38. Eaton and Haas, *Titanic*, 116; Marion Diamond, "The Titanic's Menus and What They Can Tell Us," Wordpress, July 4, 2012, http://learnearnandreturn .wordpress.com/2012/04/07/the-titanics-menus-and-what-they-can-tell-us/.

39. Eaton and Haas, *Titanic*, 116.

40. Ibid.

41. Ibid.

42. Eaton and Haas, *Titanic*, 116; Diamond, "The Titanic's Menus."

43. Eaton and Haas, *Titanic*, 116.

44. Eaton and Haas, *Titanic*, 116; Diamond, "The Titanic's Menus"; Archbold and McCauley, *Last Dinner on the Titanic*, 112–14.

45. Archbold and McCauley, *Last Dinner on the Titanic*, 94–97.

46. Ibid.

47. Diamond, "The Titanic's Menus."

48. Ibid.

49. Ibid.

50. Diamond, "The Titanic's Menus"; Eaton and Haas, *Titanic*, 116; Archbold and McCauley, *Last Dinner on the Titanic*, 66, 94, 97, 106.

51. Titanic-titanic.com, First class breakfast menu, April 11, 1912, "Titanic Dining," http://www.titanic-titanic.com/titanic_dining.shtml.

52. Ibid.

53. Diamond, "The Titanic's Menus."

54. Titanic-titanic.com, "Titanic Dining"; Archbold and McCauley, *Last Dinner on the Titanic*, 66.

55. Ibid.

56. Ibid.

57. Ibid.

58. Ibid.

59. Ibid., 40–58

60. Edington, *The Captain's Table*, 51.

61. James Burke, *Connections* (Boston: Little, Brown, 1978), 239–40.

62. Ibid., 241–42.

63. Ibid.

64. Ibid., 238–43.

65. Ibid., 241.

66. Archbold and McCauley, *Last Dinner on the Titanic*, 22.

67. Yvonne Hume, *RMS Titanic: "Dinner Is Served"* (Catrine, UK: Stenlake, 2010), 12.

68. Edington, *The Captain's Table*, 23.

69. Ibid., 21.

70. Traditional. Author's own repertoire.

Chapter 8

1. British Royal Navy, *Brinestain and Biscuit: Recipes and Rules for Royal Navy Cooks*, 1930 (Surrey, UK: National Archives, 2006), 60.

2. Ibid., 60.

3. Nathan Miller, *The U.S. Navy: An Illustrated History* (New York: American Heritage; Annapolis: United States Naval Institute Press, 1977), 252.

4. Ibid., 256.

5. Ibid., 252–56.

6. Navy Department, USS *Arizona* Dinner Menu, July 4, 1935, author's collection.

7. Charles J. Gibowicz, *Mess Night Traditions* (Bloomington, IN: AuthorHouse, 2007), 75.

8. Ibid., 77–78.

9. Ibid., 76.

10. Daniel Orkent, *Last Call: The Rise and Fall of Prohibition* (New York: Scribner, 2010), 219.

11. Ibid., 218.

12. Bob Dickinson and Andy Vladimir, *Selling the Sea: An Inside Look at the Cruise Industry* (New York: John Wiley & Sons, 1997), 16.

13. Ibid., 8–9.

14. Ibid., 19–20.

15. Ibid., 19.

16. John A. Fostik, *America's Postwar Luxury Liners* (Hudson, WI: Iconografix, 2011), 105–8.

17. Dickinson and Vladimir, *Selling the Sea*, 18.

18. Orkent, *Last Call*, 217.

19. Ibid.

20. Dickinson and Vladimir, *Selling the Sea*, 19.

21. Ibid.

22. Orkent, *Last Call*, 217.

23. Ibid.

24. Richard E. Miller, The *Messman Chronicles: African Americans in the U.S. Navy: 1932–1943* (Annapolis, MD: Naval Institute Press, 2004), 5–11.

25. Ibid., 172–94.

26. Ibid., 310–11.

27. David Miller, *The Illustrated Directory of Submarines of the World* (London: Salamander Books, 2002), 10–19.

28. Lothar-Gunther Buchheim, *U-Boat War* (New York, Alfred A. Knopf, 1978)

29. John W. Alexander, *United States Navy Memorial: A Living Tradition* (Washington: United States Navy Memorial Foundation, 1987), 149.

30. British Royal Navy, *Brinestain and Biscuit*, 12.

31. Ibid., 10–12.

32. Agostino von Hassell, Herm Dillon, and Leslie Jean-Bart, *Military High Life: Elegant Food Histories and Recipes* (New Orleans: University Press of the South, 2006), 106.

33. Sharon Poole, and Andrew Sassoli-Walker, *P&O Cruises: Celebrating 175 Years of Heritage* (Gloucestershire, UK: Amberly, 2011), 37.

34. Fostik, *America's Postwar Luxury Liners*, 5.

35. Ibid., 81.

36. Ibid., 5.

37. Ibid., 8–16.

38. Brian J. Cudahy, "The Containership Revolution—Malcolm McLean's 1956 Innovation Goes Global," TR News 246 (Washington: Transportation Research Board of the National Academies, September–October 2006), http://www.worldshipping.org/pdf/container_ship_revolution.pdf.

39. Dickinson and Vladimir, *Selling the Sea*, 24.

40. Ibid., 26–27.

41. Ibid., 29.

42. Ibid., 35.

43. Ibid., 29.

44. Ibid., 32–33.

45. Ibid., 28.

46. Ibid., 49.

47. Poole and Sassoli-Walker, *P&O Cruises*, 133.

48. Sandy Pukel and Mark Hanna, *Greens and Grains on the Deep Blue Sea Cookbook: Fabulous Vegetarian Cuisine from the Holistic Holiday at Sea Cruises* (New York: Square One, 2007), 1–3.

49. Dickinson and Vladimir, *Selling the Sea*, 52.

50. Viking Cruise Line and Manne Stenros, *Sea & Food* (Finland: Studio Avec Audiovisual, 2003), 2–3.

51. Pukel and Hanna, *Greens and Grains on the Deep Blue Sea Cookbook*, 47.

52. Dickinson and Vladimir, *Selling the Sea*, 53.

53. Ibid.

54. Ibid., 87.

55. Ibid.

56. Pukel and Hanna, *Greens and Grains on the Deep Blue Sea Cookbook*, 76–77, 83.

57. Silver Donald Cameron, *Sailing Away From Winter: A Cruise from Nova Scotia to Florida and Beyond*, 2nd ed. (Toronto: McClellan & Stewart, 2008), 365.

58. John Masefield, *Salt-Water Ballads*, 1902, in Alexander, *United States Navy Memorial*, 176.

Bibliography

Abbey, Charles A. *Before the Mast in the Clippers: The Diaries of Charles A. Abbey, 1856 to 1860.* Edited by Harpur Allen Gosnell. 2nd ed. New York: Dover Publications, 1989.

Abulafia, David. *The Great Sea: A Human History of the Mediterranean.* New York: Oxford University Press, 2011.

Adams, Ian, and Meredyth Somerville. *Cargoes of Despair and Hope: Scottish Emigration to North America: 1603–1803.* Edinburgh: John Donald Publishers, 1993.

Alexander, John W. *United States Navy Memorial: A Living Tradition.* Washington, DC: United States Navy Memorial Foundation, 1987.

Almgren, Bertil et al. *The Viking.* Gothenberg, Sweden: Tre Tryckare, Cagner & Co., 1966.

Amadas, Philip, and Arthur Barlowe. *The First Voyage Made to the Coasts of America, with Two Barks, Where in Were Captaines M. Philip Amadas and M. Arthur Barlowe, Who Discovered Part of the Countrey Now Called Virginia, Anno 1584.* Virtual Jamestown Project. http://etext.lib.virginia.edu/etcbin/jamestown-browse?id=J1014.

American Seamen's Friend Society. *The Sailor's Magazine and Seamen's Friend* 38, No. 7 (March 1866). http://books.google.com/books?id=59kaAAAAYAAJ&pg=PA200&lpg=PA200&dq=trotter+grog+1781&source=bl&ots=PQw3pjW4Rk&sig=xHku5dcCIL_p1DNMYAMz_iFHJJc&hl=en&sa=X&ei=dmMvU8RSy6HSAdfGgcAB&ved=0CC4Q6AEwAg#v=onepage&q=trotter%20grog%201781&f=false.

Andrews, Ralph W., and A.K. Larssen. *Fish and Ships: This Was Fishing From the Columbia to Bristol Bay*. Seattle: Superior Publishing Company, 1959.

Archbold, Rick, and Dana McCauley. *Last Dinner on the Titanic: Menus and Recipes from the Great Liner*. New York: Madison Press, 1997.

Bass, George F., ed. *Beneath the Seven Seas: Adventures with the Institute of Nautical Archaeology*. London: Thames & Hudson, 2005.

Bass, George F., and Frederick H. van Doorninck, Jr. *Yassi Ada*. Vol. I. College Station: Texas A&M University Press, 1982.

Beaglehole, J.C. *The Life of Captain James Cook*. 2nd ed. Stanford: Stanford University Press, 1974.

Beavis, Bill, and Richard G. McCloskey. *Salty Dog Talk: The Nautical Origins of Everyday Expressions*. London: Adlard Coles, 1983.

Bowen, E.G. *Britain and the Western Seaways*. London: Thames & Hudson, 1972.

Bradford, Ernle. *The Story of the Mary Rose*. London: W. W. Norton, 1982.

British Royal Navy. *Brinestain and Biscuit: Recipes and Rules for Royal Navy Cooks, Admiraly 1930*. Surrey, UK: National Archives, 2006.

Bruzelius, Lars. "Kenilworth." The Maritime History Virtual Archives. December 30, 1998. http://www.bruzelius.info/Nautica/Ships/Fourmast_ships/Kenilworth(1887).html.

Buchheim, Lothar-Gunther. *U-Boat War*. New York, Alfred A. Knopf, 1978.

Burke, James. *Connections*. Boston: Little, Brown, 1978.

Burrows, Edwin G., and Mike Wallace. *Gotham: A History of New York City to 1898*. New York: Oxford University Press, 1999.

Cameron, Silver Donald. *Sailing Away From Winter: A Cruise from Nova Scotia to Florida and Beyond*. 2nd ed. Toronto: McClellan & Stewart, 2008.

Casson, Lionel. *Ships and Seamanship in the Ancient World*. 2nd ed. Baltimore: Johns Hopkins University Press, 1995. First published in 1971 by Princeton University Press.

Chapelle, Howard Irving. *The Baltimore Clipper: Its Origin and Development*. 2nd ed. New York: Dover Publications, 1988.

Choi, Charles Q. "Ingredients for Salad Dressing Found in 2,400-year-old Shipwreck." Livescience.com. November 8, 2007. http://www.livescience.com/2024-ingredients-salad-dressing-2-400-year-shipwreck.html.

Cipolla, Carlo M. *Guns, Sails, and Empires: Technological Innovation and the Early Phases of European Expansion, 1400–1700*. New York: Minerva Press, 1965.

Columbus, Christopher. *The Log Book of Christopher Columbus: His Own Account of the Voyage That Changed the World*. Translated by Robert H. Fuson. Camden: International Marine Publishing Company, 1987.

Commager, Henry Steele. *The Blue and The Gray*. 2nd ed. New York: Fairfax Press, 1982.

Cudahy, Brian J. "The Containership Revolution—Malcolm McLean's 1956 Innovation Goes Global." TR News 246, September–October 2006. Transportation

Research Board of the National Academies, Washington, DC. http://www.world
shipping.org/pdf/container_ship_revolution.pdf.

Diamond, Marion. "The Titanic's Menus and What They Can Tell Us." Wordpress,
July 4, 2012. http://learnearnandreturn.wordpress.com/2012/04/07/the-titanics
-menus-and-what-they-can-tell-us/.

Dickens, Charles. *American Notes for General Circulation*. 1842. Reprinted with introduction and notes by John S. Whitley and Arnold Goldman in 1972. Reprinted
with note by Angus Calder in 1985. London: Penguin Classics, 1985.

Dickinson, Bob, and Andy Vladimir. *Selling the Sea: An Inside Look at the Cruise
Industry*. New York: John Wiley & Sons, 1997.

Dugan, James. *The Great Iron Ship*. New York: Harper & Brothers, 1953.

Dunmore, John. *Mrs. Cook's Book of Recipes for Mariners in Distant Seas: Boiled Jellyfish, Stewed Albatross, and Other Treats for Sailors*. London: Quercus, 2006.

Eaton, John P., and Charles A. Haas. *Titanic: Triumph and Tragedy*. 2nd ed.
New York: W. W. Norton, 1994. http://books.google.com/books?id=uia8zK
fX1koC&pg=PA116&lpg=PA116&dq=specimen+third+class+bill+of+fare
&source=bl&ots=26t96mUtWa&sig=0fQ169M1pW7csGHkLPXxQDYbV
ro&hl=en&sa=X&ei=CvYgU8-SMsnq0gHk_oDIBg&ved=0CCcQ6AEw
AQ#v=onepage&q=specimen%20third%20class%20bill%20of%20fare&f=false.

Edington, Sarah. *The Captain's Table: Life and Dining on the Great Ocean Liners*. London: National Maritime Museum, 2005.

EyeWitness to History. "Aboard a Slave Ship, 1829." 2000. http://www.eyewitness-
tohistory.com/slaveship.htm.

Ellmers, Detlev. "The Hanseatic Cog of Bremen AD 1380." Deutsches Schiffahrtsmuseum, Bremen. http://www.raco.cat/index.php/Drassana/article/viewFile/106096/
132585.

Foss, Richard. *Rum: A Global History*. London: Reaktion Books, 2012.

Fostik, John A. *America's Postwar Luxury Liners*. Hudson, WI: Iconografix, 2011.

Fury, Cheryl. *The Social History of English Seamen: 1485–1649*. Woodbridge, Suffolk,
UK: Boydell Press, 2013.

German, Andrew W. *Voyages: Stories of America and the Sea: A Companion to the
Exhibition at Mystic Seaport*. Mystic, CT: Mystic Seaport Museum, 2000.

Gibowicz, Charles J. *Mess Night Traditions*. Bloomington, IN: Author House, 2007.

Graham, Winston. *The Spanish Armadas*. London: Collins, 1972.

Grant, Gordon. *Sail Ho: Windjammer Sketches Alow and Aloft*. New York: William
Farquhar, 1930.

Gregory, Hugh McCulloch. *The Sea Serpent Journal: Hugh McCulloch Gregory's Voyage Around the World in a Clipper Ship, 1854–1855*. Edited by Robert H. Burgess.
Charlottesville: University Press of Virginia, 1975.

Grenville, Richard. *The Voiage Made by Sir Richard Greenville, for Sir Walter Ralegh,
to Virginia, in the Yeere 1585, Part 1*. Virtual Jamestown Project. http://etext.lib
.virginia.edu/etcbin/jamestown-browse?id=J1015.

Grossman, Anne Chotzinoff, and Lisa Grossman Thomas. *Lobscouse and Spotted Dog: Which Is a Gastronomic Companion to the Aubrey/Maturin Novels*. New York: W. W. Norton, 1997.

Harlow, Frederick Pease. *The Making of a Sailor, or Sea Life Aboard a Yankee Square-Rigger*. Salem, MA: Marine Research Society, 1928. Reprint, New York: Dover Publications, 1988.

Haugen, Einar, trans. *Voyages to Vinland: The First American Saga*. New York: Alfred A. Knoff, 1942. http://www.archive.org/stream/voyagestovinland013593mbp/ voyagestovinland013593mbp_djvu.txt.

Henriksen, Louise Kaempe. "Journeyman Cook." Viking Museum. Roskilde, Denmark. March 12, 2007. http://www.vikingesskibsmuseet.dk/en/the-sea-stallion-past -and-present/the-ships-crew/crewmembers-in-the-viking-age/matsveina/# .UypKWyjDPdk.

Hibberd, Isaac Norris. *Sixteen Times Round Cape Horn: The Reminiscences of Captain Isaac Norris Hibberd*. Edited by Frederick H. Hibberd. Mystic, CT: Mystic Seaport Museum, 1980.

Hoexter, Corrine K. *From Canton to California: The Epic of Chinese Immigration*. New York: Four Winds Press, 1976.

Howarth, David. *The Voyage of the Armada: The Spanish Story*. 2nd ed. New York: Penguin Books, 1981.

Hugill, Stan. *The Bosun's Locker: Collected Articles, 1962–1973*. Todmorden, UK: Herron, 2006.

Hugill, Stan. *Shanties from the Seven Seas*. 2nd ed. London: Routledge & Kegan Paul, 1984.

Hugill, Stan. *Songs of the Sea*. Maidenhead, England: McGraw-Hill, 1977.

Hulton, Paul. *America 1585: The Complete Drawings of John White*. Chapel Hill: University of North Carolina, British Museum Publications, 1984.

Hume, Yvonne. *RMS Titanic: "Dinner Is Served."* Catrine, UK: Stenlake Publishing, 2010.

Jackson, Helen Hunt. *The Helen Jackson Yearbook*. Edited by Harriet Perry. Boston: Robert Brothers, 1895. http://books.google.com/books?id=ELk3AAAAYAAJ &pg=PP1&lpg=PP1&dq=helen+hunt+jackson+the+helen+hunt+jackson+ yearbook&source=bl&ots=RN-kGOyyB4&sig=QMjLF0bE7ss4owc_qL-pxon ofIM&hl=en&sa=X&ei=D1UvU7usKqXB0gHd7YGgCw&ved=0CDUQ6 AEwAg#v=onepage&q=sails%20anchors&f=false.

Johnstone, Paul. *The Sea-craft of Prehistory*. 2nd ed. London: Routledge & Kegan Paul, 1988.

Kirsch, Peter. *The Galleon: The Great Ships of the Armada Era*. London: Conway Maritime Press, 1990.

Kurlansky, Mark. *Salt: A World History*. 2nd ed. London: Penguin Books, 2003.

Lai, Him Mark, Genny Lim, and Judy Yung. *Island: Poetry and History of Chinese Immigrants on Angel Island: 1910–1940*. 2nd ed. San Francisco: HOC DOI Project, Chinese Culture Foundation of San Francisco, 1986.

Lallanilla, Mark. "Ancient Roman May Hold 2,000-Year-Old Food." Livescience .com. August 12, 2013. http://livescience.com/38814-ancient-roman-shipwreck .html.

Landstrom, Bjorn. *The Ship: An Illustrated History*. New York: Doubleday, 1961.

Lavery, Brian. *Nelson's Navy: The Ships, Men, and Organisation, 1793–1815*. 2nd ed. London: Conway Maritime Press, 2012.

Macdonald, Janet. *Feeding Nelson's Navy*. 2nd ed. London: Chatham, 2006.

Mackenzie, George A., ed. *From Aberdeen to Ottawa in Eighteen Forty-Five: The Diary of Alexander Muir*. Aberdeen: Aberdeen University Press, 1990.

Maddocks, Melvin. *The Atlantic Crossing: The Seafarers*. Amsterdam: Time Life Books, 1981.

Marcus, G.J. *The Conquest of the North Atlantic*. New York: Oxford University Press, 1981.

Masefield, John. *Sea Life in Nelson's Time*. London: Conway Maritime Press, 1984.

Mattingly, Garrett. *The Armada*. Boston: Houghton Mifflin, 1959.

Maxtone-Graham, John. *The Only Way to Cross*. New York: Macmillan, 1972.

Mayers, Kit. *North—East Passage to Muscovy: Stephen Borough and the First Tudor Explorations*. Gloucestershire, UK: Sutton, 2005.

Melville, Herman. *Redburn: His First Voyage*. New York: Doubleday Anchor Book, 1957.

Menzies, Gavin. *1421: The Year China Discovered America*. 3rd ed. New York: Perennial: 2004.

Miller, David. *The Illustrated Directory of Submarines of the World*. London: Salamander Books, 2002.

Miller, Nathan. *The U.S. Navy: An Illustrated History*. New York: American Heritage; Annapolis: United States Naval Institute Press, 1977.

Miller, Richard E. *The Messman Chronicles: African Americans in the U.S. Navy: 1932–1943*. Annapolis, MD: Naval Institute Press, 2004.

Morison, Samuel Eliot. *The European Discovery of America: The Northern Voyages, AD 500–1600*. New York: Oxford University Press, 1971.

Mott, Lawrence V. "Feeding Neptune: Food Supply and Nutrition in the Catalan-Aragonese Fleet," Paper presented at the Forty-Third International Congress on Medieval Studies, 2008.

Mott, Lawrence V. *Sea Power in the Medieval Mediterranean: The Catalan-Aragonese Fleet in the War of the Sicilian Vespers*. Gainesville: University Press of Florida, 2003.

Nagle, Jacob. *The Nagle Journal: A Diary of the Life of Jacob Nagle, Sailor, from the Year 1775 to 1841*. Edited by John C. Dann. New York: Weidenfeld and Nicolson, 1988.

Navy Department Library. "Living Conditions in the 19th Century U.S. Navy." http://www.history.navy.mil/library/online/living_cond.htm.

Navy Department, Naval History Division. *Civil War Naval Chronology: 1861–1865*. Washington, DC: U.S. Government Printing Office, 1971.

Okrent, Daniel. *Last Call: The Rise and Fall of Prohibition*. New York: Scribner, 2010.

Oliver, Sandra L. *Saltwater Foodways: New Englanders and Their Food at Sea and Ashore in the Nineteenth Century*. Mystic, CT: Mystic Seaport Museum, 1995.

Oriental University Institute. *The Imperial and Asiatic Quarterly Review and Oriental and Colonial Record* 11, Nos. 21 and 22, 1901. http://books.google .com/books?id=1RYoAAAAYAAJ&pg=PA409&lpg=PA409&dq=trotter +grog+1781&source=bl&ots=d9eK2gtZ1c&sig=kUq77VpOnqzNIoia4nc YNRW07fo&hl=en&sa=X&ei=dmMvU8RSy6HSAdfGgcAB&ved=0CDYQ 6AEwBQ#v=onepage&q=trotter%20grog%201781&f=false.

Parry, J.H. *The Age of Reconnaissance: Discovery, Exploration, and Settlement 1450 to 1650*. 2nd ed. London: University of California Press, 1981.

Phillips, Carla Rahn. *Six Galleons for the King of Spain: Imperial Defense in the Early Seventeenth Century*. Baltimore: Johns Hopkins University Press, 1986.

Poole, Sharon, and Andrew Sassoli-Walker. *P&O Cruises: Celebrating 175 Years of Heritage*. Gloucestershire, UK: Amberly, 2011.

Pukel, Sandy, and Mark Hanna. *Greens and Grains on the Deep Blue Sea Cookbook: Fabulous Vegetarian Cuisine from the Holistic Holiday at Sea Cruises*. New York: Square One, 2007.

Rediker, Marcus. *The Slave Ship: A Human History*. 2nd ed. New York: Penguin Books, 2008.

Rifkin, Jeremy. *Beyond Beef: The Rise and Fall of the Cattle Culture*. 2nd ed. New York: Plume, 1993.

Ringle, Dennis J. *Life in Mr. Lincoln's Navy*. Annapolis: Naval Institute Press, 1998.

Rodger, N. A. M. *The Wooden World: An Anatomy of the Georgian Navy*. 2nd ed. New York: W. W. Norton, 1996.

Rose, Susan. *Medieval Naval Warfare*. New York: Routledge, 2002.

Rossetti, William Michael. *The Stacions of Rome . . .: And the Pilgrims Sea-voyage . . . with Clene Maydenhood . . . A Supplement to "Political, Religious, and Love Poems," and "Hali Meidenhad."* Edited by Frederick James Furnivall. Early English Text Society, 1867.

Rutz, Meryl. "Salt Horse and Ship's Biscuit: A Short Essay on the Diet of the Royal Navy Seaman During the American Revolution." http://www/navyandmarine .org/ondeck/1776salthorse.htm.

Semmes, Raphael, Admiral CSN. *Memoirs of Service Afloat*. Seacaucus, NJ: Blue & Grey Press, 1987.

Severin, Tim. *The Sinbad Voyage*. New York: G.P. Putnam, 1983.

Smith, Hervey Garrett. *The Arts of the Sailor*. Edited by Eugene V. Connett. New York: D. Van Nostrand Company, 1953. Reprint, New York: Barnes & Noble Books, 1979.

Smith, John. *A Sea Grammar: With the Plaine Exposition of Smiths Accidence for Young Sea-Men*. 1627. Gale Digital Collections: Sabin Americana Print Editions 1500–1926.

Smith, Ken. *Turbinia: The Story of Charles Parsons and His Ocean Greyhound*. Newcastle Upon Tyne, UK: Tyne and Wear Museums, 1996.

Snodgrass, Mary Ellen. *Encyclopedia of Kitchen History*. New York: Fitzroy Dearborn, 2004.

Snow, Elliot. *Adventures at Sea in the Great Age of Sail: Five Firsthand Narratives*. Salem, Massachusetts: Marine Research Society, 1925. Reprint, New York: Dover Publications, 1986. Originally Published as *The Sea, The Ship and The Sailor*.

Tannahill, Reay. *Food in History*. 2nd ed. New York: Stein and Day, 1974.

Teonge, Henry. *Diary of Henry Teonge, Chaplain on Board His Majesty's Ships Assistance, Bristol, and Royal Oak: 1675–1679*. London, 1825. https://archive.org/details/diaryofhenryteon00teon.

The Trident Society. *The Book of Navy Songs*. 3rd ed. Annapolis: Naval Institute Press, 1955.

Tucker, Spencer, C. ed. *Almanac of American Military History*. Santa Barbara, CA: ABC-CLIO, 2013. http://books.google.com/books?id=TO2mx3l4ST0C&pg=PA553&lpg=PA553&dq=Robert+Fulton+steam+powered+defense+vessel+1812&source=bl&ots=LdoUjKJ79l&sig=s1f_yGIydKvGsGNTHTqP0m8GiVs&hl=en&sa=X&ei=0DwZU96CB4ySkQeG4oGYCA&ved=0CDgQ6AEwAw#v=onepage&q=Robert%20Fulton%20steam%20powered%20defense%20vessel%201812&f=false.

Tucker, Spencer, C., ed. *The Civil War Naval Encyclopedia*. Santa Barbara, CA: ABC-CLIO, 2011. http://books.google.com/books?id=Ho_8ONL5UgsC&q=food#v=onepage&q=food&f=false.

Twain, Mark. *The Innocents Abroad*. Hartford, CT: American Publishing Company, 1869. Project Gutenberg. http://www.gutenberg.org/files/3176/3176-h/3176-h.htm.

Viking Cruise Line, and Manne Stenros, *Sea & Food*. Finland: Studio Avec Audiovisual, 2003.

Villiers, Alan. *The War with Cape Horn*. London: Pan Books, 1971. Wordpress.com blog. http://ageofsail.wordpress.com/category/naval-food/.

Von Hassell, Agostino, Herm Dillon, and Leslie Jean-Bart. *Military High Life: Elegant Food Histories and Recipes*. New Orleans: University Press of the South, 2006.

White, John. *The Fift Voyage of M. John White into the West Indies and Parts of America Called Virginia, in the Yeere 1590*. Virtual Jamestown Project. http://etext.lib.virginia.edu/etcbin/jamestown-browse?id=J1019.

White, John. *The Fourth Voyage Made to Virginia with Three Ships, in the Yere 1587*. Virtual Jamestown Project. http://etext.lib.virginia.edu/etcbin/jamestown-browse?id=J1018.

Williams, Neville. *The Sea Dogs: Privateers, Plunder & Piracy in the Elizabethan Age*. London: Weidenfeld and Nicolson, 1975.

Index

About the Author

Simon Spalding is a maritime historian as well as a writer, lecturer, teacher, and performer. He has created educational programs for museums throughout the United States and Europe. Mr. Spalding holds a BA from the University of California at Berkeley, and he has performed and lectured in festivals, concerts, and museums throughout North America and twelve European countries. Mr. Spalding has served as a working crew member aboard two schooners, a sloop, a barque, a brig, and in transatlantic and Baltic voyages in the Polish sail training vessel *Zawisza Czarny*. Mr. Spalding's previous writings include articles on history and education, museum manuals, and a play script "The Constitutional Convention of 1836" for the Texas Historical Commission. Mr. Spalding grew up in San Francisco but he now lives in New Bern, North Carolina, with his wife Sara and their two children. *Food at Sea* is Mr. Spalding's first full-length book.